Marques of America

Lincoln & Continental:
The Postwar Years

Publishers & Wholesalers Inc
Osceola, Wisconsin 54020, USA

Paul R. Woudenberg

© 1980 by Dr. Paul R. Woudenberg
ISBN: 0-87938-063-2
Library of Congress Number: 80-12242

Printed and bound in the United States of America
Book and jacket design by William F. Kosfeld

Motorbooks International is a certified trademark,
registered with the United States Patent Office.

1 2 3 4 5 6 7 8 9 10

Library of Congress Cataloging in Publication Data

Woudenberg, Paul R
    Lincoln and Continental.

    (Marques of America)
    Includes index.
    1. Lincoln automobile. 2. Lincoln
Continental automobile. I. Title. II. Series.
TL215.L5W68   629.2′222   80-12242
ISBN 0-87938-063-2

Acknowledgments

The Lincoln-Mercury Division has been generous in their help in preparing this book and thanks should be given to Vice President Walt Oben and Public Relations Manager Edward S. Gorman. In particular James R. Olson and Carol Bowie have provided photographs and data. Eugene Bordinat, twenty-year styling director for Ford, was very helpful as were John Najjar, John Reinhart, David Ash and public relations man Bill Carroll. The Henry Ford Museum and archives remain the major resource for historical research and thanks are due President Frank Caddy, Archive Director John Conde, Winthrop Sears, Jr. and especially to David Crippen who manages to "arrange" discoveries for writers. The Petersen Publishing Company library supplied photographs and other material and thanks go to Erwin M. Rosen and librarian Jane Barrett. The photographs located on page 12 (right), 14, 28, 64 (left and right), 74, 75 (left and right), 76 (left and right), and 93 are courtesy of John Oren. Patricia H. Montgomery, Director of Public Relations at Cadillac, was helpful. Lincoln authorities William F. Schmidt and Rob Wiren read the manuscript and made many valuable suggestions. Thanks also are due Richard T. Davis and typists Pearl Pike and Margaret Young.

Dr. Paul R. Woudenberg
Carmel, California
May, 1980

Table of Contents

CHAPTER 1
Zephyr Saves The Company — 1937-44
page 6

CHAPTER 2
Postwar Reorganization — 1945-48
page 20

CHAPTER 3
New Engine-New Image — 1949-51
page 30

CHAPTER 4
Lincoln Becomes a Champion — 1952-54
page 44

CHAPTER 5
Seeking Another Image — 1955-57
page 58

CHAPTER 6
Cost No Object — The Mark II
page 68

CHAPTER 7
Misunderstood Giant — 1958-60
page 78

CHAPTER 8
The Continental Bullseye — 1961-65
page 88

CHAPTER 9
New Triumph For Mark III — 1966-68
page 102

CHAPTER 10
King Of The Hill — 1969-73
page 114

CHAPTER 11
Final Big-Car Fling — 1974-77
page 126

CHAPTER 12
Versailles And Reducing Pains — 1978-80
page 136

APPENDIX
page 148

INDEX
page 150

CHAPTER 1

Zephyr Saves The Company—1937-44

IN 1936 THE LINCOLN Zephyr burst upon the American automobile scene, a car of revolutionary styling and body construction, and it was easily the most dramatic and successful automotive product of the decade. But automotive revolutions are often short-lived, especially in styling. The thirties saw the appearance of numerous sensations such as the 1932 Graham Blue Streak, the 1934 LaSalle and Chrysler Airflow, and the 1936 Cord. The Lincoln Zephyr, however, was that rare example of an all-new car which was an immediate commercial success, a claim none of its rivals could match. The Zephyr, in its original body form, lasted four years, and with the 1940 reshaping continued through the spring of 1948. This styling triumph saved the Lincoln Division from extinction and made possible the tremendous postwar success story. Even the LaSalle, the most successful and targeted competitor of the Zephyr, was redundant by the end of 1940. Chrysler tried hard with the Airflow, but the car remained Chrysler's major and costly error of the thirties. That the Lincoln could succeed as a fresh new car sold by an organization showing serious signs of decay is all the more remarkable.

By 1936, the Ford Motor Company was widely regarded as conservative to the point of being moribund. Mr. Ford's last great technical achievement was the V-8 engine; from then on very little innovation took place. Ford engineers were ready with many good ideas including hydraulic brakes in 1936, a six-cylinder engine, conventional distributors, a 1937 Mercury prototype which abandoned transverse springs, and numerous other ideas—all of which were vetoed. When change finally did come, such as the column shift and hydraulic brakes, Ford was usually last. To be sure, such conservatism helped the firm avoid short-lived novelties such as freewheeling and the startix system. The curious fact is that the Lincoln Zephyr was built within the general mechanical design limits of the Ford Motor Company yet it managed to be defiantly new and fresh.

The credit for the Zephyr must certainly begin with Edsel Ford who placed the original order for development of the Tjaarda prototype in 1932. John Tjaarda was a Dutch engineer who had worked at the Fokker Company. After emigrating to the United States he was employed by the Locke Body Company and then in 1931 was hired by Ralph Roberts at the LeBaron Studios in the Briggs Manufacturing Company. Tjaarda had done some private sketches for Fred Duesenberg on a rear-engined car, a project scrapped when financing appeared for the Model J from E. L. Cord. The LeBaron studios were familiar to Edsel and since Briggs

The 1940 Lincoln Continental with a perfection of line seldom equaled. It was the car which later Lincoln stylists looked to for inspiration. E. T. Gregorie deserves credit for the theme.

The Chrysler Airflow and the Lincoln Zephyr have often been compared but there can be little doubt which of the two cars was esthetically successful. Only 6,275 of this 1936 Airflow were produced while the brand-new Zephyr sold 14,994 units. In 1937 Zephyr production doubled but Airflow sank to 4,600 and was finished.

The brilliant basic design of this 1938 Cadillac 60 Special can still be seen beneath the gewgaws and chrome bits tacked all over it. As a trend-setter the 60 Special had few rivals. In particular, the center door-post treatment would reappear on the Continental in 1975 as the colonnade-style greenhouse.

was a major supplier for Ford, it was a natural liaison. Tjaarda was the right man at the right place at the right time when Edsel's encouraging order for development appeared. The fact that such an idea could generate from Edsel during one of the worst years of the depression is indicative of his vision and characteristic of his foresight. Despite the introduction of the new KB, without doubt the grandest Lincoln ever built up to that moment and the beginning of the final great line of America's greatest car, Edsel was well aware of technological developments which put even the superlative Model K into proper perspective.

Edsel's artistic gifts had found ample expression in the coachwork mounted on the Models L and K. The fine coachbuilding houses of America found in Edsel both sensitivity and rare encouragement, and the great Lincoln bodies were quite likely the finest in the world. Edsel's interest in coachwork kept him in touch with European trends and prepared him for more radical approaches to design and engineering in 1938. When he asked Eugene T. Gregorie to design his new Zephyr with a 'Continental' flair it was a term which had depth by virtue of his

travels and experience. The Tjaarda rear-engined experimental car was completed by October 1933 and was put on display at the Ford Exposition of Progress at Convention Hall in Detroit. In 1934 the exhibit was relocated at the Chicago World's Fair where Tjaarda's ideas received further display and acclaim.

Work was begun at once to explore the production possibilities. The sophisticated rear engine suspension, a good deal better than Hans Ledwinka's simple swing axles on the contemporary Tatra rear-engined Model 77, used double universals, and parallel arm suspension not unlike the later Studebaker planar system of the 1939 Champion. The whole concept, however, was wildly beyond Mr. Ford's engineering vision so the Tjaarda ideas were quickly translated into a more conventional front-engined job utilizing production Ford components. The modifications worked very well and the new car had great possibilities. Not the least advantage of the Tjaarda achievements was light weight, the first production Zephyr of 1936 coming in at only 3,300 pounds. (The Airflow of that year was over 4,100 pounds—a severe handicap.) Mr. Ford's constant search for light weight was commendable and the Zephyr's brilliant unit construction, which did so much with so little, was a strong argument for his early approval.

Tjaarda's design was wonderfully roomy and the six-passenger-capacity advertising claim was no casual boast. The most striking feature of the Zephyr was the front seating position, directly behind a large flat windshield. Because the glass was flat, the instrument panel

This magnificent 1939 Model K Lincoln was given a special parade touring body by LeBaron and was used by the king and queen of England on their United States and Canada tour. Time was running out for the Model K; only about 133 were produced in 1939. Perhaps no car in production at that time could match the K for sheer quality without regard to cost.

Only six of these Willoughby panel broughams were built in 1938 and the great coachbuilding firm of Utica would last just another year. At $7,400, it was the highest-priced Lincoln available on normal order. Few customers were left in the super-luxury market; most found good alternatives from Cadillac or Packard at half the price.

dropped vertically from the lower edge of the windshield, which allowed the seat to be positioned forward and thus provided extraordinary panoramic visibility for the driver and front-seat passengers. This splendid interior and body shell was not changed by stylist E. T. Gregorie's grille and new prow, necessary when the engine was placed forward. Gregorie, with his usual skill, beautifully integrated a V-shaped grille of fine horizontal bars, the fine bars being an identifying Lincoln feature through 1942. The headlamps were neatly faired into the front fenders. The front and rear bumpers were not unlike those of contemporary Ford production.

Edsel was determined that the new car would be built in 'his' Lincoln Division, perhaps the only way to insure its production. This suggested that if the Lincoln nameplate were to be used, the car should have twelve cylinders and thus was determined the general outline of the engine that would be used in the Tjaarda car. Frank Johnson, the distinguished designer of both of Lincoln's V-12 engines, was called in and given clear direction about what he was to do. The new car was to have light weight, be sold at a competitive price and be in harmony with general Ford engineering philosophies. There would be no giant and weighty K components. Johnson went to work using the Ford V-8 as his base and what emerged was a seventy-five-degree V-12 which,

happily, took advantage of the low production costs associated with the Ford engine. The exhaust ports, for example, were routed through the block, though Johnson wisely placed the water pumps on the block instead of the head so that they shoved cool water rather than sucked hot, as Ford was still doing in 1936.

The engine design had advantages not only by doing away with costly exhaust manifolds cradled in the center of the vee, but by insuring rapid warm-up in cold climates. This was one of the reasons why Mr. Ford embraced the design on the V-8 in the first place and, in the winter climate of Michigan, it made a great deal of sense. But in an Arizona summer, the problems were severe. A giant twenty-seven-quart radiator was fitted which was increased to thirty quarts in 1938.

The V-12 crankshaft was some eight inches longer than the Ford's, a size increase of thirty-three percent, with weight up twenty percent to seventy-three pounds. One might expect a loss of torsional rigidity, but stress was lighter because the bore was down to 2.75 inches and the overlap was much greater. The result was an exceptionally smooth engine, a revelation to new owners. The Lincoln Zephyr offered a motoring experience unknown before in the thirties except to the wealthy owners of the super luxury V-12's and V-16's and those rare buyers who discovered the Auburn twelve. Long induction passages radiating from the single dual-downdraft carburetor helped to make for good gas flow. The engine performed like an electric turbine. One of the characteristics that endeared it to new owners was a full-power torque figure of over 180 pounds-feet at near-idle 400 rpm. If there ever was a car with total high-gear performance, the Lincoln Zephyr was it. Unlike the heavier V-12's of the classic era, the Zephyr was vastly more responsive at the low end of the rev scale because of the car's light weight. Furthermore, the V-12 engine had an unusually high power-peak of 3900 rpm, higher than any unblown American engine. Coupled with a 4.33:1 or 4.44:1 axle ratio, it is likely that the Zephyr had the widest usable high-gear performance of any current production car. Top speed of the Zephyr was nearly 90 mph and the crawling speed was determined only by the insensitivity of the driver. Indeed, numerous Lincoln owners regarded their car as virtually a one-gear automobile. That the torque curve was still 180 pounds-feet at 3500 rpm tended to support this brutality.

Any new engine requires time to 'settle down' and the Lincoln Zephyr unit was no exception. Owners soon complained of excessive oil consumption. Johnson had placed the ring grooves high in the piston and used a cast-iron oil ring. The rings may have been too close to the combustion chamber and, though the design flaw remained, the switch to steel section rings helped somewhat. Early Zephyr engines under heavy use or abuse would sometimes require new rings as early as 20,000 miles. As was the case with the early V-8's, reliability improved with production modifications.

The oiling system was never the Zephyr's strong point. The original oil pump was none too large and if clearances opened up anywhere, pressure fell. There were simply more places for oil to go in a twelve-cylinder engine. A large oil pump with bigger passages was fitted in 1946 to correct the problem. Larger crank journals were fitted in 1942 and, unless matched with the bigger pump, often caused trouble.

Solid lifters were used in 1936 and 1937 and were reliable in the Ford tradition. The first hydraulic lifters were used in 1938 and were supplied with oil drawn directly from the sump. The lifters could tolerate very little dirt and careless owners who failed to change oil regularly reported trouble. In 1939, the whole oiling system was revised so that lifter oil was bled off directly after filtration, which worked well unless owners neglected filter changes.

The new Lincoln Zephyr was presented in November 1935 with a two-door price of $1,275 and a four-door at $1,320, almost the same as the LaSalle which Edsel had targeted as principal competition. The Chrysler Airflow eight was $1,246 and the Buick Models 50 and 60 bracketed the Zephyr in price. It was a fast track on which to compete but the Zephyr was met with resounding acclaim and first-year sales were 17,715, easily beating LaSalle and the Airflows. The public rightly sensed that the car was different in many fresh ways. The styling, though radical, avoided the functional ugliness of the Airflow. The seating, especially in the front, was a revelation. The incredibly smooth engine was unmatched at the price. Top speed was at the very front of the competition. The quality of trim and finish was the finest.

Early problems were quickly corrected by alert engineers. The Zephyr shared the transverse spring layout of the 1936 Ford and their dimensions were virtually identical. Load rates for the Zephyr were increased by the addition of two leaves, both front and rear. The Zephyr, however, had a ten-inch-longer wheelbase and six hundred pounds more weight than Ford. Furthermore, advertising stressed that the new car could carry six passengers with ease. Taken together, the weight of the new Zephyr when loaded could be nearly half a ton above that of the Ford. The chassis hung all too freely on the shackles at the end of the springs and the car swung from side to side under any centrifugal force or road camber. The Zephyr shared the new Ford cross steering in which the drag link was parallel with the front axle and transmitted steering effort to the right side of the car. This new steering layout inadvertently converted the link into a stabilizing strut which transmitted sideways motion directly to the steering box. A true stabilizing rod was hurriedly introduced in mid-1936 to control lateral axle motion.

The success of the Zephyr was anything but transitory and the sales moved upward in 1937 to 25,243. Sales were helped by the introduction of the handsome three-window coupe which accounted for 5,199 units. The new Lincoln dashboard was a trend-setter in that it was the first effort at a console or center pillar area which would be used to house radio components, and later to conceal the floor-mounted gear shift.

The Ford design team led by E. T. Gregorie gave a major revision to the front styling of the Zephyr for 1938 and it was to have a profound effect on Detroit thinking. The grille was relocated into the lower half of the front of the hood using fine horizontal bars. The prow of the hood was gracefully rounded and the whole ensemble was exceptionally smooth. It will be remembered that 1938 was a year of sharp vertical grilles, especially in the General Motors line where both Buick and

Cadillac were using very tall, narrow units. The Chrysler line was strong in the vertical motif, too. The Lincoln Zephyr focused attention downward, which tended to give the whole car a lower and smoother expression. The following year Buick and Studebaker followed Lincoln's lead, as did the whole Chrysler line to some extent. In 1940 the new look was nearly everywhere except for LaSalle.

Lincoln profited mightily from its styling leadership and though sales slipped to 19,111 in 1938, the rest of the industry fell much further behind in percentage declines. Again the body offerings were expanded with two new convertibles, a coupe and a four-door. The town limousine, essentially a trim option on the four-door introduced in 1937, was continued for the second and last year. A hypoid axle was introduced in 1938, a fine unit which might have been used with profit in the forthcoming Mercury lineup. The new blocker synchronizers were used in the transmission, and needle bearings replaced bushings in the universal joint. Hydraulic self-adjusting valves appeared. The engineers were steadily refining the car.

One curious aspect of the Zephyr was its brakes. The original brakes were cable self-energizing units by Bendix, similar to the Ford Lockheed-Wagner system except that the linings were shorter, though thicker. The Lincoln specification for brake lining area was 168 inches, same as the Model A, while the concurrent Ford brakes offered 186 square inches of lining.

The highly successful Lincoln Zephyr grille received minor changes for 1939; the fine grille bars were now vertical and the hood prow was raised and squared. It was even better than the splendid 1938 grille. The air opening was enlarged to help cooling—a problem in 1938. The interior console remained for the last year, with the gear-shift lever winding its way around behind the console in imitation of the convenience features of a column shift. Hydraulic brakes appeared finally and were excellent. The wheel bolts were changed from the periphery of the brake drums to a more normal central position with a bolt circle diameter of 5.5 inches, which Ford and Mercury would follow in 1940. Again the five basic body types of 1938 were offered and production continued strong at 20,905.

Edsel Ford could well have been pleased after four years of the new Lincoln Zephyr. Sales had been steady and the Lincoln Division had been saved as the Model K faded from the scene. The new car found general acceptance amid a highly competitive area of the market. The Zephyr's advanced styling helped to project a new image of the Ford Motor Company. And finally, at the close of 1939 an altogether new triumph was in the making.

Edsel's love of beautiful cars had resulted in at least two specials constructed under E. T. Gregorie's supervision, none of which appeared

The original Lincoln Continental used by Edsel Ford on his Florida trip. Two hundred orders were reported in hand if the car would go into production. The go-ahead was given in April and on October 3, 1939, the first production car was ready; 25 were completed in 1939.

The four-door convertible sedan was offered in 1938 and 1939 in the Zephyr lineup. There were 461 units produced of this 1938 model while only 302 were built in 1939.

to have production possibilities. Another such special was ordered in September 1938 following Edsel's return from the Continent. The new car was to be prepared for Edsel's winter vacation in Florida and was to be 'Continental.' A clay model was ready in November and it was Edsel who asked that the spare tire be left exposed. The car was based on the 1938-39 Lincoln Zephyr convertible which was sectioned at the beltline and 'squared up.' A particularly important styling feature was the raised trunk area, which suddenly conveyed a marvelous 'hunched' look, a technique used later by L. David Ash on the first Mark III with brilliant success and also widely copied in the seventies. The front fender of the Zephyr was lengthened while the rear was scarcely changed. The results were dazzling and the car was constructed in time for Edsel's March 1939 trip to Florida.

Reaction to the new car among Edsel's friends was so enthusiastic that reportedly two hundred orders were in hand if the car was to go into production. Edsel at once ordered Gregorie to prepare a second car as a possible production prototype. By April, Edsel was so confident about the new car that he ordered production to begin with the 1940

model. On October 3, 1939, the first Continental was turned out, using metal-faced wooden forms for those parts of the sheet metal different from normal production. Much handwork was involved, including the addition of the section in the front fender and laborious hand fitting and filling of the various panels. By the end of 1939, twenty-five Continentals had been manufactured and demand was building rapidly for a car that was instantly recognized as one of the finest designs of the decade.

During the 1940 model year, which concluded in September, 350 cabriolets and fifty-four coupes were built. The coupe price was about $2,800, with the cabriolet one hundred dollars higher.

The 1940 Lincoln Zephyr was given a major restyling and set the body contours that would continue through the end of production in 1948. The magnificent grille design was revised, though continuing 1939 themes, and the Tjaarda body was expanded and heightened. Windows were larger, rear fender outlines were subdued, and the whole car was smoother in outline. Despite an increase in bulk, very careful attention to design resulted in little weight increase and, in the case of the coupe, for example, a decrease in weight of over 200 pounds. The two 1940 Continentals were the heaviest bodies in the line at 3,760 pounds for the cabriolet and 3,740 for the coupe.

The instrument panel on the 1940 car lost the center console though instruments were still grouped in a giant circular panel. A steering-column shift was finally fitted. Prices for the 1940 Zephyr were under

Convertible coupes of most cars would seem to be rarer than coupes, which has led several writers to confuse the 1940 Continental production. The coupe shown here is much rarer, only 54 produced while there were 350 cabriolets.

$1,500 for closed cars at the factory with the one convertible club coupe at $1,850. Sales continued evenly with 21,536 Zephyrs produced. The new club coupe began well with 3,500 units, replacing the coupe sedan of the Tjaarda body, which had been in essence a two-door sedan and had never achieved much of a following with but 800 units sold in both 1938 and 1939.

The 1940 Zephyr retained all of the fine features of the first series, including the great flat windshield. The Zephyrs remained defiantly different, their unique mechanical performance in high gear matched by the unequaled spaciousness of the front seat so close to that panoramic windshield. The mechanical problems of early production had been somewhat eased though competitors never tired of talking about Zephyr oil consumption and twelve-cylinder gasoline consumption.

The 1941 car was little changed in outward appearance. The track was slightly widened and spring rates were softened. Push-button door

handles were used. The cabriolet received an electric lift mechanism in line with the Ford and Mercury convertibles. Zephyr interiors were, if anything, more plush than before, setting high interior standards which were to mark Lincolns throughout the postwar period.

Prices rose slightly in that last feverish prewar year but the sedan and club coupe were still a bargain at $1,541 f.o.b. Detroit. Zephyr sales of 20,094 maintained the exceptionally steady production rate of the previous three years.

The Continental became a separate model in 1941, no longer a special Zephyr body type. The name Lincoln Continental appeared on the spare hubcap and on the cowl side. The mechanical changes of the Zephyr naturally found their way into the Continental. Prices were virtually unchanged. Demand was strong and production, though much

The new body on this 1940 Lincoln Zephyr sedan was used until the end of twelve-cylinder production in 1948. The rear door has been squared-off, making entry much easier. The increased bulk of the car has been beautifully handled by Gregorie in his continuation of basic Zephyr themes.

increased, was never able to keep up. Eight hundred fifty coupes and four hundred cabriolets were turned out, all soon to be worth far more than their new price; such were the inflated market conditions. The Office of Price Administration (OPA) ceiling price for the 1941 Continental coupe would be $3,700.

Production of the mighty Model K Lincoln had dribbled to a close in 1939, the few chassis left over being presented as 1940 models with black Lincoln medallions, a fitting funereal color to commemorate what many believe to be the finest-quality car produced in America in the thirties.

One segment of the market which the big K had never really reached was the commercial limousine as used by the executive and funeral trade. It is true that federal use of the Lincoln at the presidential parade level was a quiet testimony to the supreme quality of the car. But Lincoln Model K's were very expensive; in 1939 the cheapest production seven-passenger sedan, 407A, listed at $5,000. Such an investment was not lightly undertaken by a corporation when faced with the alternatives of Packard Super Eights selling for as little as one half the price and Cadillac 75's at $3,200. That the Lincoln K was still being built to lofty standards then largely ignored by the industry was no argument when viewed in a very tough, commercially competitive environment.

Thus, in 1941, Lincoln made a beginning effort to enter the commercial limousine market with the Custom series in two models, a limousine and a sedan. The car was built on a 138-inch wheelbase, essentially a stretched Zephyr sedan with a slightly higher roof arch. Trim and finish were superb, not beneath comparison with the K. The best news was the price, the limousine at $2,836 f.o.b. and the sedan at $2,704. Here was a brand-new car which could compete with the Cadillac 67, Packard 180 and Chrysler Crown Imperial eight directly on price.

The Custom did well in 1941, selling 355 sedans and 295 limousines, which outsold the eight-passenger Chryslers and came close to the Packard 180's. Cadillac's grip on this market was already tight with 900 model 67's and 2,104 of the 75's in 1941; nevertheless, as a first-year showing the Lincoln effort was remarkable.

The 1942-model Lincoln production began in early October and lasted only until February 10, 1942, as World War II brought automobile production to an end. This new Lincoln was radically restyled by Gregorie and his team and introduced motifs which would carry through to 1948. The principal change was the adoption of a boxy look, quite the reverse from Tjaarda's original streamlining. The front of the grille was vertical with a pronounced bulbous nose and no semblance of the 1941's V-shaped prow. It was an idea that Gregorie had tried on the 1941 Ford and Mercury with success and which had been used also on the 1941 Cadillac. Gregorie's horizontal-bar radiator grille was attractive, but the most noticeable novelty was a new lip or protrusion in the lower half of the grille which added a massive appearance, and

with it some seven inches of additional length. The great mass of horizontal bars obliterated the sense of streamlined flow of the 1941 grille but Gregorie wisely squared off the fenders in a further move to completely change the 'feel' of the car. When used on the Continental, these body changes reflected an already developed angularity on the windshield outline, window trim and rear trunk outline. As a styling ensemble the result was harmonious. But the new square look, when applied to the Zephyr sedan and coupe sheet metal, was less suited to the great sweeping curves and was at odds with the fundamental concept that Gregorie had laid down in 1939. The problem was most obvious in the club coupe and the short-lived three-window coupe where convex surface development on the rear deck was quite unrelated to the boxy fenders.

Weight had risen over the years, a normal penalty of development, but the 1942 car was up nearly 400 pounds, an increase that could not be ignored. Particularly vexing was the premium weight of the Continental, caused by the high amount of lead filling, handwork and shaping which amounted to not less than 300 pounds in 1940. The 1942 Continental weighed over 4,000 pounds in both coupe and cabriolet

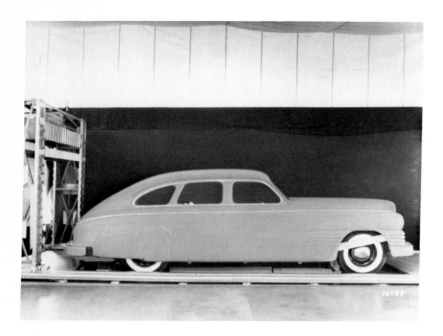

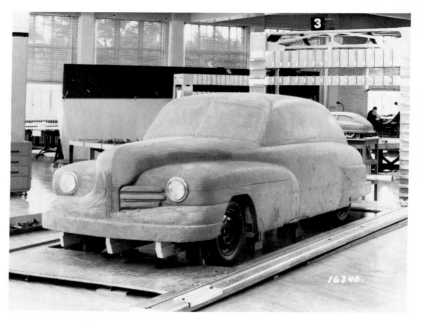

The side view of a Lincoln clay with a Packard Clipper-like grille dated September 15, 1941. The body outline could be taken straight from a Pontiac. Gregorie's 1949 Cosmopolitan could tolerate few of these straight lines because it was a design of voluptuous curves.

A possible Ford clay dated August 13, 1941, with a hint of the 1946 Ford grille and the 1949 small Lincoln front fender. E. T. Gregorie was certainly fascinated with the heavy lower grille, about to be introduced in the 1942 car.

forms. A horsepower increase was needed and so the V-12 engine was bored out a sixteenth of an inch to produce a displacement of 305 cubic inches and a horsepower increase from 120 to 130. This modification began late in the 1942 production run, on January 6, 1942, and ended on January 28, so that little experience in the field was available. The big engine continued in early postwar production but it was soon recognized that the cylinder walls were too thin and any core shifting during casting of the block caused trouble. The bore was reduced to the original specification in 1946 after some 1,797 of the 305-cubic-inch engines had been built.

With over 100,000 Zephyr V-12 engines in the field by the end of 1941, much experience had been gained on the engine. The oil pump insufficiency was noted and soon to be corrected. The engine would tolerate oil pressure as low as ten or fifteen pounds provided wear was even and stresses were kept down. The oil consumption problem was also noted but the problem was not simply rings. A main cause was poor crankcase ventilation coupled with the substantial piston area of the twelve-cylinder engine. Pressure was high and fumes in a worn engine were driven out of the breather cap and sometimes fanned back into the passenger compartment. High manifold vacuum also sucked oil up the valve guides when wear caused increased clearances. The high crankcase pressure forced oil through every possible leak and there were several, such as the rear main bearing, the fuel pump tower and at the pump itself. These problems were attacked by Frank Johnson and the engineers and much improvement was made, but the engine's reputation suffered from these early problems.

In the fall of 1941, few shoppers were in any mood to criticize. The 1942 Lincolns were snapped up by eager buyers who were all too aware

A town limousine (a sedan with a division) had been offered in the Zephyr line beginning in 1937. A true seven-passenger limousine appeared in 1941 in the Custom series along with a seven-passenger sedan, both on a 138-inch wheelbase. This 1942 Custom limousine was listed at just over $3,000. Only 66 were produced before the war stopped production on January 28, 1942.

This slightly scarred veteran is the 1941 Continental used by Edsel Ford until his death in 1943. The handsome driving lights may have reduced radiator efficiency, a real problem in hot climates.

of what the war would mean to new car production, which at Lincoln was pitifully small—6,118 Zephyrs until the close of the line on February 10, 1942. The Continental production was 136 cabriolets and 200 coupes. Only forty-seven Custom seven-passenger sedans were built and sixty-six limousines.

The Lincoln Division on the eve of the war was caught in the maelstrom of the general decay of the Ford Motor Company. Mr. Ford suffered a stroke in 1938 from which he had apparently recovered with nearly full strength. He still exercised absolute control throughout the company, and as Allan Nevins put it, was "reluctant to define spheres of authority." After 1938, Mr. Ford paid less attention to many areas of company operation, one of which was the Lincoln Division, which had been operating under Edsel's increased direction. Thus the relative success of the Lincoln Zephyr in the late thirties, the debut of the brilliant Continental and the rather graceful exit from the Model K were principally the work of Edsel.

In 1941 Mr. Ford suffered another stroke, much more severe and debilitating. The casual nature of Ford administration could work with strong leadership, but Mr. Ford was never the same after 1941 and without his steady attention the company moved aimlessly. A more serious blow for Lincoln was Edsel's declining health, culminating in his tragic death in May 1943. The key man responsible for Lincoln's forward momentum was gone.

A power struggle was under way by 1942 with the opening rounds won by Harry Bennett who entrenched his associates in key positions. The casualties of Bennett's victories were the men who had guided the

 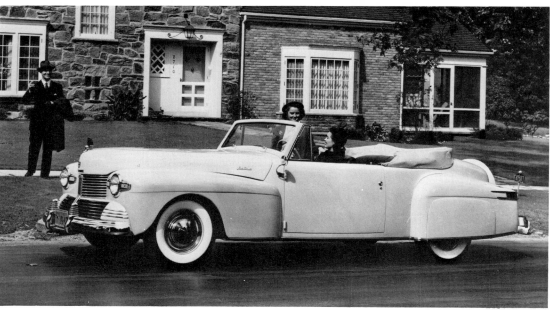

At left a Lincoln stylist carefully prepares the full-size clay of the 1942 Continental. The new boxy fenders harmonized particularly well with the angular Continental body. Only 136 Continental cabriolets (right) would be built for the 1942 model year. It weighed 4,020 pounds and on January 6, 1942, the engine was bored out a sixteenth of an inch to increase horsepower to 130. After 22 days of production, car building ceased. Only in 1946 did the weaknesses of the larger bore become apparent and the smaller bore was restored after 1,797 postwar engines.

growth and development of the company from the earliest days. A. M. Weibel, a first-class executive in charge of purchasing, was relieved in April 1943. Laurence Sheldrick, chief engineer who had done so much with the V-8, left soon after, followed by E. T. Gregorie though Gregorie would return a year later. After Edsel's death even mighty Charles Sorensen could not prevail and he left in March 1944.

The Lincoln Division felt these losses severely, especially that of Gregorie who had been responsible for Lincoln's styling triumphs. The remaining leadership of the company was confused and uncertain and those executives of the second rank were pondering the fate of the company if Bennett and his followers would capture all of the

administrative control. The struggle for power was to continue straight through the war until September 1945 when Henry Ford II took over absolute leadership of the company.

The Lincoln Division faced another problem in merchandising which had not been resolved by 1942 and was, if anything, worse by 1945. The traditional image of the Lincoln in the thirties was that of a supremely elegant and prestigious motor car whose principal sales were in the major cities. Showrooms commensurate with the style of the car were very rare—in part because volume was so low and few dealers were interested in constructing the mini-Versailles palace which was *de rigueur* in the late twenties. The dealer network for the Lincoln was thus very small. To be sure, Ford dealers throughout the United States had access to the Lincoln and were occasionally shipped one, sometimes against their will. Some dealers embraced the Lincoln business with a will but most saw the Lincoln as a merchandising problem, particularly as the depression took hold. And few dealers were interested in maintaining any realistic inventory of parts to service the big Lincoln.

The Zephyr network of 1935 was thus dependent upon Ford dealers who opted for the new car, not upon what few Lincoln exclusive dealers remained. A new car meant new inventory and investment on a slow-moving item, admittedly better than the K but a very long way from the popular Ford. Furthermore, the Ford dealers were often unprepared for the sort of merchandising required to sell a car in the upper-middle price range. Thus the Zephyr was often resisted by Ford dealers and did not receive the sort of stylish merchandising effort that was instinctive to the Packard dealers and the Buick or Cadillac-LaSalle agencies.

John R. Davis, the gifted new sales manager, took over in 1937 and helped immeasurably to strengthen the dealer network. By 1939 Davis had linked the Zephyr to two of the four types of dealerships, namely, the 'all' Ford products group—major dealers who would include the new Mercury; and the 'quality cars only' group—Lincoln-Mercury paired dealerships. This helped to sharpen sales techniques for the Zephyr. The central selling force, even under Davis's plan, remained the big major dealerships who could afford the capital investment necessary to handle the line. The Lincoln-Mercury paired dealership in 1939 was risky, especially after the bad year of 1938, and in the light of the unproved sales potential of the new car.

By 1942, the sales network was strengthened but a very long way from the sort of prestige operation common to Cadillac and Packard. The great single dealerships housed in magnificent buildings (such as that of Alvin Fuller in Boston or Earle C. Anthony and Don Lee in California), which had been identified with one make for years, had easily survived World War II and were ready to promote the postwar models in proper style, but were simply too few and far between in the Lincoln network. It was one of the reasons why, as we'll see, Lincoln sales in the postwar period were to lag.

CHAPTER
2

Postwar Reorganization—1945-48

THE FINAL ALLIED victory was clearly in sight following the collapse of Germany in early May 1945. On May 25, the War Production Board granted the automobile industry permission to make 200,000 vehicles before the end of the year, of which Ford's quota was 39,910. Ford start-up was exceptionally quick and on June 3 the first car appeared—a facelifted version of the 1942 model. Production climbed slowly in the face of serious material shortages and the new model announcement was delayed until October 26. The company managed to produce 34,439 Fords in 1945.

The early Ford start-up belied the revolution going on in the company. Henry Ford II had been a vice president since December 1943 and had gradually drawn around him trusted advisors including Mead Bricker, Logan Miller, John S. Bugas and John R. Davis. An intense power struggle began with Henry Ford II and his men against Harry Bennett and his numerous aids, culminating in the dismissal of Bennett on September 21, 1945, and Henry Ford II assuming the presidency of the company at the age of twenty-eight.

The Bennett group was soon ousted and reorganization began. The new management team was first announced on September 27 and convened on October 3. On October 18, young Ford suggested a separate Lincoln Division and T. W. Skinner was appointed its head.

In November, a young group of Air Force officers headed by Charles B. 'Tex' Thornton was hired to begin administrative analysis of the company. These men, known as the Whiz Kids, began work on February 1, 1946, and included George Moore, Wilbur R. Andreson, Charles E. Bosworth, J. E. Lundy, Robert S. McNamara, Arjay Miller, Ben David Mills, Francis C. 'Jack' Reith and James O. Wright.

The Thornton group provided a reservoir of talent for the new company but its members were little older than young Ford and lacked automotive experience. What was needed at once was an experienced executive, and on July 1, 1946, Ernest R. Breech took office as vice president and chief operating officer. Breech had been lured from the presidency of Bendix Aviation and had an impressive business career, including a stint with General Motors. Breech, in turn, recruited Lewis D. Crusoe in management, Harold T. Youngren in engineering, Delmar S. Harder in operations and Albert J. Browning in purchasing. It was the beginning of the new team that would carry the company for the next generation. No little credit must be given to Henry Ford II for the wise

The 1946 Lincoln four-door sedan. The absence of fog lamps means this car was built in late 1945 and may well be one of the very first off the line. The fenders, bottom door flaring and very heavy bumper and lower grille combine to give the car a somewhat squatty appearance.

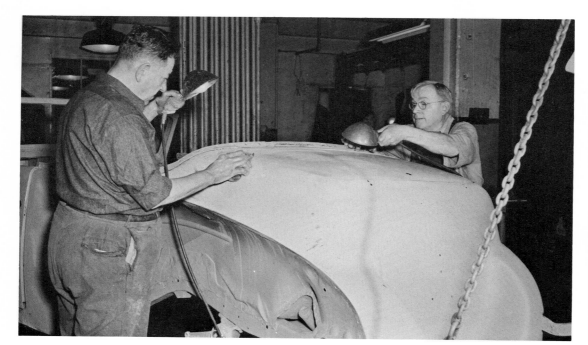

Handwork was still the rule when the 1946 Continentals were put back into production (left). Hand sanding was helped by the electric lamp which revealed imperfections. The lack of heavy tooling always made the Continental an expensive proposition. The earliest Lincolns built in the fall of 1945 did not have fog lamps, and the end of the lower grille was covered with a decorative plate. Beginning in January 1946, regular production included the lamps. Instructions for retrofitting included this picture (right) which shows the early cover plate.

choices he was making despite virtually no experience at the center of the company.

In the fall of 1945, as these first rumblings of the reorganizing were being felt, the new Lincoln had still not appeared. Production began slowly on November 1 and by the end of 1945 only 569 units had been built, not even enough to supply a token car to each dealer. The announcement could not be delayed much longer and on January 6, 1946, the new car was unveiled. All early postwar cars were warmed-over 1942 models and some were virtually indistinguishable, such as the Studebaker, Pontiac, Chevrolet and Cadillac. Other cars were given

considerable restylings such as Oldsmobile and Chrysler. The Ford, Mercury and Lincoln received substantial grille changes. Gregorie was looking for new boldness and a move away from the fine grille bars so typical of the late thirties. The new Ford was an excellent example of the simplification of a fussy grille, though the 1946 Mercury was anything but simple. For the Lincoln, Gregorie made a very bold change, a design which he had completed in late summer of 1941 and which was probably intended for the 1943 model.

The Lincoln grille was a heavy die-cast egg-crate type, accentuated by a thick additional lower grille band just above the bumper. The emphasis on the bumper area may be seen in many of Gregorie's wartime clays. As initially produced in November 1945 the grille band tapered at each end into a flat chrome cover, but in January 1946 a fog lamp was introduced, replacing the cover.

The egg-crate idea was to prove very popular in the early postwar years. Introduced by Cadillac in 1941, it was used by Dodge and

Chrysler in 1946 followed by Pontiac, Frazer, the 1949 Nash, Checker and some of the Studebakers. The Lincoln design, however, was exceptionally strong and, when created in 1941, accurately forecast Cadillac trends in 1946 and 1947. Thus the first postwar Lincoln look was up-to-date and trendy.

The Lincoln body outline was continued without change in the four-door sedan, club coupe and convertible. The three-passenger three-window coupe was discontinued because in 1941, the last normal production year, it had sold only 1,150 units, less than a third of club coupe production. Gregorie's new grille worked well with the unchanged 1942 sheet metal and the heavier bumper combined to give the car an imposing image.

The fine Lincoln trim quality was continued and the slow start-up helped early quality control. The unique front seat position—well forward with the large flat windshield very close—continued to be one of the most charming features of the car. There had been little opportunity for mechanical revisions, not simply because of the war but because of low production of the 1942 model and the limited service information feedback. The big-bore engine was thus used in early 1946 production, but after some 1,797 units the bore was reduced one sixteenth of an inch to 1941 dimensions in the interest of more consistent cylinder-wall thickness. Brake horsepower was quoted at 125, up because of a very slight compression increase to 7.2:1 from 7.1:1.

One specification of 1942 was not repeated, that of the ill-fated Liquamatic transmission. The Liquamatic was an abortive effort to match both Chrysler's and GM's new automatic transmissions but was plagued from the beginning by complexity and a lack of development. A liquid vane-type coupling unit was attached to a conventional clutch which was used when reversing and when starting on steep grades. A conventional transmission was vacuum-shifted and was combined with an overdrive. The driving procedure was to place the gear-shift lever in high; the car would then start in second gear and, with release of the throttle, the conventional transmission would shift to third between 12 and 23 mph. When the throttle was again released above 23 mph, the shift would be made to overdrive. Down-shifting by depressing the accelerator first took the ratio from third overdrive to second overdrive and then, upon a second punch of the accelerator, to normal second gear. Two vacuum-shifting units working in series (and dependent upon varying throttle openings) were difficult to coordinate and all too often power could be reapplied with one or both of the units midway in a shift. Low gear was used for emergency power. The former second gear position was also usable and simply locked out the overriding clutch and the self-shifting mechanisms.

A puzzling picture of what appears to be a post-war Custom limousine. None were cataloged and there is no evidence of production. It may be a 1942 model with the postwar grille. The red light, siren, and front and rear grab handles suggest government work with provisions for standing Secret Service men, yet there is no evidence of step plates. The heavy-duty truck-type wheels suggest armor plating.

When confronted with a transmission requiring an anti-stall carburetor device, as well as two governors, two solenoids, vacuum cylinders, throttle stops and switches, few mechanics could orchestrate the whole system into any sort of permanent harmony. The average owner was understandably puzzled and no doubt irritated by the capricious whimsy of the Liquamatic drive. Few were sold and almost all were replaced by the reliable and clean-shifting standard Warner three-speed box; it is unlikely that any Liquamatics have survived.

Rear-end ratios of the Zephyr had always been on the high side to take advantage of the high rpm of the engine and to enhance its superb flexibility. In 1936 the original Zephyr pulled 4.33 gears, but the ratio

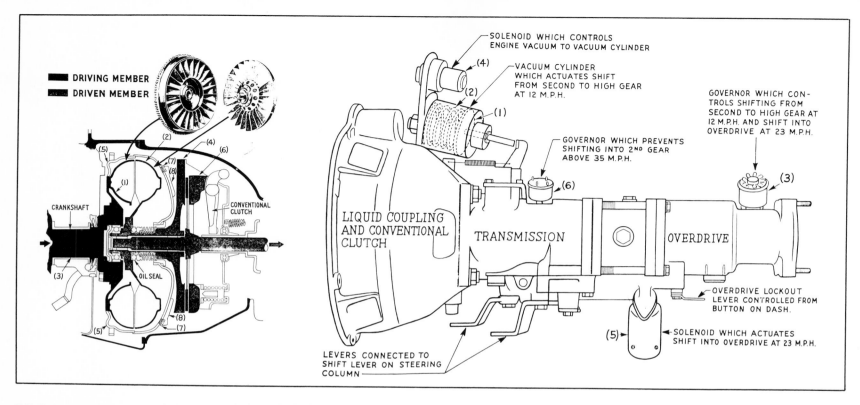

DRIVING MEMBER
DRIVEN MEMBER

(5)
(2)
(4) (6)
(7)
(8)
(1)
CRANKSHAFT
CONVENTIONAL CLUTCH
(3)
OIL SEAL
(8)
(5)
(7)

SOLENOID WHICH CONTROLS ENGINE VACUUM TO VACUUM CYLINDER
(4)
VACUUM CYLINDER WHICH ACTUATES SHIFT FROM SECOND TO HIGH GEAR AT 12 M.P.H.
(2)
(1)
GOVERNOR WHICH CON-TROLS SHIFTING FROM SECOND TO HIGH GEAR AT 12 M.P.H. AND SHIFT INTO OVERDRIVE AT 23 M.P.H.
GOVERNOR WHICH PREVENTS SHIFTING INTO 2ND GEAR ABOVE 35 M.P.H.
(6)
(3)
LIQUID COUPLING AND CONVENTIONAL CLUTCH
TRANSMISSION
OVERDRIVE
OVERDRIVE LOCKOUT LEVER CONTROLLED FROM BUTTON ON DASH.
(5)
SOLENOID WHICH ACTUATES SHIFT INTO OVERDRIVE AT 23 M.P.H.
LEVERS CONNECTED TO SHIFT LEVER ON STEERING COLUMN

If this liquid coupling of the Liquamatic Drive (left) had been fitted to a standard transmission as Dodge was to do, the Lincoln might have made it. The vacuum shift of the transmission was the problem when coupled to an overdrive which also depended on vacuum for shifting. When everything worked (right) this combination of units produced five forward speeds in the following ratios for 1942: low 10.3, second 7.0, second overdrive 4.9, high 4.44 and high overdrive 3.11. Everything rarely worked right and the Liquamatics were replaced by conventional transmissions. Few if any survived.

was raised to 4.44:1 as weight climbed. The 1942 car with the bored-out engine pulled 4.22 gears and the Liquamatic version used the 4.44:1 ratio. Both of these ratios were used postwar, the higher mated with overdrive.

The dealers greeted the new Lincoln with jubilation on January 6, 1946, for it ended four long and lean years. The demand was phenomenal for anything that ran and waiting lists were long. Early

buyers got a bargain if they were able to buy the car at list price. For example, the earliest West Coast delivered base price was $2,176.40 for the four-door sedan exclusive of equipment. The Office of Price Administration's ceiling price on the 1942 Lincoln four-door was $2,183 and the cars were selling right at ceiling. The situation was clearly without logic and Henry Ford II made several public challenges to the OPA, noting that the deregulation of some ceilings on auto parts and the low man-output as start-up occurred throughout the industry made for substantial losses on each car produced. The postwar world was indeed a different world and the OPA allowed price increases on March 11 and May 22 so that the stabilized Lincoln f.o.b. Detroit price ended up at $2,337.

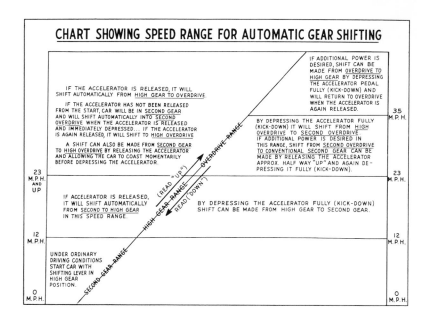

CHART SHOWING SPEED RANGE FOR AUTOMATIC GEAR SHIFTING

IF ADDITIONAL POWER IS DESIRED, SHIFT CAN BE MADE FROM OVERDRIVE TO HIGH GEAR BY DEPRESSING THE ACCELERATOR PEDAL FULLY (KICK-DOWN) AND WILL RETURN TO OVERDRIVE WHEN THE ACCELERATOR IS AGAIN RELEASED.

IF THE ACCELERATOR IS RELEASED, IT WILL SHIFT AUTOMATICALLY FROM HIGH GEAR TO OVERDRIVE.

IF THE ACCELERATOR HAS NOT BEEN RELEASED FROM THE START, CAR WILL BE IN SECOND GEAR AND WILL SHIFT AUTOMATICALLY INTO SECOND OVERDRIVE WHEN THE ACCELERATOR IS RELEASED AND IMMEDIATELY DEPRESSED.... IF THE ACCELERATOR IS AGAIN RELEASED, IT WILL SHIFT TO HIGH OVERDRIVE

A SHIFT CAN ALSO BE MADE FROM SECOND GEAR TO HIGH OVERDRIVE BY RELEASING THE ACCELERATOR AND ALLOWING THE CAR TO COAST MOMENTARILY BEFORE DEPRESSING THE ACCELERATOR.

BY DEPRESSING THE ACCELERATOR FULLY (KICK-DOWN) IT WILL SHIFT FROM HIGH OVERDRIVE TO SECOND OVERDRIVE.
IF ADDITIONAL POWER IS DESIRED IN THIS RANGE, SHIFT FROM SECOND OVERDRIVE TO CONVENTIONAL SECOND GEAR CAN BE MADE BY RELEASING THE ACCELERATOR APPROX. HALF WAY "UP" AND AGAIN DEPRESSING IT FULLY (KICK-DOWN).

35 M.P.H.

23 M.P.H. AND UP

IF ACCELERATOR IS RELEASED, IT WILL SHIFT AUTOMATICALLY FROM SECOND TO HIGH GEAR IN THIS SPEED RANGE.

BY DEPRESSING THE ACCELERATOR FULLY (KICK-DOWN) SHIFT CAN BE MADE FROM HIGH GEAR TO SECOND GEAR.

23 M.P.H.

12 M.P.H.

12 M.P.H.

UNDER ORDINARY DRIVING CONDITIONS START CAR WITH SHIFTING LEVER IN HIGH GEAR POSITION.

0 M.P.H.

0 M.P.H.

(READ "UP")   OVERDRIVE RANGE
HIGH-GEAR RANGE   READ "DOWN"
SECOND-GEAR RANGE

The used-car market remained very firm. In January 1947 the 1942 Lincoln four-door was still selling for over $2,100 at West Coast average retail. By this time, the parallel base price for the new 1947 Lincoln four-door was $2,578. Six months later the used-car market was falling and the 1942 car was down to $1,600 while the postwar sedans were at the $2,700 level.

The superheated market of these early postwar years prevents any analysis of the competitive position of the Lincoln against its principal rivals. As time went on and normal market conditions returned, the weakest makes gradually showed falling used-car values and easier new-car availability. In 1946, the new Lincoln four-door listed slightly above the comparable Cadillac 62. By mid-1947, this same 1946 Lincoln had an average used retail price of $2,755 while the 1946 Cadillac 62 commanded $4,200. This was an unfavorable comparison yet the 1946 Packard Super Clipper, selling at fifty dollars below the Lincoln and measured by the same circumstances, had an average retail of only $2,500, surely a serious danger signal for Packard management. The Chrysler New Yorker, however, $250 below the Lincoln when new, was averaging $2,725, while the Buick Roadmaster, priced slightly above the Chrysler, had an average retail of $2,575.

This chart may have seemed clear to the engineer who designed it. The fact that two gear changes were possible with a kickdown from high overdrive, i.e. to normal high gear or to second overdrive, made a downshift at approximately 35 mph unpredictable. The same confusion presented itself when upshifting over 23 mph.

Benson Ford, second son of Edsel, died on July 28, 1978. He joined the Ford Motor Company in 1940 and was elected vice president and appointed director of the Lincoln-Mercury Division on January 30, 1948, a position he held until April 1955, when he was appointed group director of Mercury and Special Products Division.

25

The Continental in its first postwar guise. The new grille with the bold bars rivets attention to the face of the car. The lower grille adds even more weight to the very heavy bumper. Litheness has given way to aggression.

These figures represent a fair reflection of the public's acceptance or perhaps measurement of the postwar luxury cars. Cadillac had clearly established a command of the high-priced market, followed in order by Chrysler, Buick, Lincoln and Packard. The comparison is slightly flawed because the Chrysler was not yet targeting the top market apart from a long-wheelbase limousine bearing the Imperial name, and Buick traditionally sold slightly beneath Cadillac. These two cars would thus benefit from a slightly better depreciation curve, as would be the case with all lower-priced cars. By 1947, the price structures of the Cadillac 62, Lincoln and Packard Super were within two percent of each other while the Buick Roadmaster and Chrysler New Yorker sold at thirteen percent less.

One Lincoln seemed always above any sort of competitive pressure and that was the great Continental. Production began very slowly at the beginning of 1946 because the Continental had never been fully tooled and required an inordinate amount of handwork. Skilled workmen were in short supply. It was also apparent that the Continental made no money for the company and had to be viewed as a prestige loss-leader. Rising labor costs were particularly hard on the Continental.

In the turbulent 1946 market, Ford could sell anything that moved yet still lost money steadily through September 1946. Under these circumstances there was little pressure to build the Continental and without the urging of an Edsel Ford the whole project was something of an orphan. Thus, in 1946 only 265 coupes and 201 cabriolets were built, sharing the mechanical and styling changes of the Lincoln line. They were expensive, with the cabriolet at $4,472 and the coupe at $4,392, but the public lined up to buy them. No American production 'personal' car exceeded the Continental in price.

The 1946 Continental was an effective design because the boxy fenders harmonized well with the sharp lines of the original Continental body. The new grille added a much stronger impact to the fine-barred 1942 front style, a fact proven so effectively by the 1941 Cadillac grille which had replaced the fine-barred horizontal grille of the 1939 and 1940 Cadillacs. Altogether it was a unified and strong look, better than the standard Lincoln bodies because the added heaviness at the front was better balanced by the rear trunk and spare wheel treatment. No amount of facelifting could change the fact that the 1940 Zephyr body was never quite a successful mate with the 1942–48 box fenders.

The 138-inch-long-wheelbase Custom limousine was unlisted in 1946 and appears not to have been offered again in the postwar V-12H series. Yet some may have been built to special order, reputedly for White House service.

In 1946, automobiles of the various major corporations were vastly different technically and the Lincoln was a standout of novelty. The V-12 engine delivered its power with unmatched smoothness, offsetting in some measure the refinement of the Cadillac V-8 and the fine straight-eights from Packard and Chrysler. The Lincoln's flat torque curve also provided an answer to the Hydra-matic transmission, Lincoln's flexibility coming close to making it a high-gear car. The Chrysler FluidDrive was slow-shifting and costly in performance and fuel and, apart from clutchless driving, was awkward.

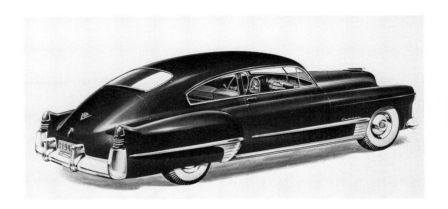

The new body of this 1948 Cadillac was a trend setter and bucked the slab-sided design of Kaiser-Frazer, Nash, Packard, Hudson and the new Lincoln. Within a year the verdict was in and the slab side was finished, but Lincoln was committed with the style through 1951.

Lincoln novelty persisted in the transverse springs although they were well behind industry standards in 1946. The transverse springs did have the virtue of stable front-end geometry not easily knocked out of adjustment by abuse. On the smooth roads where these big luxury cars were usually used, the Lincoln suspension was no handicap when measured by riding comfort. An argument could be made that the firm Lincoln suspension on winding roads at high speeds was superior to the conventional unequal parallel-arm independent front suspension.

The L-head engine reigned supreme in the luxury group for reasons of silence and the persistence of prewar designs. The Lincoln engine was as silent and efficient as its competitors though the heating problem remained with exhaust gasses passing through the block.

On fit and finish, the Lincoln remained a first-class job, equal or better than its competitors. Interior fabrics may well have been the best in the industry, a tradition for Lincoln from the thirties when cost analysis on the big K's meant little and the only policy was 'buy the finest.' Cradled in silent luxury, the Lincoln owner was still awed by that superb windshield with a tastefully designed instrument panel underneath, avoiding the note of garishness that was creeping into Chrysler interiors and the plastic look of the Packards. The 1946 Lincoln

Very few of these 1946 Lincoln convertible coupes were produced and they would seem now to be much rarer than the Continentals. This unit had a factory-delivered price of $2,883 but few would find their way into owners' hands for much under $3,500 with taxes, delivery and equipment.

was a distinctive car which conveyed to its owner the image of individual good taste and discrimination.

Lincoln production was remarkably good in 1946, considering the material shortages which plagued all the manufacturers and the difficulty in finding the skilled workers necessary to build a high-priced luxury car. Lincoln production compares favorably with the principal competition:

Lincoln (all)	16,645
Cadillac (all)	29,194
Packard Eight	14,901
Chrysler Eight	11,000 (approx.)

Prices for late 1946, f.o.b. base, without extras, were as follows:

Lincoln sedan	$2,337
Lincoln club coupe	2,318
Lincoln convertible	2,883
Lincoln Continental coupe	4,392
Lincoln Continental cabriolet	4,474

And for price comparisons:

Cadillac 62 sedan with Hydra-matic	$2,519
Packard Eight Super Clipper sedan	2,290
Packard Eight Custom Super	3,047
Chrysler New Yorker sedan	1,963

In the light of these production figures and prices, it will be observed that Lincoln market penetration in the top price category was second only to Cadillac and, since sales were hardly a problem in 1946, reflects production capacity more than public acceptance.

As 1947 opened, every U.S. manufacturer stood pat on existing designs except Studebaker. Demand continued heavy and production was unable to develop inventories for most dealers. Faced with insatiable demand, Lincoln changes were minor, including pull-out-type door handles, new hubcaps with 'Lincoln' in script, and a new color on the horn button.

By mid-1947 the first signs of the return to normal market conditions appeared as the weaker makes such as Hudson began to show both inventories and falling used-car values. It was natural that the high-priced cars would show the first weakness, and a comparison of West Coast retail used-car values as percentages of new car f.o.b. prices is instructive:

1947 Cadillac 62 sedan	189%
1947 Lincoln four-door	123%
1947 Lincoln Continental	114%
1947 Packard Super Clipper	104%
1947 Packard Custom Super	83%

Only the Packard Custom showed real dollar depreciation but both the Lincoln Continental and Packard Custom suffered from very high new-car prices, illustrated by the fact that used Cadillac 75 limousines in 1947 were nearly all selling below one hundred percent of their new price.

Production figures for 1947 show that Lincoln had regained its normal prewar pace:

Lincoln	21,460
Packard Eight	36,137
Cadillac (all)	61,926

In October 1947 the Lincoln-Mercury Division was reorganized and on January 30, 1948, Benson Ford was named general manager of the division and vice president of the Ford Motor Company. The 1948

Lincolns appeared on November 1, 1947, with virtually no changes.

Change was in the wind for 1948, however, and Cadillac led the way with an all-new car featuring the first rear fender fin and a slightly pinched waistline. The Packard slab-sided body was very clean but seemed heavy by comparison. Lincoln dealers were understandably restless at the sight of the new competition and, by spring of 1948, the Lincoln showrooms were full of cars to sell. Soon, however, the all-new Lincoln would appear, the earliest 1949 models presented in the industry and the first cars of the 'new' company reorganized by Henry Ford II.

In the very short production year for 1948, only 6,119 twelve-cylinder Lincolns were built. But Continental production was strong and 1,299 units were produced in five months of production from November 1947 to April 1948, a rate nearly double that of the 1947 model. It seems probable that as production of the twelve-cylinder Model H wound down, more chassis were diverted to the ever-popular Continental where production could be finished without disturbing the set-up for the all-new car. It was an appropriate finale to one of the most beautiful cars ever made.

CHAPTER 3

New Engine-New Image—1949-51

E.T. GREGORIE HAD returned in the spring of 1944 as chief designer to continue development of the new car line. His small and able staff began with Thomas L. Hibbard, who had led the design work during Gregorie's brief absence. Martin Regitko was the surface layout manager, a veteran from the Willoughby Company of Utica, New York, where he had been factory manager until 1938. It was Regitko who would 'measure' the clays and develop initial body drafts. Robert Doehler was another excellent studio layout man along with Joseph Farkas and artist Ross Cousins.

Following the closing of the Brunn plant in Buffalo, Hermann C. Brunn joined the styling department in October 1944 and in the summer of 1945 made a series of custom coachwork studies on the forthcoming new chassis. Brunn gradually moved into interior design and for many years was in charge of trim and color development until his retirement in 1970. Victor Lang, formerly the Brunn factory superintendent, joined Hermann Brunn at Ford.

Gregorie's team worked in relative isolation because of the death of Edsel, the weakening of Mr. Ford, and the departure of the old leadership caused in part by the Bennett attempt at administrative

takeover. Photographs and drawings that have been preserved from the styling department during the war years show Gregorie's fine handling of the round shapes so identified with Ford styling. In particular, the fastback idea had taken deep hold in Gregorie's mind. Ford had used this style since 1938 on sedans and had even offered a truncated, fastbacked sedan in 1937, but the short wheelbase never allowed the theme its optimum development. The success of the Pontiac Streamliner series, with the advertising theme of 'Torpedo' styling in 1940 and especially in 1941 and 1942, verified Gregorie's ideas and no doubt encouraged him in his wartime clays. The sad part is that the 1949 Lincoln designs were clearly in hand before the war was over and, given normal circumstances, the Cosmopolitan might well have appeared in 1945 or 1946. The Ford Motor Company, however, was in disarray and decision-making on new products was at a standstill. By the time the Cosmopolitan finally appeared, design fashion had moved on and the fastback style was passé.

The first critical appraisal of existing prototypes came from Breech as he viewed and drove the proposed 1948 Ford in April 1946. The car was large in the 'full' Gregorie style and Breech asked young Ford its

E. T. Gregorie planned this body as the first new postwar Ford. Ernest Breech thought it too big and moved it up to become the 1949 Mercury and Lincoln as shown. As the Lincoln it was mounted on the 121-inch wheelbase and weighed over 4,000 pounds. With 152 hp, it was a fast car and Johnny Mantz drove one to tenth place in the first Carrera Panamericana. The 1949 Mercury weighed 3,430 pounds and the Ford 3,033. Breech was right!

weight. Ford thought it was a bit heavy and conversation with the engineers brought veiled answers. Breech said simply, "That's a big car."

On July 17, Breech reported to the Policy Committee and joined engineer Harold T. Youngren in the opinion that the proposed Ford weights were too high. General Motors was concerned with keeping weight down and Ford ought to do the same. Youngren, formerly an engineer with Oldsmobile and chief engineer of Borg-Warner, held opinions not to be lightly disregarded. There were certainly some present on the Policy Committee who could remember old Mr. Ford's constant fight against weight. Then a fateful decision took place: Youngren suggested that the company should not "place all our hopes on Mr. Gregorie" and that an outside consultant should be called in.

That outside consultant was George W. Walker, an industrial designer who had worked for many firms including the Nash Motor Company.

Dissatisfaction with the existing Ford prototype crystalized and, on August 23, Crusoe proposed to the Policy Committee that the Gregorie Ford become the new Mercury and the Mercury, in turn, become the new Lincoln. On September 3 this proposal was passed. The absence now of a new Ford was crucial and Breech ordered a crash program. Youngren set the dimensions of the new Ford and both Gregorie and

A design dated November 27, 1941, which already hints at the front fender line of the small 1949 Lincoln and Mercury, though the oval indentation above the grille suggests that this was a Ford (left). The window treatment is very GM while the grille anticipates the 1946 Oldsmobile. Gregorie's low grille-bulge, about to be seen publicly on the 1942 Lincoln, is clearly present. A Mercury clay (right) of November 19, 1941, with an unusually heavy bumper and a mesh grille. The fully covered headlamp was used by DeSoto in 1942. Heavy brow over the front wheel arch would be used on the 1949 Cosmopolitan. There are even hints of an Edsel in that strong center prow.

Walker proceeded with competitive clays which were finished on November 22. On December 11 the Products Committee, in a blind test, approved Walker's model which was to be the revolutionary 1949 Ford. Four days later Gregorie resigned again.

With Gregorie's departure there was a general reorganization and Breech brought in further new personnel. In 1947 John Oswald was hired, soon to be chief body engineer. Charles Waterhouse was added to the design section. Earle S. MacPherson was put in charge of engineering and research and soon became the vice president and chief engineer of the Lincoln-Mercury Division. William M. Schmidt, a Ford employee since 1940, was assigned responsibility for styling at Lincoln-Mercury's newly-created separate design section.

With these changes the Lincoln development team was somewhat clarified and work went forward on the 1949 cars. The new 1949 Mercury (ex-Ford) was proposed for a 118-inch wheelbase while the Lincoln was set for a 121-inch wheelbase. It did not take long for agreement to be reached on using the same body shell for both cars with different sheet metal from the cowl forward.

The original Gregorie Lincoln, with long fastback lines, became the Cosmopolitan town sedan on a 125-inch wheelbase. The unique shell was the final statement of the Gregorie philosophy and beautifully clean in the rounded idiom. Chrome moldings over the front wheel arches, the absence of any sculpturing on the front fender and the long, smooth slab sides set the car apart from the smaller Lincoln. A splendid styling touch was the stainless-steel window trimmings, reminiscent of the 1939 Mercury club coupe. A one-piece curved windshield was fitted to the Cosmopolitan, unlike the conventional flat split windshield of the smaller Lincoln.

Gregorie was aiming for an exceptionally smooth design in the large Lincoln series and hidden headlamps were scheduled, an idea used on the 1936-37 Cords and briefly by DeSoto in 1942. The mechanical reliability of the lamp doors was never satisfactory so a chrome tunnel was prepared to hide the space from the lamp to the fender surface. Lincoln fanciers found this solution highly individualistic and pleasing, while critics saw a passing resemblance to a pair of deep-set eyes which would soon be linked to the image of a whale. The taillights were placed in a similar attractive chrome surround, the theme more successful at the rear because the lenses were not so deeply set.

The fastback town sedan was paired with a notchback sport sedan, altogether more conventional in appearance. The public seemed to prefer the notchback styling and the town sedan was dropped after one season. A club coupe completed the body lineup along with a convertible which, at 4,419 pounds, was the heaviest Lincoln offered.

An early wartime clay dated April 20, 1942, in which a fabric-covered hardtop coupe demonstrated Gregorie's fascination with the fastback style. The window frames accentuate the convertible effect and recall the highly successful 1939-40 Mercury club coupe. The front fender again shows the thinking which led to the 1949 Mercury and small Lincoln design.

A much refined clay dated January 3, 1943, clearly pointing to the 1949 Lincoln. The frowning grille is taking shape and the front fenders are close to production. This greenhouse shows marked similarity to the rare 1949 Cosmopolitan two-door sedan.

The notched-back Cosmopolitan dated June 26, 1945, still with a grille like the 1949 Mercury. The chevron-like trim on the fender pods would be used in 1951 and the rear fender pod would be introduced on the 1950 Cosmopolitan Capri. The bar in the middle of the front window would go.

The small Lincoln, with the shared Mercury shell, was much more conventional and weighed about 250 pounds less than the Cosmopolitan. The slightly longer and heavier-appearing front end of the Lincoln added nice balance to a rather compact body design. Three body styles were offered, the notchback sedan, club coupe and convertible coupe. A fastback small Lincoln was designed but the rather modest reception of the Cosmopolitan town sedan and the inevitable esthetic problems of this style on a short wheelbase soon put an end to the idea.

Gregorie's massive front grille for the 1949 Lincoln reflected his clays of the early forties. The grille outline tapered downwards from the center point to the sides, a daring idea which was well worked out and

dramatic in its power. Numerous makes used the basic theme of this grille outline, often with vertical bar relief as in the Buick or big bold bars as in the 1948 Oldsmobile, but none with the consistency and drama of the Lincoln. Gregorie was committed to curves, and what no one seemed to notice was that one effect of the Lincoln design was to present a 'sad' or a 'frowning' frontal appearance. It was the first thing that William Schmidt restyled for the 1950 car, moving immediately to horizontal lines—not a smile but certainly no frown.

A nice styling touch was the continued use of the knight's head logo, first applied in 1942 to the front of the hood, then in 1946 and 1948 at the top of the grille and again in 1949 above the grille. The big bowl hubcaps of 1949, very dramatic and well suited to Gregorie's design, sported a center crest.

The Lincoln Cosmopolitan was not the only 1949 car that had whale-like characteristics. This Golden Anniversary Packard shows how **slab** sides could ruin the original graceful Clipper design. The model is wisely posed in the middle of the car to break up the unrelieved flat sheet metal.

An early assignment for Hermann C. Brunn at Ford was to work out possible custom coachwork for the new Lincoln line to appear in mid-1948. There was concern that the Continental would be dropped at the end of the 12-cylinder Model H production, and the Custom series was initially given the term 'Continental.' In truth, the designs had no real relationship to the Continental shapes of 1946-48 and were skillful expressions of pre-war Brunn coachwork design. These drawings were made in July and early August of 1945.

The Lincoln interiors were rich and beautifully crafted, a tradition long established in the marque. Foam rubber was laid over the coil springs and hydraulic front-seat adjustment was offered. Hydraulic window lifts were also available but these hydraulic systems were prone to oil leaks and occasional mechanical failures.

The instrument panel was no more gaudy than the rest of the industry's offerings for 1949 although the long row of golden-faced control buttons resembled the stop-pulls of a church organ and required concentration in their use. The quality effect was everywhere, not only in these controls, which were neatly made, but in the instruments themselves. However, early assembly problems were somewhat concentrated in the complicated new instrument panel which had both electrical and mechanical faults.

The heavy windlacing at the door edges, rubber molding work and quality carpeting spoke volumes for the good intentions of the stylists and engineers. In practice, however, as is the case with any new car, the 1949 Lincoln received numerous changes in the early months of

The famous frowning grille of the 1949 Cosmopolitan, so named by H. H. Gilbert, chief engineer. It was the first thing removed by Schmidt and Hibbard when they restyled the 1950 car. The recessed headlamps were altogether novel, a last-minute effort which replaced little doors covering the concealed lamps. The door-opening mechanisms proved unreliable and had to be abandoned. The big 1949 Cosmopolitan club coupe convertible (right)—at 4,505 pounds, the heaviest Lincoln in standard production. On a 125-inch wheelbase, this car was 220 inches long, a length accentuated in the convertible body style. It may have been Gregorie's finest design.

production designed to correct the problems that appeared. Among the twenty-nine improvements in the body, eleven were directed against rattles and noise through the use of felts, rubber bumpers, grommets and asphalt deadeners. A more ominous correction was an improved mounting plate to prevent the hydraulic window regulator switch from falling out. Window winding mechanisms were improved to prevent glass breakage. Water leaks at the windshield and backlight were stopped with additional screws to increase pressure on the seals. The outer lip of the door scuff-plate was eliminated to prevent binding. There were several little touches to improve appearance with new moldings, linings and the moving of the rainshield from the roof rail to the window frame.

The chassis layout was entirely new and was a complete abandonment of the Ford transverse spring system. A new K-type frame with Hotchkiss drive and independent front suspension matched contemporary U.S. practice and brought Lincoln ride and handling up to par with competition. Again, the engineers were sensitive to early problems and the frame was beefed-up at critical joints and brackets, plus there was a change in side-rail gauge from .104 to .119 inch to increase general stiffness. The early suspension was too soft and bigger shock absorbers and new rubber bumpers were fitted to reduce front bottoming.

Brakes were of the duo-servo type and, with only 204 square inches of lining area, depended heavily on the 'self-energizing' effect. The brake linings were modified very early in production to counter sudden action, a common problem in U.S. braking for the period.

Another long tradition of three-quarter floating axles in Ford products was broken by the use of a semi-floating axle in which the rear wheels were bolted directly to the flanged axle-shaft ends. Little trouble seemed to result despite what might be seen as a retrogressive design, though the elimination of hubs may have helped reduce unsprung weight. The abandonment of the torque tube also helped to lower unsprung weight and improve the ride. The standard differential ratio in the Cosmopolitan was 4.27:1 and, since all were fitted with overdrive, a final cruising ratio of 3.07:1 resulted.

The engineers were well aware of the problems with the Lincoln V-12 even before the war and work on a big new V-8 had started in 1941. All development stopped with the onset of the war but a curious aluminum V-8 surfaced briefly in December 1943, with overhead cams driven by worm gears. Al Esper, manager of Ford's Dearborn proving grounds, tested this engine on the road but it was disappointing in so many respects that it was destroyed in January 1944.

In 1945, work was resumed on the big V-8 under the direction of C. C. Johnson. The dimensions of the basic Ford block were expanded to produce an engine with a bore and stroke of 3½ by 4 3/8 inches,

This 1949 Cadillac, the first of the de Ville coupes, appeared in July 1949. The pronounced rear fender line and the taillight fin had caught on, making Lincoln's slab siding awkward and outdated. Lincoln dealers had 18 months with their 1949 model—after introduction of the Cadillac with a new OHV engine—and an uphill fight.

President Truman seems to be enjoying himself in the Cosmopolitan convertible coupe, a 1949 model. The bubble-top was not yet ready on this January inaugural day of 1949.

giving a displacement of 337 cubic inches. The new block was heavy and tough, without novelty but exploiting all the best of Ford successes in V-8 design. With 7.1:1 compression the engine produced 152 bhp at 3600 rpm and 265 pounds-feet of torque at 1800 rpm. The old V-12 gave about 225 pounds of torque at the same rpm.

The engine was introduced in January 1948 in the F-7 and F-8 truck lines and used a slightly lower compression ratio of 6.4:1. For truck use, the big V-8 was long overdue and marked the beginning of new Ford success in the commercial field.

This new V-8 engine was the obvious answer for the replacement of the V-12 and announcement was made on February 24, 1948. The interchangeability of the 337-cubic-inch block between the Lincoln and Ford trucks simplified service and hastened development. The new engine promised to be beautifully smooth and quiet. Some early harshness was improved by a redesign of the motor mounts while the engine itself was steadily improved through twenty-one minor production changes aimed at correcting camshaft scuffing, poor idling, noisy air cleaner, exhaust valve corrosion and sticking, cylinder head cracking, and a buzzing noise in the oil filter line.

This fine new engine was mated to an entirely conventional transmission with a 1.518:1 second gear and a 2.526:1 low. Lincoln engineers were simply unable to come up with any automatic in the face of pressing time problems and Youngren sent to his old firm of Borg-Warner, quite naturally, for some answers. Two years later Borg-Warner units began to appear in the Ford lineup but these units were too small to cope with the 337-cubic-inch engine. The lack of an automatic transmission for the new Lincoln was a serious problem when it is realized that ninety-seven percent of the 1948 Cadillacs were fitted with the Hydra-matic unit. It was to General Motors that Youngren finally had to turn and the Hydra-matic was offered on the Lincoln after June 26, 1949.

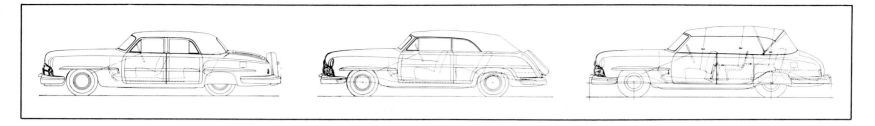

Robert Doehler drew this Sportsman sedan (left) on a 128-inch wheelbase combining elements of the Cosmopolitan, the Continental roofline and wood siding—a Lincoln equivalent to the Chrysler Town and Country. Once the 1949 Lincoln design was frozen, the imagination of the artists was given a fresh base from which to depart. On June 10, 1947, John Cheek submitted this convertible station wagon (middle), a mixture of the 1949 Mercury station wagon and the current production Mercury Sportsman convertible. Martin Regitko headed a project team which produced this parade phaeton on a 125-inch wheelbase (right). This May 1948 drawing by Mr. Allward has distinct commercial possibilities and is not unlike the parade cars Lincoln supplied to the White House.

The new Lincoln was introduced on April 22, 1948, the first of the 1949-model cars. Dealers were understandably delighted because the new Lincoln was the first Ford product in over a decade that could be compared directly against the competition in favorable terms. No longer did dealers have to defend transverse springing and a twelve-cylinder engine with a reputation for heavy oil consumption and wear. Lincoln dealers still had some of the V-12's on their showroom floors in early 1948, the 1940 body shell harder to sell than ever. Now they had a brand-new car with dramatic styling and the dealers believed they were genuinely ahead of the competition for the first time since 1936. It was a happy moment for the Lincoln organization and an early victory for the new management team.

Sales started well, as befits any really new model, especially one introduced so early in the season. Production picked up quickly with the Los Angeles plant beginning on May 6; the Metuchen, New Jersey, plant on June 14; and St. Louis on September 21. Engineering was quick to correct early production problems and quality control increased rapidly. Total production for 1948 was 43,668, only a fraction of which were the last of the old Model H V-12's.

The competition was mixed in mid-1948. Buick and Chrysler continued to market the 1946 car with little change. The twenty-second series Packard introduced in September 1947 was selling well, but the slab-side restyling of the original Clipper body was not successful and, though sales were strong, trouble was in the wind.

It was the new Cadillac body for 1948 that was changing the public's taste. When applied to the Oldsmobile Futuramic 98 the new GM shell was well balanced, but when used on the Cadillac with the rear fender fin it was clearly an innovation of dramatic importance. Cadillac mechanics were long-proven and virtually trouble-free, the old flathead engine and Hydra-matic a hard match to beat.

The 1949 Lincoln's début was in the middle of one of Cadillac's most successful years, three months after the new fins appeared. The contrast between the two cars could not have been more dramatic. Whereas the Cosmopolitan had gone to the slab side in what seemed an industry trend, the new Cadillac body, handled so ably by Harley Earl and Julio Andrade, had retained a rear fender outline which accentuated a litheness of line, even on the big 60 Special. Suddenly the 1948 Hudson, the Kaiser-Frazer, the Packard and the 1949 Nash, along with the Cosmopolitan—all with vast, unbroken expanses of side sheet metal—seemed awkward. Of the slab-sided group, the Lincoln, by virtue of its sheer size, was most noticeable in comparison and white Cosmopolitan fastback town sedans were early referred to as 'Moby Dicks,' especially with the inset headlamps. The smaller Lincolns escaped these criticisms because of the rudimentary front fender sculpturing that Gregorie had developed so skillfully.

Though sales started off well, the early introduction made the Lincolns especially vulnerable as the other 1949 models appeared in the fall of 1948. For the six months prior, Lincoln dealers had been selling a '1949' model against 1948 competition. Now, all too suddenly, the tables were turned and it was the competition's turn to take advantage of Lincoln's stand-pat position. For another whole year the Lincoln dealers would continue to offer their 'new' car. By early 1949 the dealers were beginning to grumble and new-car sales fell off badly.

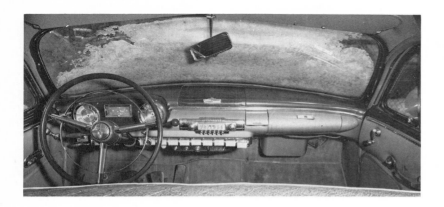

The 1949 Cosmopolitan instrument panel, in the best juke-box style of the time. The quality was high but the row of rectangular buttons was confusing. The 1950 panel was redesigned "to prevent operating the wrong control accidentally," according to H. H. Gilbert, chief engineer.

The 1950 Lincoln instrument panel was much simplified. Legibility was improved with new contrast between figures and background. Controls most frequently used are lettered on the panel above and illuminated at night.

Registrations for 1949 totaled 37,691, a rate far lower than the second half of 1948.

Dealer frustration rose to a boiling point by mid-1949. Zone by zone, the dealers got together and went to Dearborn to vent their discouragement and anger. Little could be done to help them. The commitment to body dies could not be less than three years and the only prospect for improvement was the announcement of the 1950 models, made rather late on January 27, which had meant a single-model run of some twenty-one months.

The 1950 was a much-improved car, not only by virtue of production experience but because of careful attention to many subtle problems. Schmidt, with Tom Hibbard, attacked the most obvious styling questions, beginning with a new grille which was at once simpler, cleaner and horizontal. H. H. Gilbert, chief engineer, noted that the front bumper was "rotated upward to eliminate the frown effect."

The instrument panel was completely redesigned, not only to enhance beauty but to provide easier reading of instruments, day or night. Controls were rearranged "to prevent operating the wrong control accidentally," a tacit admission by Gilbert of the basic problem of the

1949 layout. Lettering above the most-used controls received illumination for night use.

The door locks, not a strong point on the 1949 cars, were completely redesigned. Courtesy lamps now operated from right or left front doors. Fiberglass was added to the firewall insulation to reduce heat flow into the passenger compartment. The center door pillar was now upholstered instead of being a metal strip. Plastic lenses appeared in the various auxiliary outside lamps to improve optics and reduce breakage. The radio control system was improved. The steering column was isolated by rubber from the instrument panel to eliminate squeaks and rattles. The basic weakness in the stickshift collar for 1949 was eliminated by the conversion to Hydra-matic controls. The Lincoln heater was completely redesigned for 1950 with new controls, relocation of ducts, equalization of discharge temperatures on both sides of the passenger compartment, and better blowers.

Of more concern to Lincoln stylists was the emergence of a new body style, the hardtop convertible, introduced by General Motors in 1949 and followed by Chrysler Corporation in 1950. Lincoln elected not to mount a fixed top on the convertible body but instead offered two specially trimmed coupes introduced on July 5, 1950, the Lincoln Lido and the Cosmopolitan Capri. Both cars offered padded tops and a choice of vivid interiors. The Capri coupe had the bright fender spear over both front and rear wheel arches, a design idea which was picked up by Mercedes for the 1954 300 SL.

On the mechanical side, the 1950 Lincoln offered a new handbrake lever of fifty percent greater efficiency. The choke was redesigned to

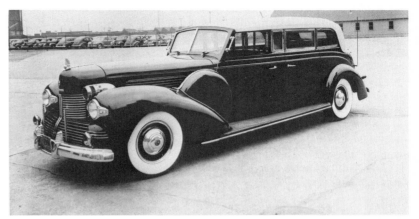

The famous 1950 bubble-top presidential parade car. Nine other Cosmopolitan limousines were delivered to the White House. The No. 1 limousine was on the same 145-inch wheelbase as the parade car. It worked from 1950 until 1961 and weighed 4,662 pounds—about one half of the old Sunshine Special.

The mammoth 1939 Lincoln Model K Sunshine Special with the well-integrated 1942 grille. The 9,300-pound weight was caused by considerable armor plating.

coordinate with the characteristics of the Hydra-matic transmission, plagued initially by excessive creep while warming up. A new dipstick made oil checking easier. The oil filter was removed from the mounting on the head because it had effected torque of the head bolts. The speed of the fan was reduced sixteen percent to lower noise. Of fundamental importance was the introduction of improved balancing for the engine in mid-year, finally clearing up persistent vibration problems.

The 1949 Lincoln V-8 engine produced 152 bhp, and when mounted in the small-bodied Lincoln was capable of new high speeds. Tom McCahill reported that the Lincoln and the Cosmopolitan were both able to top 100 mph using the overdrive. The announcement of a new Mexican road race for the spring of 1950, a 2,178-mile road event from Juarez to El Ocotal, whetted the imagination of a host of entrants, fifteen of whom chose Lincolns. Among them was Bob Estes in Los Angeles, who believed that the new Lincoln had possibilities as a road car, and he engaged Johnny Mantz as his driver. Most of the Lincoln entries were by Mexican drivers, the best of which finished fourteenth out of fifty-three. Mantz managed to finish eleventh, brought down by disastrous tire troubles in the last leg of the race over unpaved roads. The heavy Lincoln was a punisher of tires. Yet, on the paved sections earlier, Mantz showed clearly that the Lincoln, at least under his driving, was the fastest car of the race and he enjoyed an 11½-minute lead upon arrival at Mexico City. His average speed of 91 mph held at

bay the brilliant Hershel McGriff in what turned out to be the winning Oldsmobile. Mantz, in this section, beat a pair of Alfas, one driven by Taruffi, and a Delahaye and numerous Cadillacs. Mantz was delayed for an hour and thirteen minutes by a brake lock-up, but managed to regain the lead. He finished on three well-worn tires and one bare wheel worn down to the brake drum. The speed and stamina of the first-generation V-8 Lincolns is entirely in the tradition of the early Ford cars—rugged, uncompromising engine integrity with a chassis equally tough. The remarkable fact of this early performance was that the flathead Lincoln, virtually undeveloped, was able to beat a variety of modern OHV engines and OHC European engines on flat-out speed. It was a good omen for triumphs yet to come.

Few potential Lincoln buyers noticed the results of the first Mexican road race in the summer of 1950. The Lincoln had as yet no image of speed and road handling. What was more important to many was price. Here the Lincoln was well placed amid the competition. Four-door

The 1950 Cosmopolitan sport sedan, model 74. The redesigned grille fitted nicely into Gregorie's body design. Factory base price was $3,248, fourteen dollars more than the Cadillac 62 sedan. Production totaled 8,341 of this body type.

The fine, big 336.7-cubic-inch 1EL V-8 engine as fitted to the 1951 Lincoln. With a 3.5-inch bore and a 4.375 stroke the unit produced 154 bhp at 3600 rpm. Maximum torque was 275 pounds-feet at 1800 rpm. The compression was 7:1. Oil pressure when new was 50 psi at 40 mph and the sump held 6½ quarts. The Holley 885-FFC carburetor was fitted, a dual downdraft model with automatic choke. Exhaust gases still passed through the block following normal Ford practice and a 34½-quart cooling system was necessary. A solid, tough engine, though without novelty.

sedans of various makes are listed here with advertised delivered prices for 1950:

Lincoln	$2,574
Buick Roadmaster	2,633
Packard Super Eight	2,633
Chrysler New Yorker	2,758
Cadillac 61	2,866
Cadillac 62	3,234
Cosmopolitan	3,248
Cadillac 60 Special	3,797

It can be seen that the Cosmopolitan was selling directly against the Cadillac 62 but once again the competition was stiff because Cadillac had appeared with another new body after only two years. The new shell was marked by a return to squared window lines surrounded by heavy stainless-steel moldings, a Cosmopolitan theme, though Cadillac salesmen would prefer to recall the very early 60 Specials of 1938. The other luxury makes were little changed, and thus Cadillac was able to score a major restyling at the expense of the competition. The 1950 registrations compared to 1949 tell the story:

	1949	1950
Cadillac (all)	80,880	101,825
Packard (all)	97,771	73,155
Lincoln	37,691	34,318

Lincoln sales were relatively steady from 1948 to 1950 but Cadillac's exploding volume forced Lincoln's percentage of sales, when compared to Cadillac, down from fifty-four percent in 1948 to thirty-three percent in 1950. Packard's volume derived from the low-priced lines; the more expensive Super series constituted but fifteen percent of production and offered only modest competition for the Lincoln.

The interior of the No. 1 White House Cosmopolitan limousine (left) had gold-plated fixtures, lizard-skin-fitted cases in the armrests, two thermos bottles, a writing portfolio, tobacco humidor and a radio control panel. One of the nine White House Cosmopolitan limousines delivered in 1950 (right). These cars were well equipped, including bulletproof glass, running boards for Secret Service personnel, vanity cases, writing desks, communications systems and gold-plated fittings.

Though Lincoln did not lead the sales race for luxury cars in 1950, in one area it held a conspicuous and lasting success. In March 1950, ten new Cosmopolitans were put into service at the White House, continuing a tradition that had begun with the famous Sunshine Special, a V-12 convertible sedan ordered in 1939. Lincolns had not always been in White House service. Pierce-Arrows were in use in the 1920's and Herbert Hoover was seen in a Cadillac V-16 in 1930. The Sunshine Special was a tremendous parade car on a 160-inch wheelbase covered with armored plate and fitted with one-inch bulletproof glass. The usual parade equipment was fitted including sirens, flashing red lamps, step plates and outside grab-handles for Secret Service men, a gun compartment, two-way radio and flagstaff sockets. The car weighed 9,300 pounds.

The Brunn Company updated the front of the car in 1942 with a pleasing amalgam of the current grille against the 1939 K body. The car worked steadily during the war and President Roosevelt used it at Yalta,

Malta, Teheran and Casablanca. In 1946 the car traveled to South America with Admiral William Leahy. So formidable was this great Sunshine Special that it remained in service until 1950.

The 1950 Cosmopolitan fleet was composed of nine limousines and a new parade car built by the Henney Company in Illinois on a 145-inch wheelbase and weighing 6,450 pounds. All of the Lincoln fleet were equipped with bulletproof glass, vanity cases, writing desks, communications systems and gold-plated fittings. In 1954, President Eisenhower had the parade car returned to Dearborn for a clear plastic bubble-top. He had noted that in inclement weather, with the regular canvas top up, the waiting parade crowds could not see the President at

The final statement of Gregorie's small Lincoln in 1951, the 74 sport sedan. Extending the rear fender did not help the basic design and served only to emphasize the small greenhouse. The body stripe integrated nicely into the rear fender crease. Lincoln lovers missed that rear wheel skirt which helped the small car's popularity when it was introduced in 1949.

Comparing the 1949 Cosmopolitan instrument panel will reveal how advanced this 1951 panel really was. Instrument legibility is vastly improved. Controls are easy to find and use, and the sense of space in the whole front seat area is much more obvious. A good design which pointed ahead to new functional interiors of 1952-54.

all. The bubble-top parade car continued in service until March 1961 after more than 100,000 miles of use. It was brought out again in the summer of 1963 for President Kennedy's European tour. Thus the Lincoln association with the White House was firmly cemented by the Cosmopolitan order.

The final rework of Gregorie's 1949 body took place for the 1951 cars, introduced on November 15, 1950. Faced with yet another year of the same body shell and with the corporate energy now focused on the 1952 models, the facelift for 1951 was expectedly minor. The rear fender had become a new focus for the stylists—thanks to Cadillac's fins—and Schmidt, Hibbard and company lengthened the rear fenders, which, on the small Lincoln, destroyed whatever unity Gregorie had originally planned. The tail lamps were new and fresh, perhaps the best

idea at the rear of the car. The Cosmopolitan suffered less from rear fender elongation because the fenders did not protrude so far and they added strength to the rear quarter view. The front grille was simplified a bit more, further accentuating the new rear fender line.

By 1951 the mechanical problems had been thoroughly sorted out and the Lincoln was a model of smooth and refined luxury transportation. The engine was up to 154 bhp and torque was 275 pounds-feet. The rear-end ratio had dropped to 3.31:1 with overdrive producing an astonishingly low final ratio of 2.38:1. It was this combination that Les Viland used in making his remarkable 25.448 mpg record in the Mobilgas Economy Run on March 8, winning the Grand Sweepstakes Prize.

Griff Borgeson did a road test of the 1951 Lincoln for *Motor Trend* and was able to duplicate Viland's mileage at a steady 45 mph. Top speed was 100.67 mph with a four-run average of 97.08 mph, while 0-60 mph was 15.8 seconds. Borgeson found the 3.31:1 ratio perfectly adequate for good performance and economy. Steering was slow with 5½ turns lock-to-lock. The 8.00x15 tires shrieked in agony when pressed by the soft front suspension. The hydraulic tappets and the forged crank with "excellent crankcase ventilation" were outstanding features. These were fitting tributes to the last year of the flathead engine.

The 1951 Lincoln was the first Ford Motor Company postwar car to receive the full treatment from the marketing specialists. Accessories were grouped under headings such as 'utility,' which included a tank lid lock, vanity mirror, license plate frame, exhaust pipe extension deflector and a utility extension light that plugged into the cigar lighter.

Cosmopolitan for 1951, with the grille further simplified and stronger. The body molding is borrowed from the smaller Lincolns and replaced the pod over the front wheel arch. The big round hubcaps have given way to a more modest sculptured design. Many think that the 1951 Cosmopolitan was the best looking of the series because the trim and grille were more integrated.

In the 'safety' group one received an outside rear-view mirror, backup lights in the trunk lid, button-operated windshield washers and a flashing parking brake signal light.

Available also were curb buffers, chrome rear-door guard, seat covers, exterior visor on the Lincoln only, seeing-eye sportlight, road lamps, tripod jack, engine compartment light, under-coating and porcelainizing. Accessories which have been rediscovered recently but were offered long ago in 1951 by Lincoln included a rear window wiper and a vanity mirror light.

The Lincoln radio offered four tone ranges: normal, bass, hi-fidelity and lo-noise. The antenna could be vacuum-powered and a rear speaker was available.

Despite the highest quality interiors, a mechanical refinement better than any previous Lincoln, performance worthy of winning a road race, and a new sales slogan 'There's nothing quite like a Lincoln,' the public stayed away. Registrations fell to 25,816, little more than one quarter of Cadillac's 97,093. The Korean War hurt production for all manufacturers—it was a mediocre year.

On the used car market 1949-51 Lincolns did not age gracefully. At the close of 1955 the retail price for a 1949 Lincoln in the *Kelley Kar Blue Book* was $380. Cadillacs of the same year were selling for twice as much and a 1949 de Ville could still command $1,000. Public esteem for Packard in 1955, however, had vanished, perhaps in anticipation of the early demise of the once mighty firm; used Packards retailed around $250.

Junking came too early for the 1949-51 Lincolns. Their good performance was overshadowed by the 1952-54 Lincolns. The Gregorie style dated rapidly and all the quality in the body could not help. The great 'Moby Dicks' looked increasingly like beached whales and they were hauled off to the furnaces, the molten residue soon to be transformed into the steel of another generation of cars. The nobility and grandeur of the last of the big flathead Lincolns would never again be duplicated.

CHAPTER 4

Lincoln Becomes A Champion—1952-54

HAROLD T. YOUNGREN HAD completed his basic engineering reorganization in 1947 and at once began building a new engineering center near Greenfield Village which would cost $50 million. Personnel were added quickly and whereas in 1939 the engineering staff totaled 800, by the end of 1947 there were 2,600 on the job. No longer would Ford products emerge from a relative handful of talented and brilliant men whose output could only be matched by their versatility. The new team, headed by Chief Engineer Earle S. MacPherson, was equally brilliant but proper organization allowed new concentration on design development. Furthermore, the sometimes whimsical leadership of old Mr. Ford no longer acted as a brake upon novelty.

MacPherson soon built a splendid research program which was set to work on the 1952 Lincoln. As an expert on suspensions, he saw to it that the new car was properly underpinned and it was hardly an accident that the first truly postwar Lincoln design was a technical masterpiece which would quickly establish itself as the finest road car of the time.

The importance of the development of the new Lincoln line was emphasized by the assignment of Benson Ford on January 30, 1948, as vice president in charge of the Lincoln-Mercury Division. The introduction of the 1949 models only four months later added excitement and new hope for the division. But as the strong early sales momentum faded in late 1949 and the more somber competitive picture began to be revealed, a new urgency in the development of the 1952 car became apparent.

George Walker's great success with the 1949 Ford made him the logical man to plan the next major body line. The Ford family of cars was to have new unity in 1952 and Walker came up with the general theme. His ideas were clean and simple, angularity now replacing the Gregorie curves. At the Lincoln-Mercury studios, stylists William Schmidt and Don DeLaRossa developed the senior cars with emphasis on a new grille which was in truth a massive mid-height bumper. This bumper-cum-grille made the 1952 car much more lithe and replaced the rather scow-like appearance of the 1951. The Lincoln grille would be widely copied, the 1955 Pontiac being a particularly obvious example.

The hood was very low, little above the front fender line, and the headlamps were moved to a forward and high position, peaking the fender crowns. The car was aggressive and seemed to lean forward, eager to move. The vestigial rear fender was set off at the forward edge

Chuck Stevenson (left) and Clay Smith were the winners of the big-stock class in the 1952 Carrera Panamericana. Their average speed was 90.982 mph for 1,934 miles.

There were Lincolns at the very beginning of the Carrera Panamericana in 1950. Jesús Nava Gonzales drove this 1949 model with spirit and manages to become airborne; he finished 14th.

The basic sedan body of the 1952 Lincoln was compact and sharply edged. The high placement of the headlights and the forward-leaning trim stripe delineating the rear fender gave the car an aggressive look.

by a slash-strip which angled forward and added to the lithe feel of the new car. Minor touches showed brilliant engineering, such as new molded taillight lenses that had horizontal parallel flutes which were self-cleaning in wet weather. This idea would be rediscovered by Mercedes many years later with much fanfare.

The 123-inch wheelbase of the new Lincoln fell squarely between the Cosmopolitan's 125 inches and the small Lincoln's 121 inches. The overall length of 214.1 inches was one-half inch shorter than the small 1951 Lincoln. It was a new and much more compact car and though the angularity was helpful to interior dimensions, the cavernous interior size of the Cosmopolitan was gone. Glass area was up thirty-three percent and the high fender crowns made for superb driver visibility of the car's edges.

The Lincoln's fine new styling was matched by MacPherson's engineering. The key chassis change was the ball-joint front suspension, the first in America. Two sturdy, fully rotating sockets replaced the kingpin and various bushings, the simplicity of the new system making possible a reduction of grease fittings from sixteen to four and eliminating much unsprung weight. Walt Woron, writing for *Motor Trend*, was enchanted: "Without a doubt, the most outstanding characteristic of the Lincoln is its handling ability. It doesn't heel excessively on sharp, high-speed turns, and it doesn't feel like you're guiding a couple of sponges around a turn." MacPherson, using his

Lincoln's 1952 ball-joint front suspension (left), a brilliant simplification of the standard ifs, was one reason for the superb roadability of these cars. The 1952 instrument panel (right) with black-on-white legibility, positive heater controls and good separation of other switches making a very functional layout.

substantial suspension expertise, so improved the tautness of the chassis, both front and rear, that Woron could not refrain from commenting on the positive traction of the inside wheel on turns. Furthermore, the car no longer bottomed out when challenged by severe road bumps.

Matching MacPherson's new chassis was Lincoln's first OHV engine with very oversquare dimensions of 3.8 by 3.5 inches bore and stroke. Displacement was down to 318 from 337 cubic inches in the old flathead V-8. Horsepower moved up to 160, a good initial output though the horsepower race was now on and Buick, Chrysler and Cadillac had moved up to 170, 180 and 190 respectively. The engine had a wedge combustion chamber, avoiding the complexity and cost of Chrysler's fine hemi-head unit. Lincoln torque was 284 pounds-feet.

The Lincoln engine was very compact, nearly one hundred pounds lighter than the Cadillac unit, and of good thermal efficiency. The radiator volume fell from 34.5 to twenty-four quarts for 1952. The wedge head was of clean design and it was apparent that development had just begun. In fact, more than one observer noted that the horsepower of the engine was modest. Tom McCahill put it pungently to Lincoln: " . . . you made the pants too small."

The Dual-Range Hydra-matic was fitted to Lincoln as standard with a 3.15:1 axle ratio, though 3.07:1 remained as the stickshift standard ratio. The extreme overdrive ratio which Les Viland had used to such good effect in the Mobilgas Economy Run was gone. Woron was able to report 16.5 miles per gallon at 60 mph, about average for similar American cars of the period.

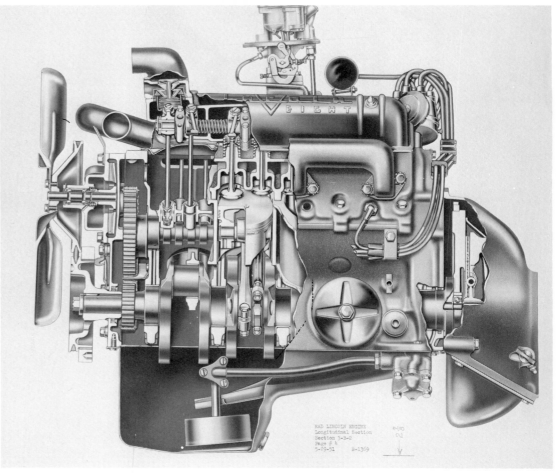

The 1952 Lincoln engine was one of the finest powerplants of the fifties. In this form it delivered 160 bhp. Even when horsepower moved up to 205 in 1953 it was perfectly reliable at maximum speeds in the Mexican road races. Small carburetor suggests low state of tune initially offered. This tough engine had few equals.

Engineering advances did not stop with the engine and drive train. The troublesome hydraulic system that had been used in window lifts and seat adjustments was abandoned. In its place was an extravagant use of electric motors for each window, the seat adjustment and the convertible top mechanism. They worked beautifully and were typical of Lincoln's quest for quality with cost a secondary consideration.

The new Lincoln was offered in two models; the Cosmopolitan was the standard car and the Capri the deluxe version. A sport coupe and sedan were offered in both models, with the convertible available only in the Capri line. The price differential was $225 for the coupe versions and $133 for the sedans.

The new Lincoln was offered in fourteen colors, with lacquer paint used in Detroit and baked enamel elsewhere. Two metallic colors were offered in baked enamel only. All these colors were then combined in twenty-seven two-tone options. There were five convertible-top colors, and eight interior leather colors and combinations. Six frieze cloths, three broadcloths and two nylons, for interiors, rounded out enough choices to keep a salesman at his homework. Everything in these new interiors was of the highest quality and was a tribute to stylist Don Beyreis. Lincoln was moving resolutely toward the finest interior layouts in the industry. The dashboard was all new, tastefully designed by L. David Ash, who would add so much to Lincoln styling in the years just ahead.

For the first time since the war, Lincoln advertising was ready for the exciting challenge of a new car. The previous sales themes, 'Nothing could be finer' (1948) and 'There's nothing quite like a Lincoln' (1951), were basically negative statements and presented no design philosophy at all. For 1952 the theme became 'Modern Living' and the idea was interwoven with magnificent photography into several sales applications: modern living and the home; women; publications; merchandising force; and *Lincoln*. A twentieth-century revolution was taking place in 'modern living' and Lincoln was at the forefront with cars that were "luxurious yet functional," with "ample room but not so much that it is oversized, heavy and hard to park." The advertising also stressed modern living and car design, the Lincoln being that car which "completely matches the characteristic of modern living," with "big windows" and "luggage space." Dealers were instructed that "Modern Living - Sells Lincolns for *You*."

The theme was creative and well developed but the truly dazzling part of the sales brochures for 1952 was the photography. Car brochures had usually been presented with line drawings and renderings, often in color, and with proportions altered when necessary to enhance styling. For the first time, Lincoln used direct color photography with the cars in gorgeous settings. The advertising was as fresh as the car.

The new Lincoln made its debut in February 1952 and the delighted cheers of the dealers were matched by the rave reviews of the motor journalists. Harry Walton accurately noted in *Popular Science* that "hardly anything but the name remains of the Ford Company's upper bracket automobiles." Walton was impressed with the new frame in

The 1952 Lincoln Capri convertible—superb compact design, ready for action.

which the cross member was further strengthened. Walton found the car some five hundred pounds lighter than the 1951 Cosmopolitan, in part because the car was six inches shorter, despite only a two-inch drop in wheelbase.

Walt Woron did a Research Report for *Motor Trend* with an emphasis on performance and handling. After a 2,486-mile trip Woron found the performance beyond the capacity of the tires, an observation confirmed by MacPherson who said, "Passenger tires, particularly, are one weakness—they're not built for speeds of 100 mph." The Lincoln certainly had that speed in hand, Woron's test producing 100.33 on the fastest one-way run with a 98.31 average for four runs in both directions. Steering effort was greatly reduced from 1951, not only because of the ball joints but because of the lower unsprung weight. Woron found little to criticize on handling though the large 8.00x15 tires caused swerving on parallel road-irregularities and much squeal. Steering effort for parking was also high.

Fuel consumption went up in 1952, despite new efficiency and lighter weight, because of the higher 3.31:1 axle ratio used with the Dual-Range Hydra-matic, though at steady speeds mileage approached that of the 1951 car. Aggressive driving in everyday use brought about consumption levels below 10 mpg.

The big 1952 Chrysler Imperial, still in the most conservative styling dictated by K. T. Keller. But underneath that hood was the fine hemi-head V-8 engine. Imperial sales virtually equaled Lincoln's in 1952 but Chrysler trends were down and Lincoln's were up.

Tom McCahill tested the 1952 car and with his usual wit accurately sensed the changed characteristics of the Lincoln. He called the Lincoln "one of the finest handling American cars I have ever driven and in the luxury and comfort department . . . unbeatable." But McCahill found the car underpowered and the engine "too small." He was eager to "hop it up." McCahill's comparisons of the Lincoln with the other 1952 cars are significant. Buick's handling was very poor; Chrysler's fine hemi-engine was unmatched by its styling and handling; Cadillac's superb engine was mated to a mediocre chassis layout; and Oldsmobile was an "agile barge." The Hudson Hornet excited McCahill, apart from styling and size, while the Packard had settled into a comfortable and silent luxury slot. All the Lincoln needed was increased performance.

The Detroit f.o.b. prices began at about $3,730 and went up to $4,146, comparable to Cadillac 62 prices. The increasingly complicated ways of figuring optional equipment made comparisons difficult, especially when 'options' included universally fitted items such as power brakes and steering, heaters, radios and electric seat adjusters. The delivered price could balloon upwards by $1,000 on 'loaded' cars. The Chrysler Imperial was approaching the $3,900 level in stripped form

while the comparable Packard would be the highest-priced 400 model. Lincoln's model year production for the 1952 car totaled 27,271, down from 32,574 for 1951 but representing a very short production year of around nine months. Registrations through the calendar year including the opening sales of the 1953 model were 29,110, up from the 1951 total of 25,816. There was no question in the dealers' minds that the 1952 car was a tremendous improvement and morale soared.

Ford's management gains and corporate restructuring took hold in 1952. Personnel changes included the appointment of R. E. Kravre as executive assistant to Benson Ford in January and as general manager of the Lincoln-Mercury Division in July. Ground for the Romulus plant, some ten miles southwest of Dearborn, was broken on March 31. The late introduction was not repeated and an elaborate press presentation of the new models was held at Warner Brothers studios on October 18 to prepare for the November 30 introduction. And on November 19 the Lincoln went racing in Mexico with astounding results.

The third Carrera Panamericana began at Tuxtla Gutierrez and was to prove a major turning point in both Lincoln's fortunes and image. Walt Faulkner and Ray Crawford had participated with a Lincoln in the 1951 race, with Crawford finishing a creditable eighth—but far from the unbelievable finish of Troy Ruttman who managed a fourth in a 1948 Mercury, only twenty minutes behind the winning Ferrari driven by Piero Taruffi. Ruttman was quick to give much of the credit to Clay Smith who had prepared the car with off-the-shelf items such as Edelbrock heads and manifolds, a Kong distributor, four additional shock absorbers and some vents in the brake backing-plates. Top speed of the Mercury was 115 mph.

The incredible result of such careful preparation was not unnoticed by Lincoln management. It seemed possible that this new car, praised on every side for handling and roadability, might stand a good chance of finishing well up in the 1952 race. Of particular importance was that the 1953 cars could be used by virtue of the early introduction and these cars were to have the new high-performance engine. The 1952 engine was easily modified and started with a compression increase from 7.5:1 to 8.0:1. Breathing was much improved with larger intake manifold runners, a 1.98 intake valve and higher intake lift. A four-barrel carburetor was fitted. Horsepower jumped to 210 at 4200 rpm and torque went up to 305 pounds-feet over a rev range of 2300 to 3000 rpm. Here was an engine that could outpower anything in the industry and could pull at peak torque over a most usable rev range. Though the Cadillac bhp was upped to 210 for 1953, the 19.8 pounds per horsepower of the Lincoln was the lowest in the industry and its bhp per cubic inch was the highest. Engine durability was also virtually without limit.

Lincoln's 1953 chassis as used for the hardtop and convertible. There is a tube cross-member under the engine. A special cross-member ties the center of the X-members to the side rails. This fine chassis provided exceptional rigidity—one of the reasons for the success of these cars in the Mexican road races.

The first Cadillac Eldorado of 1953 would meet its match in the Mark series Lincolns. The wire wheels, cut-down doors and 210 bhp made this car very special. It cost more than twice the price of a Lincoln and opened up the possibility of new markets for Lincoln planners.

The racing-team Lincolns were delivered to Bill Stroppe's shop in Long Beach, famous for tuning Ford products and highly respected by the personnel of the Long Beach Ford plant. There Clay Smith, Stroppe and their able staff quietly prepared the Lincolns using their experience of the prior year. Heavy-duty and export options were used, plus insulating gaskets to keep carburetors cool, and matched manifolds and ports. The Lincoln brakes, already good, were given additional air scoops with rear blowers mounted in the trunk. Cop-Sil-Loy was used on drums and linings to aid heat dissipation. The lowest axle ratio was fitted, likely the cataloged 3.07:1 of 1952 though it was rarely used and was uncataloged in the November 18, 1952, Automobile Manufacturers' Association specifications. One hundred tires were put in the racing inventory and were critically important since tire life averaged one day's run despite stiffer carcass construction. These magnificently prepared Lincolns had a top speed of around 130 mph at 5000 rpm and were dead reliable. No other domestic car could touch them on speed.

The race began at Tuxtla on November 19. Some scrambling during the early legs over mountain terrain and bad road conditions helped to equalize the performance of the Chryslers, Oldsmobiles and Lincolns. But once the race moved onto the flatter northern regions, the Lincolns walked away from the competition. The winning Lincoln averaged over 115 mph on the fastest leg.

The Lincolns finished 1, 2, 3, 4 in the stock division, driven by Chuck Stevenson, Johnny Mantz, Walt Faulkner and Bob Korf. Stevenson's winning time was 21 hours, 15 minutes, 38 seconds. Overall the Lincolns finished 7, 8, 9 and 10, the leading cars being two

Mercedes, a Ferrari, a Lancia and two more Ferraris. Behind the Lincolns by some eighteen minutes was Reginald McFee's fine Chrysler, followed by the Evans Chrysler and the Marshall Teague Hudson. Stevenson in the first-place Lincoln had averaged 90.982 for 1,934 miles. Exactly one week later, the 1953 Lincolns were introduced.

The 1953 car continued to be offered in two models, the standard Cosmopolitan and the deluxe Capri, both in two- and four-door bodies. The Capri also continued the convertible coupe. Lincoln stylists tidied up the front end, the Lincoln name now in block letters at the base of the hood and the 1952 hood medallion now moved down into the grille opening. The interior color display of fabrics and leathers was, if anything, expanded for 1953 and new richness of textures was evident.

The big news for 1953 was the whopping power increase from 160 to 205 bhp. Sales themes seized on this increase with slogans such as 'Completely powered for modern living.' The power theme was passed along into promoting the various power options available including power steering, vacuum power brakes, electric seat adjustments and the window lifts. A special 'power' catalog was issued stating that "Lincoln power offers a new concept of driving ease."

The V-insignia on the rear fender of the 1953 Lincoln Cosmopolitan sedan commemorated the golden anniversary of the Ford Motor Company.

Buick's Skylark was introduced in 1953 with a $5,000 price tag, much higher than the Lincoln Capri convertible. This Skylark prototype on the 1952 Roadmaster chassis showed the general styling of the series. Lincoln management was startled by the car's success, selling at a price higher than Capri and with volume two thirds of the Lincoln convertible.

The 1953 Continental Nineteen Fifty-X show car was a Ford exercise and had little influence on the Continental Mark II.

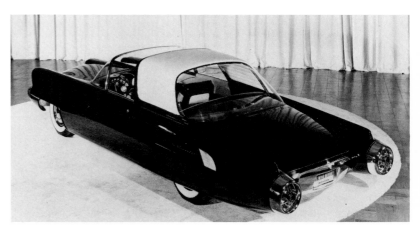

For once Lincoln sales timing was perfect and, coupled with virtually no price change, sales were heavy. Dealer inventory was nonexistent and, by March 1953, assembly plants were running second shifts at Metuchen; St. Louis; and Wayne, Michigan. May sales of 5,009 were the highest in Lincoln history. However, a fire at GM's Hydramatic plant on August 13 crippled output and prevented the final exploitation of a tremendous sales year. The success of the 1953 car prompted the expansion of the Metuchen plant, begun on October 30.

For the Fiftieth Anniversary Show at Chicago, a special Capri was prepared in white, dubbed the Maharajah. Four thousand dollars worth of gold was plated on the brightwork of the car. It was a dazzling car but buying maharajahs were in scarce supply.

Testers were unanimous in declaring the 1953 Lincoln the finest and fastest road car in America. John Bond of *Road & Track*, testing a car with an all-up weight of 5,040 pounds, produced a standing quarter mile in just under twenty seconds and a 0-60 time of 14.4 seconds. He had no doubt that a top speed of 110 to 115 mph was attainable and Bond was especially impressed with the 2,500 feet-per-minute piston speed at 4300 rpm for 110 mph. Said Bond, "Thus the car can be cruised at any speed desired, up to the maximum, without concern for the engine."

Somewhat spartan 1953 Lincoln sedan interior (left) is not helped by the puckering seat seams. But the quality of the materials was outstanding. The front hood was cleaned up on this 1953 Capri (right) and a new ornament accentuated its aggressive styling. Simple block letters also replaced the hood insignia of 1952. Strong, protruding bumper guards at the front were typical of the stylists' efforts to lengthen the car through the early fifties. The hardtop coupe was especially handsome.

Bond was also surprised at the 17 mpg he averaged while doing 60 to 70 mph, which fell to 13.5 mpg at higher speeds while utilizing the car's maximum performance. But Bond did not care for the power steering; he felt it should not need four turns lock-to-lock and required too much effort. The power brakes, on the other hand, were without fault.

Walt Woron repeated the *Motor Trend* Research Report on the 1953 Lincoln and found little to criticize in the car's handling and speed. He clocked 110.42 mph on a four-run average. Despite only forty-two percent of the weight on the rear wheels, the front end did not feel mushy and the rear broke away only on soft dirt and gravel. Woron, however, was even more impressed with the new emphasis on refinement exemplified by both the complete array of power-assist accessories and the generally high quality of upholstery and trim materials. He described the Lincoln as a car of "compact but unstinting luxury," offering "ease and comfort of handling." Woron's automatic seat adjustment failed on his test Lincoln, which gave him slight pause in his tribute to the 'new age,' but it was clear that the car could only be described in superlatives.

Production of the 1953 Lincoln totaled 40,762, two thirds of which was the deluxe Capri series. It was the highest volume so far in the decade. The facelifted Cadillac 62, the model directly opposite the

Lincoln in the luxury market, had a production of 85,446. Lincoln sales approached fifty percent of the principal Cadillac model, a remarkable recovery from the poor showings since the war. After such a triumph, changes were obviously going to be minor for 1954. The stylists were hard-pressed to improve on the clean lines of 1953 and the changes which were made did little to enhance the appearance of the car. The rear bumper was extended around to the sides of the rear fenders, destroying the very crisp fairing used in 1952 and 1953. The slash-strip of brightwork on the rear fender was abandoned in favor of a stainless panel at the base of the fender. A second running bright stripe extended rearward from this panel and was typical of the sort of 'slap on' modifications done in the mid-fifties. At the grille all ornamentation was removed, but a large V-insignia appeared on the front of the hood. The front bumpers were much heavier with guards jutting forward much like the Cadillac's. The Lincoln was beginning to grow.

Lincolns at Oaxaca in the fourth Carrera Panamericana. They very nearly finished as close, the
elapsed time between the four winning Lincolns
being under two minutes.

Not all the Lincolns were successful. Roger Ward
smashed this car in the 1953 Carrera Panamericana road race.

There were some neat touches. The back-up lamps were integrated
into the taillights. Those stainless side moldings did help to lengthen
the car, an answer to the comparisons that were now beginning to be
heard about the too-compact size of the Lincoln when compared to
luxury competition. And Lincoln interiors continued to be more
sumptuous than ever. A Dinoc decal was used to provide little blue
stars on the dash panels, which were, in turn, coordinated with the
colored interiors. The interior pleating was deeper and richer. Little

extras available included a prism to attach to the windshield pillar,
enabling the driver to see overhead stoplights. A rear window defroster
was offered and a compass appeared in the option list for confused
travelers.

Mechanical changes were minor refinements. The carburetor
received a vacuum control for cutting-in the second set of barrels in an
effort to improve economy. A magnetic fuel filter with a new fuel bowl
improved an already excellent system. Of more importance was the
increase of brake-drum diameter to twelve inches, bringing lining area
up from 202.34 to 220 square inches.

The tremendous success in the Carrera Panamericana in 1952
dictated that Lincolns would again appear. The race was scheduled
precisely one year later, beginning on November 19 at Tuxtla. The
Lincoln factory team was composed of three cars prepared by Stroppe
and Smith in the same meticulous manner of 1952. Jack McGrath of
Pasadena entered his own Lincoln, using preparation techniques similar
to Stroppe's. The race results were also similar to 1952, for the
Stevenson-Smith car was first in the big-stock division with a time of 20
hours, 31 minutes, 32 seconds, nearly forty-five minutes faster than
1952. Faulkner was second, McGrath third, and Mantz fourth with the
elapsed time difference between them all under one minute, fifty-eight

A 1954 Lincoln Capri sedan. Its heavier chrome trim increases the sense of body mass. Redesigned rear fender chrome and rocker panel brightwork lengthens the car's appearance.

seconds! The next big-stock car was an Oldsmobile driven by Jim Rathmann, over forty-two minutes behind, but the car was disqualified for having polished ports. The Chrysler entries of E. C. Kiekhaefer were driven by John Fitch, Reggie McFee, Bob Korf and Frank Mundy and on paper looked like major challengers. Three of the Chryslers dropped out with transmission trouble and the fourth was disqualified for exceeding the time limit into Durango. Of the first ten big-stocks, seven were Lincolns, two were Chryslers and the tenth car was a Packard. The Lincoln triumph was overwhelming.

Dealer showing was on December 3, again nicely timed to take advantage of the Mexican road race victory. Walt Woron tested the Lincoln for *Motor Trend* and pronounced the car "virtually the same." The brakes were much improved, however, and the average stopping distances from 30, 45 and 60 mph, a novel *Motor Trend* method of measurement, fell from 136 to 101 feet for the 1954 car. Woron did, however, note severe brake fade after high-speed decelerations. The tire squeal of 1952 and 1953 was reduced by a change in tire design in which 'squeal suppressors' were cast into the tire in the form of rubber

buttons between the ribs. The superb roadability, great forward vision, high quality-level of trim and finish, and all-around comfort continued to describe America's finest luxury road car.

An outstanding advertising program was designed for 1954, based upon a series of photography sessions near Traverse City, Michigan, at Sleeping Bear Dunes. Chauncey F. Kotten, of the Kenyon and Eckhardt agency, designed the project which involved placing the 1954 cars in various settings on the dunes. It was an extraordinarily difficult project because bulldozers and tractors were required to position the cars. Lake winds relentlessly blew the sand away from the wheels and the cars would settle. In the end, the sand had to be raked into place, and even the models pitched in to help. The result was a masterpiece of automotive photography by Cle Clark which was the talk of the industry. For sheer high style, the 1954 Lincoln brochures set standards for a decade.

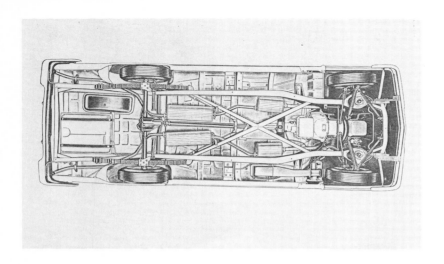

The 1954 Lincoln chassis—straight-forward, strong and beautifully matched to engine and running gear.

Lincoln prices for 1954 at the factory and without accessories were:

Cosmopolitan four-door	$3,537
Cosmopolitan sport coupe	3,640
Capri four-door	3,726
Capri hardtop coupe	3,884
Capri convertible coupe	4,045

The Hydra-matic was standard. Extra cost options were:

Power steering	$145
Power brakes	40
Heater	113
Air conditioning	647
White sidewall tires	37
Power windows	65
Power four-way seat	165
Radio	122

A fully equipped Capri coupe was thus over $4,900 at the factory.

The 1954 Cadillac was completely restyled, with a three-inch-longer chassis, 230 bhp, a new wraparound window, and the first hint of the grotesque rear-fin emphasis. It was a big car and the new fine-meshed grille and trim emphasized the massiveness in front while the flat rear deck seemed to extend forever. In only nine months of production, Cadillac manufactured 96,680 cars, 77,345 of which were Model 62's.

Despite a weight of 5,100 pounds, its big 230-horse engine was able to do 0-60 mph in eleven seconds, down from 13.2 in 1953.

Lincoln production for 1954 totaled 36,993, the big fall-off being in the Cosmopolitan series. The shortage of Hydra-matics hurt both Cadillac and Lincoln. Packard production plummeted to 30,965, a disastrous year. Chrysler had trouble and was discounting heavily through the year. Still saddled with the conservative styling dictated by K. T. Keller, sales had lagged. As a corporation, Chrysler had lost second place in overall sales to Ford in 1952.

The Lincoln-Mercury Division faced the end of the three-year body cycle in 1954 and, on balance, the car had been very successful. The new Lincoln image of the best-engineered road car in America had been firmly established and the car had taken on a youthful spirit. It had been the right move at the right time because both Packard and Chrysler, following more conservative styling, had seriously fallen behind, despite quality engineering and performance. Chrysler had squarely placed its future on sensible and upright styling and had watched its market penetration decline. Packard, in grave trouble by 1954, was unable to change the public's growing doubt about its future and despite good, even great, cars could not break the crushing dominance of Cadillac's hold on the luxury market. Lincoln had won by turning away from the top luxury market, in essence leaving it to Cadillac to exploit. There were no limousines in the Lincoln lineup. Packard built only one hundred long-wheelbase jobs in 1954 while Cadillac turned out 1,500.

Though the decisions leading to the 1952-54 Lincolns had been correct, it was evident to Benson Ford and the policy-making team of the corporation that changes must be made. These changes were predicated on the idea that prestige and luxury were equated with size. Within the Ford corporate model mix, the 1954 Ford, with ball-joint suspension and virtually every luxury option of the Lincoln, had drawn sufficiently close to the prestigious Lincoln image as to be embarrassing. The Walker styling idiom was evident in every Ford, Mercury and Lincoln. It was becoming apparent that the Lincoln must draw away from the Ford, and even the Mercury, in order to establish itself as a true competitor of Cadillac.

The image of the new big Cadillac for 1954 and its obvious success was there for all to see. Furthermore, the small-Ford project, which had reappeared from time to time, had always been shelved in the face of the growing success of the ever-bigger Ford. What was needed were new products in the middle and upper ranges of the car market to take advantage of the growing affluence of the nation. It was that sort of reasoning that spawned the Edsel and which prepared the way for the radically changed Lincoln of 1958, a car which would be defiantly, perhaps overwhelmingly, large.

The postscript to the exciting Lincoln racing story was the final Carrera Panamericana of 1954. Again the starting date was November 19 and the Lincoln team was on hand with full factory support. Clay Smith had died but Bill Stroppe's shop continued to provide the meticulous preparation that was critical for success. The engines were dynamometer tested in Stroppe's shop, even the engine used in the transporter. All replacement tires were mounted on prebalanced wheels which were color-coded to painted lug nuts to insure perfectly matched balancing. Spares and tools were color-coded as well. Two-way radios were fitted. A complete movie of the 1952 race was filmed from the copilot's seat and used for the driver's final familiarization. Roller charts covering each kilometer were provided, giving speeds for every bump and turn. Refreshments for the crew were carefully planned, including pure spring water and even cigars. The drivers and the cars were so meticulously prepared that the final level runs of some 500 kilometers were done with the Lincolns traveling only a few feet apart.

The Lincolns were again victorious and finished first and second with a best time of 20 hours, 40 minutes, 19 seconds. A factory car was not first; instead a private entry driven by Ray Crawford, though prepared by Stroppe, crossed the finish line first. One minute, forty-eight seconds later came the Faulkner factory entry. Only a minute and seven seconds behind Faulkner was Keith Andrews in a Cadillac, followed by yet another Cadillac. The crushing Lincoln dominance was clearly over and there was no walkaway team triumph. Of the seven factory entries, only two finished and the same proportion of the seven private Lincoln entries survived. A 1955 race would have been highly competitive but casualties in Mexico (and the tragedy at the Le Mans 24-Hour Race) brought an end to this spectacular event.

Lincoln outsold Packard for the first time in 1954. This Packard Caribbean was but a shadow of the original clean design. Only 400 Caribbeans were produced; Lincoln convertibles totaled 1,951.

CHAPTER 5

Seeking Another Image—1955-57

THE 1955 MODEL year remains one of the unforgettable moments in Detroit history, when factories worked feverishly to keep up with the greatest sales volume recorded to that time. Ford managed to register 1,473,276 units, exceeding Chevrolet's previous all-time record. In this hectic sales race Chevrolet, in turn, pushed sales to 1,640,681, a further high. In such grinding competition Kaiser died, Hudson stumbled badly and Willys ceased production of their Aero models.

Unfortunately, Lincoln did not have a new model for this great sales year, and the existing dies dating from 1952 were extended for a fourth year. The Mercury received a new body with vertical windshield pillars, a wraparound windshield, and hooded headlamps setting off a massive grille; the result was a production record of 329,808 units.

The Lincoln, however, was given substantial styling changes within the limits of the existing dies. The headlight rims were extended and enlarged, a good job but held on by only four clips. Alas, the new rim was much heavier and tended to fall off when jolted. The big, black open grille area of 1954 was filled in with fine horizontal bars, a pleasing improvement. An important styling gain was on the rear side panel where the horizontal bar of 1954 no longer passed across the fender outline without any reference to the basic design. For 1955, the fender sculpturing was lowered and properly accented, the horizontal accent stripe now entirely above and unrelated to the rear fender outline. It was an excellent resolution of an awkward problem. The rear fenders were elongated with a new reverse angle taillamp, a design idea that would identify the Lincoln through 1957. The rear coupe window was revised. A neat touch was the knight's-head rear deck lid ornament, the visor of which lifted to reveal the keyhole. These good styling changes could not hide the fact that the front windshield post remained the same, in retrospect entirely right but, in terms of the styling fads of 1955, out of step.

The interiors for 1955 were again revised with a new horseshoe bolster design for the seats which extended down the sides, a great improvement. The fourteen leather colors were exceptionally bright and lovely new pastel tones. Leather in these new colors could no longer be vat dyed but the leather paintwork was of the highest quality. Lincoln interior designers had a field day with the spring 1955 show cars. The Huntsman Capri convertible was in red, white and black with the floor mat in black uncut loops and the convertible top in red trimmed with black. Another special show model sedan with the preview name

1955 Capri hardtop, fourth year of the same shell, remained clean and uncluttered, a miracle of styling restraint. Rear fender trim precisely followed the sheet metal contours. Grille was simple and effective. Yet this handsome car was a sales disappointment, overshadowed by new trends better expressed in the Mercury.

Premiere was offered in black with the rear half of the top padded in white vinyl and the front of the top fitted with a solar panel of plastic. "See the gay lights of theatre row," said the advertising copy.

Mechanical changes were also substantial. The engine was bored out fourteen thousandths to 3.94 inches and the horsepower moved up to 225. Again the horsepower race carried Packard up to 260 bhp and Cadillac to 250 (270 in the Eldorado), but Lincoln could be somewhat aloof from the horsepower competition after their third victory in the Mexican road race. The General Motors Hydra-matic was finally dropped as Youngren came up with Turbo-Drive, a beefed-up three-

speed planetary and torque converter unit similar to that used on the Ford. Low gear offered a maximum 5.04:1 ratio.

The rear-end ratio was lowered to 3.07:1, to improve economy with little performance lost as engine bhp and torque moved ever higher. An optional 3.31 ratio was available and used on air-conditioned cars. A variation of the old Bijur one-shot lubrication system was introduced

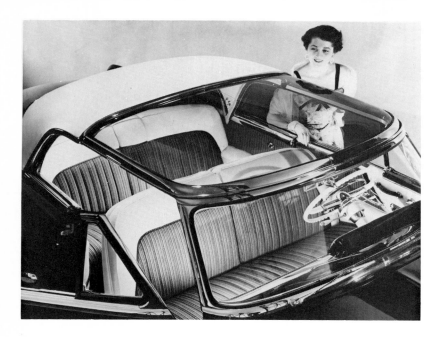

Plexiglass roofs appeared in 1954 on Fords and Mercurys and never quite caught on. Their solar heat transmission was fearful despite tinting, and the plexiglass was vulnerable to scratching. This 1955 Lincoln Premiere used the advertising theme, "See the gay lights of theatre row."

Imperial was first marketed as a separate marque in 1955, priced $900 above the cheapest Lincoln Custom sedan. The New Yorker was Lincoln's direct competition; Lincoln triumphed by moving up in image, eventually overwhelming Imperial.

Hooded headlamps, wraparound windshield and vertical A-pillars made this 1955 Monterey Montclair up-to-date. Mercury's new styling was in contrast to Lincoln's 1955 car, which had only minor revisions. Lincoln's sales were down and Mercury had a great year.

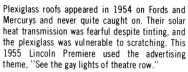

with an instrument panel button and indicator light. The splendid ball-joint suspension was retained and handling continued supreme. Observers rightly noted that the Lincoln was substantially different from the competition, more compact, more suitable to exuberant drivers, yet with the usual array of luxury options.

Though Lincoln had offered air conditioning in 1954, the 1955 unit was all-new and much improved. The four-way seat adjustment

(pioneered by Lincoln) was now pretty much taken for granted. One could still order a spotlight in 1955.

The two series of Lincolns were continued but a name changed. The Cosmopolitan was replaced by the Custom. The top-priced Capri series continued. Base prices at the factory began at $3,563 for the Custom four-door and topped out with the Capri convertible at $4,072. Options quickly pushed these prices up hundreds of dollars. By comparison, the Cadillac 62 four-door sedan was about $200 above the comparable Capri though the two-door hardtop was priced some thirty dollars below the Capri two-door hardtop. The Cadillac convertible was nearly $400 above the comparable Lincoln. Packard prices started very much lower and only the Packard line at the top of the range had comparable prices, even though the new V-8 engine was available in all models. The Imperial, offered as a separate marque by Chrysler for the first time, was priced at $4,483 for the sedan, well above Cadillac and Lincoln, in a bold strategy to establish a new superior image.

The Lincoln was a fine automobile, the steady refinement of three years' strong production showing up in a car of near-faultless assembly, in many ways superior to its rivals. The public, however, was buying ever bigger cars and the Lincoln was especially caught in an unfavorable dimension comparison with its rivals. Cadillac was mounted on a 129-inch wheelbase, the new Imperial on 130 inches. Though the overall length of the Lincoln was not much less than either Cadillac or Imperial, the general dimensions of the other cars were larger. The Cadillac was heavier by a hundred pounds, the Imperial by three hundred, a particularly galling comparison because Lincoln economy was proving troublesome.

Lincoln was the only luxury car to show declines in sales and production in 1955. The actual production for the model year was 27,222, the lowest since the V-12 days just after the war. Calendar-year registrations were 35,623, the lowest since 1952, and even at that were helped greatly by the early success of the 1956 models. Cadillac production for the model year was 118,586 Model 62's and another 18,300 of 60 Specials. Packard production totaled 55,517, concentrated in the lower-priced Clipper series, yet with over 16,000 units in the top luxury Patrician and 400 models. The new Imperial got off to a good start with 12,727 units produced.

A most honest appraisal of the success of the various 1955 models may be made by comparing retail used car values at the close of the year. As a percentage of the new-car base price, using the four-door sedan as the standard of comparison as listed in the *Kelley Kar Blue Book*, the following results appear:

Cadillac 62	+5.8 %
Lincoln Custom	−9.0 %
Lincoln Capri	−10.0 %
Imperial	−19.0 %
Packard Patrician	−25.0 %

Though Packard still looked alive in 1955 by virtue of sales volume, as well as a new V-8 engine and a merger with Studebaker which promised new resources, the public had clearly made a somber decision about Packard's future. Likewise, the new Imperial was clearly up against a critical appraisal which time alone would confirm.

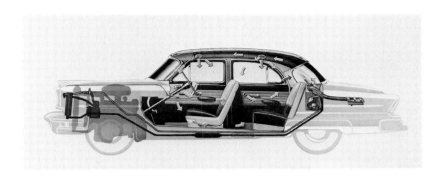

Lincoln presented this new rear blower air-conditioning system in 1955. It required awkward transparent tubes in the rear corners. The front-mounted blower system would wait until 1958.

It seems odd to recall that in 1955, economy was an important factor in the public's appraisal of luxury cars, with gasoline selling at levels that today would be considered absurdly low. Cadillac, however, had built a commanding reputation as an economical car and Cadillac owners would jokingly refer to their purchase as an economy step over cheaper cars of the GM line. The economy was so good that Cadillac was able to raise the axle ratio from 3.07:1 in 1954 to 3.36:1 for 1955 in the interest of increased performance. It was a tough act to challenge.

Another novel experimental car surfaced at the Detroit Automobile Show on January 29, 1955. The Lincoln Futura was a design exercise of the Lincoln-Mercury Division along with the engineering staff of Ford. It was built on a wheelbase of 126 inches and was almost nineteen feet long. The outstanding styling feature was a twin plexiglass canopy which pivoted upward when the doors were opened. Built at a cost of approximately $250,000, the Futura was heavy on fender blades and the complex bubble windshield had a spaceship feel. Instrument controls were located behind roll-type doors and the warning lights, speedometer and tachometer were located in an unusual steering wheel 'binnacle.'

The Futura was photographed on March 3 in Central Park, where it was driven by Benson Ford. The pearlescent blue-white lacquer was prepared with fish scales. The running gear was essentially Lincoln with a 330 bhp engine, Turbo-Drive transmission and ball-joint suspension.

The instruments of the Futura (left) were grouped in the steering column binnacle. A compass was mounted on the cowl in front of the driver and a clock in front of the passenger. A microphone on the rear deck amplified the horn signal from a car approaching from the rear—it might have been hoped that a muting switch was available. Benson Ford drives the Futura around Central Park in New York (right). The car was put on display at the Detroit Auto Show on January 29, 1955. At almost 19 feet long, seven feet wide and only 52.8 inches high, the car was entirely roadworthy. The steel body was painted pearlescent blue-white lacquer.

Lincoln management was reorganized in April 1955 when the Lincoln Division was established as a separate entity from Mercury and Ben Mills became the new general manager. (The Lincoln Division did not remain independent for long following the collapse of the Edsel and Continental Mark II projects and Mercury rejoined Lincoln in 1960.) Mills made it clear that the target for the new team was Cadillac and detailed comparisons were begun. The Lincoln engine, though bigger, was ten percent under Cadillac's advertised brake horsepower and torque was below Cadillac, perhaps a result of the extremely oversquare bore-stroke ratio which Lincoln was using. The body size differences were duly noted and it was obvious to Lincoln management that the luxury market was pulling away from the sporty Lincoln image. Uppermost in the minds of all was the fact that all of the luxury competition now outsized the Lincoln, and this reflection would give

rise to the dimensions ordered on the 1958 model, now being developed by John Najjar and his team.

The 1956 Lincoln remains one of the greatest of the postwar Lincolns, and this in spite of the fact that it was something of a short-lived *tour de force*. It was a styling prize winner. The mechanical changes were extensive, performance was brilliant, and sales set a record, but the basic design lasted only two years. It was a car which was overshadowed by the new Continental Mark II, yet, in retrospect, it has aged very gracefully, far more than the Lincoln that immediately followed. In essence, it was a final flowering of a design philosophy which would shortly be overturned, as the Lincoln Division sought yet a further avenue toward dominance of the luxury market.

The all-new car began with a three-inch increase in wheelbase to 126 inches, still compact when compared to Cadillac's 129 and Imperial's 133 inches. The design of the car, begun in 1953 by Schmidt and his group, seemed large at the time, especially when compared to the 1953 Lincoln, but it was a bold effort to move into a new segment of the market. Schmidt had to turn away from corporate direction which was still aimed at competing against the Oldsmobile in 1953 and, in truth, was building a car which would easily beat the General Motors performance champ. Schmidt's early experimental cars included the XL-

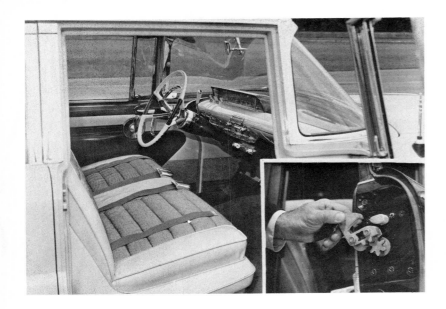

Horizontal pleats appeared on Lincoln seats in 1956. Interiors were of lavish specification with twenty-nine colors, five fabrics and leather. Rotary door latches, pioneered by Chrysler in 1940, were introduced on the Lincoln as part of a safety emphasis, which explains those seatbelts lying so neatly on the squab.

The handsome interior of the 1956 Lincoln reflected the creative brilliance of the whole car. The horizontal pleats were new and color coordination was elaborate. This convertible had a factory list base price of $4,318.

500 which showed a break from the sculptured side panels. The new Lincoln for 1956 was slab-sided again, but, unlike the Cosmopolitan, was graced with a high, crowned fender line and sharp edging at both front and rear which prevented the design from falling back into the old 'convex' school.

At the leading edge of the front fender a hooded headlamp was set, a bit like the 1955 Mercury but stronger and without the separate rim. The grille had some of the fine bars of 1955 but was altogether new and strong, a vast array of horizontal chrome of massive dimension. There was no mistaking the image of power. Trimwork on the side of the car was modest by 1956 standards and again reflected the clean styling ideas of Schmidt. The clean fender crown at the front was carried through in an unbroken line to the tip of the rear fender blade under which splendid taillamps were set. The styling group, wisely unwilling to follow Cadillac's fin game, emphasized the rear bumper in a very heavy design in which the exhaust pipes came through bumper ports. There was plenty to see at the back of the car.

The wraparound windshield was set against vertical front windshield pillars, altogether in style with the moment, but an idea which was to

be short-lived, as the stylists correctly sensed its absurdities in both function and form. This minor comment aside, the 1956 Lincoln was a superb design, whose cleanliness may be finally expressed by the beautiful concave hubcaps of remarkable simplicity.

The new body layout was matched by an all-new engine of 368-cubic-inch displacement producing 285 bhp and 401 pounds-feet of torque. Lincoln was proud of the torque and advertised it as the highest in the industry, though the Packard 374-cubic-inch engine pulled 405 pounds-feet. The big Lincoln engine could move the new car from 0-60 mph in 11.7 seconds with a top speed in the neighborhood of 105 mph, both times better than the 1955 car. Despite improved performance, economy was slightly better than 1955, varying from about 18 mpg

The instrument panel of the 1956 Lincoln was still using a basic design developed for the 1952 car. Controls were clear and functional. The ornate steering wheel resembles an optional wheel first offered on the 1949 Ford.

The 1956 Lincoln was a very handsome car with exceptionally clean styling. Production totaled 50,322, an all-time record. This Capri coupe was similar to the Premiere coupe that won the Industrial Designers Award on June 21, 1956.

under optimum steady cruising at 45 mph to about 11 mpg around a measured test course, according to Jim Lodge of *Motor Trend*.

The safety emphasis of Ford management was evident in several new features, including a recessed-center steering wheel with a 3½-inch energy-absorbing cushion between the rim and the steering column. Seatbelts were offered, anchored to a reinforced floor pan. Rotary door locks were more resistant to collision impact and the instrument panel was given a non-reflective textured vinyl covering. The rear-view mirror was vinyl-coated to resist shattering. These were nice ideas but premature—safety was still considered morbid.

An important technical improvement was the introduction of a 12-volt electrical system, useful not only in cold starting but in lowering the amperage required for the myriad power-assist mechanisms throughout the car.

The 1956 Lincoln was offered with further refinements in the air-conditioning system, the 12-volt power helping to speed blowers so that a complete change of air was achieved in one minute. The heat exchange unit was mounted in the trunk and ducts were through four headliner ports. New attention was paid to the extra loads that air conditioning placed upon so many of the car's elements, and heavier tires, springs, shock absorbers, a larger radiator, and tinted glass were part of the factory installation. Lincoln was proud of the redesigned air-conditioning system and allocated twenty percent of early production to models with air. This percentage fell back to thirteen in the fall months. Geographical distribution of air-conditioned cars showed an increased sensitivity to marketing problems. The southeastern states plus Texas were receiving over fifty percent air-conditioned cars by December. In contrast, the northeast was running about three percent. In particular, eighty-three percent of Dallas Lincolns were fitted with air, Kansas City received fifty-one percent, Los Angeles only eighteen percent and Boston 1.3 percent. Air conditioning was not yet a universal requirement in a luxury car but times were changing.

Paint and interior specifications were lavish for 1956. A range of seventeen exterior colors, thirty-five two-tone colors, and twenty-nine interior color and trim combinations were available. The Capri series, the standard line for 1956, offered the Matelasse and broadcloth trim, argent-weave, and chevron nylon interiors. Matelasse is two layers of cloth woven together to give an embossed or three-dimensional effect. The Premiere line added Lurex Tweed with interwoven metallic threads. The pleating was horizontal, a fresh idea, and the bolsters in leather

The prize-winning 1956 Lincoln Premiere reached a production total of 50,322 units, the best Lincoln year to date. The new longer 126-inch wheelbase was still three inches under Cadillac and despite the great virtues of this new model it would last only one more year, as the quest for size absorbed the planners' thoughts.

were of the finest top-grains. All-leather seats were available and almost anything the purchaser wished could be ordered out. The Lincoln interiors were marvelously color-coordinated and showed an imagination in specification unequaled in the industry.

The instrument layout was clean and uncluttered, following themes established in 1952. The power window-lift switches were now mounted on an instrument panel extension convenient to the driver's left hand plus, of course, the individual switches at appropriate locations. Town-and-country switching bars were offered on the 'travel tuner' radio which would tune in either direction on the frequency scale. Power antennas and rear speakers were now taken for granted.

The 1956 Lincoln was a most impressive car and made its debut very early on September 8, 1955; suggested list prices were as follows:

Capri coupe	$3,735
Capri four-door sedan	3,821
Premiere coupe	4,183
Premiere four-door	4,183
Premiere convertible	4,318

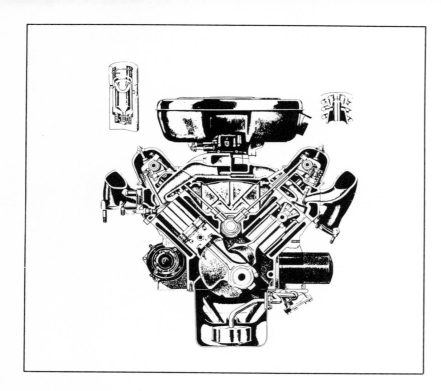

The 1957 Lincoln engine was clearly still the same block as 1952 but many detail changes had brought about much higher bhp. The carburetion and manifold were much improved while the head had undergone subtle revision.

By the time taxes, distribution, delivery, preparation plus options were added, $5,000 was closer to the delivered price.

Reaction to the new car among the motoring journalists was enthusiastic. The car was bigger, and though the sense of compact controllability was diminished, the car was faster, sure-footed and very stable. Walt Woron in *Motor Trend* noted slightly increased body lean along with a softer suspension but felt that roadability was virtually the same as the 1955 car. Tom McCahill found the 1956 car faster despite initial skepticism.

A more stunning approval of the new car's styling could not be found when the Industrial Designers Institute gave its award for design to the 1956 Lincoln Premiere hardtop coupe on June 21. The public seemed to agree, because sales were good and by the end of the production year totaled 50,322, the very best year for Lincoln to that date. The calendar year production for 1956 of 47,760 was also a record. Vice President and General Manager Mills of the Lincoln Division was understandably pleased.

By another measurement the 1956 Lincoln was a tremendous success. The number of sales compared to Cadillac advanced to thirty-three percent, up from twenty-five percent in 1955. Packard registration plummeted to 28,936 in 1956 and production ceased in Detroit, the 1957 Packard by then just a warmed-over Studebaker. Imperial registrations dropped to 10,460. Thus Lincoln's sales gains were in the face of substantial retreat by two of its rivals and were greater than Cadillac in both percentage and absolute terms.

For 1957, L. David Ash restyled the successful 1956 shell. Quad headlamps appeared for the first time—actually two headlamps under which were mounted two fog lamps. The remainder of the grille and bumper areas were given slight modifications; Ash, however, saved his major styling touches for the rear of the car. The relentless growth of the fins and blades, begun by Cadillac and now strongly followed by Chrysler and Imperial, exerted powerful styling pressure. The new Lincoln rear blades were commendably modest and resisted the more bizarre development in the GM and Chrysler studios. A new slash-strip broke the slab side panel and gave a hint of a rear fender outline, again a pure styling gimmick which did not help the basic outline of the car. David Ash's taste in the 1957 Lincoln must be complimented, however, for when compared to the growing vulgarity of its rivals, the Lincoln was a model of restraint.

The Lincoln engine was readily tuned to 300 bhp with compression rising to 10:1 and a redesigned combustion chamber and pistons. Torque moved up to 415 pounds-feet. A new option in the drive train was a limited slip differential, 'power-directed' as Lincoln called it.

Power accessories continued to multiply, including vent windows, electric door locks and a new six-way adjustable front seat. A useful new idea was a low-fuel warning light in which a red glow appeared on the fuel gauge when three gallons remained. The side mirror was remote-controlled. An automatic headlight dimmer was offered.

The air conditioner was again changed with a four-cylinder compressor now fitted and a single-knob control on the instrument panel. The engine room was getting crowded and hot and a new carburetor was fitted with a larger float bowl to counteract evaporation.

Hydro-cushion adjustable shocks allowed some changes in ride control but the adjustment had to be made at the shock and not from within the car. The ride remained superb and handling was slightly improved over 1956.

Lincolns came in eighteen solid body colors, seventy-seven two-tone combinations and forty-four interior trim patterns. One wonders how anyone made a decision and indeed it would eventually be recognized that these vast choices could create a sort of buyer numbness. Limited specifications such as the designer series of the later Mark Continentals were yet a long way off.

The Lincoln was a fine car and 41,123 were built, a satisfying record though down eighteen percent from 1956. Cadillac production went down five percent for a gross production of 146,841 units. The real surprise for 1957 was the Imperial, with a new design and fresh marketing helping to push production up to 37,577, a tremendous increase. As a total share of the luxury market, Lincoln production fell from twenty-three percent to eighteen percent. Despite the styling successes, plus the new and well received four-door Premiere hardtop and an undeniably fine reputation from both the technical and luxury standpoint, the Lincoln continued to face aggressive and able competition. It was becoming clear that the Lincoln image as a top luxury car was still not in order. Visually the car remained smaller than

Revision of the fresh 1956 Lincoln seen in this 1957 Capri shows the debasing of the original idea. The rear fins are in tune with Cadillac and Chrysler themes and the rear door slash-strip is gimmicky. The Lincoln, however, is still conservative when compared to its rivals. Sales were down.

The quad headlamps of this 1957 Premiere are really two fog lamps mounted beneath the regular lights. The car still retains the handsome body outline of the award-winning 1956 Lincoln but the tailfins have become lethal.

both Cadillac and Imperial, and Lincoln's lower weights proved it. Both Cadillac and Imperial had settled at a wheelbase of about 129 inches, while Lincoln continued to build on 126 inches. Planners at the Lincoln Division saw these size comparisons as an increasing obstacle to Lincoln's ultimate success in the luxury market, an obstacle which would soon be removed in a most dramatic manner.

CHAPTER 6

Cost No Object – The Mark II

DURING THE FIFTIES, the question of a new Lincoln Continental had never really vanished from the thinking of designers, corporate brass and merchandisers because it remained the symbol of leadership which the Lincoln organization was now struggling to affirm. The decision for the muscle cars of 1952-54 and the accompanying withdrawal from the 'carriage trade' market posed the danger of blurring the Lincoln's traditional image. Youngren's target for the 1952 Lincoln had been the Oldsmobile and not the Cadillac. Furthermore, Henry Ford II was eager to broaden the company's offerings in order to become more competitive with General Motors.

On January 29, 1952, Ford appointed the Davis Committee, headed by veteran John R. Davis who had helped launch the Mercury in 1939. Davis had already been working on product planning and was sympathetic with the product expansion ideas of Henry Ford II. Davis was joined by some of the senior leadership of the corporation and included Lewis Crusoe, Delmar S. Harder, Walker Williams, Theodore O. Yntema and Harold T. Youngren. The committee quickly concluded that there was a need for a new car in the middle and upper-middle price range, at that time only partially covered by Mercury. The car that eventually appeared to fill this need was the Edsel, though when

the Edsel finally made it to the market for the 1958 model year, the need had become obscured.

Another recommendation came from the Davis Committee and was received favorably by the Executive Committee: the reintroduction of the Continental. William Clay Ford declared his interest in this proposal and on July 1, 1952, a separate division was established with William Clay at its head.

There were several immediate reasons for pursuing the Continental project. The public memory of the old Continental remained strong and it had won a favored place in both collector and artistic circles. It was the only postwar car to be admitted into the Classic Car Club of America at that time. The Museum of Modern Art had exhibited a 1941 Continental coupe in the autumn of 1951 as an example of outstanding design. The depreciation of used Continentals compared favorably with Cadillac and dealers continued to report the requests of Lincoln customers for another Continental.

Not the least of the reasons for the Continental was the need to face Cadillac with an entirely new luxury car, especially when considering the 1952 Lincoln, a substantially smaller car than the Cadillac and smaller than the 1951 Lincoln Cosmopolitan. A head-on assault was not

The Mark II Continental convertible built by Derham in Rosemont, Pennsylvania, to the design of Gordon Buehrig and John Reinhart. It was never put into production and became the personal property of William Clay Ford.

possible, if for no other reason than Cadillac's production facilities were so much greater. A flanking action seemed to make sense, in which a new Continental of unquestioned superiority could provide a 'pass down' image for the whole Lincoln Division. Perhaps a new Continental could unseat Cadillac as the prestige leader of the industry—if not in volume, at least in image.

Yet another factor entered into the planning. By summer of 1952, the forthcoming Cadillac Eldorado was well-rumored throughout the industry and it was the "star of the 1953 line," as Maurice Hendry put it. The Eldorado had a wraparound windshield, cut-down doors and custom interiors, but what impressed the trade most was the price at the factory of $7,465, a figure more than double the usual price for a closed-bodied Model 62. First-year sales of 532 were not sensational but a price drop for 1954 opened up the market and 3,150 were sold, followed by 3,950 units in 1955. Few could have foreseen a burgeoning

market at the top price level for a personal car, and the prestige that such a car garnered for Cadillac was immeasurable.

The Buick Skylark was introduced in 1953 with a $5,000 price tag and sold 1,960 units the first year. Though the Skylark faded after two years, the fact of a Buick selling at that price level in a volume more than two thirds of the much cheaper Lincoln Capri convertible could not fail to dismay Lincoln management. Oldsmobile's Fiesta convertible for 1953 was yet another, though less successful, attempt to enter the personal market—only 458 were sold.

William Clay Ford (left), grandson of Henry Ford, was born on March 14, 1925, and joined the Ford organization in 1948. On July 17, 1952, he was appointed manager of Special Products Operations in charge of the Continental Mark II. He was vice president and general manager of the Continental Division from 1954 to 1956. Since May 1973 he has been vice president of Product Design. In June 1978 he was elected chairman of the Executive Committee and appointed a member of the Office of Chief Executive. John Reinhart (right) has had a long and brilliant history in the automobile industry. After training at the GM design school he worked on the instrument panel for the Cadillac 60 Special in 1937, Loewy's 1947 Studebaker, the postwar Rootes line in England and was chief stylist for the 1951 Packard. He was chief stylist for the Continental Mark II.

The Packard Caribbean, the last special edition of a great marque, appeared in 1953 with a base f.o.b. price of $5,309. It sold a respectable 750 units and remained in production until 1956, albeit with declining production.

The presence of these numerous specialized cars—penetrating price areas in which Lincoln was an obvious and cheaper option—was a powerful motive in reconsidering the Continental project. The Eldorado was clearly the finest-executed of the new personal cars and the target to be surpassed in Continental planning. Thus a base price for the Continental was established in the Lincoln corporate thinking at not less than $7,500. The Davis Committee initially used $8,000 as the target price. Psychological reasons dictated $10,000 as a prudent top limit, a price under which even the illustrious Rolls-Royce Silver Dawn was available in 1954. Lavish equipment was an obvious requirement with very few options necessary. Only air conditioning would be a major option for the Continental.

Who was the target buyer for a specialized car approaching a $10,000 price tag? The obvious answer might have been found by analyzing the sales of the old Continental, and though this was done on a superficial basis, a problem was overlooked. The original prewar Lincoln Continental was priced around $2,700, approximately three times the price of a Ford and far beneath the great Lincoln V-12 Model K whose closing moments briefly paralleled the brilliant new car. At that price, the 1940-41 Continental was cheaper than the Packard Custom Super Eights and Cadillac 75's, and equaled by the Chrysler C-33 Crown Imperials. In other words, the original Continental was a competitive option for wealthy buyers who sought something different and personal.

Buyers in 1941 saw in the Continental a unique automobile offering superb styling at a fair price. And it was bought by the 'solvent literati' such as Frank Lloyd Wright and John Steinbeck and artists like Duke Ellington. The coupon clippers stayed with the limousines. It was a narrow marketing target but then there were few Continentals sold and their influence was wildly beyond their numbers.

The projected price for the Continental Mark II was at the very top of the market, set initially by market design rather than by any engineering or cost studies. Such a car would have to be bought by persons of some wealth, or at least by those who were willing to invest a very substantial amount of money in a very distinctive automobile for very important personal returns. The failure of the Davis Committee and its planning successors to recognize the beguiling nature of the Continental image forestalled the hard market analysis required for commercial success. To build a new Continental seemed enough.

The question, then, was how to build an extraordinary automobile of such overwhelming quality as to justify a price double that of a Cadillac 60 Special. And what were the qualities that would make such a car truly extraordinary? The answer seemed to be in the recreation of the 'classic' beauty of the original Continental. The first Continental was not a classic in the normal sense, for it lacked the finish, fit, mechanics and sheer quality of the truly great cars. It was more Ford

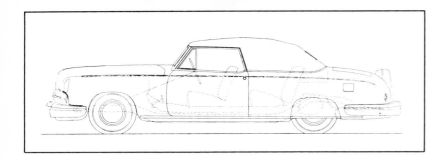 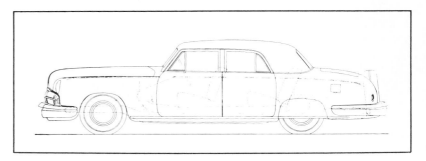

than Lincoln Model K. But it was stunning and different and that is
what had to be recaptured.

Virtually every stylist, designer, surface developer and engineer at
the Ford Motor Company had thought about the Continental. Numerous
studies were made by Doehler, Farkas, Regitko and others on the 1949
car back in 1946. These results were not happy because in all cases
elements of the 1941 car were simply applied to the stock body. A
squared roofline or rear-mounted spare doth not a Continental make.

More serious efforts were begun by William Clay Ford in the new
Special Products Division. Within ten months and a budget of a million
dollars, the new Continental had to be formed. Key men in the new
project were Harley Copp, chief engineer; Gordon Buehrig, body
engineer; and John Reinhart, stylist.

John Reinhart was a graduate of the GM design school and had
worked on the instrument panel of the Cadillac 60 Special in 1936.
After a short stint with Gordon Buehrig in Auburn, Indiana, Reinhart
moved to Packard where he worked with Werner Gubitz as a junior
designer on the first Clipper. In 1942 he was with Raymond Loewy doing
exterior design work on the 1947 Studebaker. At the close of the war he
joined Loewy in England and restyled the whole Rootes line including
the Humber, Hillman and Sunbeam Talbot. Reinhart returned to
Packard in 1947 replacing Gubitz and was the senior designer on the
1951 car. Reinhart thus came to Ford in 1951 with a breadth of
experience in numerous assignments not easily duplicated.

The Special Products Division was not allowed to draw stylists from
other divisions and so Reinhart advertised for help. Robert Thomas and
Ray Smith came from American Motors and others were from the old
Ford Trade School. Starting with the 1948 Continental, the group drew
what might have been the logical model changes for 1949 and

thereafter. The goal was to create a new car yet retain the distinctive
features of the original Continental. By late 1952, Reinhart and William
Clay Ford felt they were ready and they invited Henry Ford II along
with the Executive Committee to view the first renderings of the new
Continental. Following an awkward silence, Henry Ford was reported to
have said, "I wouldn't give you a dime for that."

Revision started at once, and Bill Ford and Reinhart hedged their
bets by calling in four outside consulting designers: Walter Buell Ford
(married to Josephine Ford and thus a brother-in-law of William Clay),
V. Gardner, the team of R. Miller and A. Grisinger, and George Walker.
These groups worked through the winter, and in April a second
presentation was made.

Each consultant prepared five views of what the new Continental
should look like—front, rear, side and two quarters. All the teams used
Honolulu blue, Bill Ford's favorite color, and all the pictures were
matted identically and hung without a hint as to their creators.

The viewing was done by the Executive Committee, one at a time
and without consultation with each other. Reinhart and Bill Ford were
delighted to discover that the Special Products team had 'won.' On May
12, 1953, William Clay became a vice president of the Ford Motor
Company.

By June 25, Reinhart had prepared a full-size clay and on July 7 the
Continental program was formally approved. Work now moved forward
at full speed. Reinhart proceeded to detail the body design, adhering

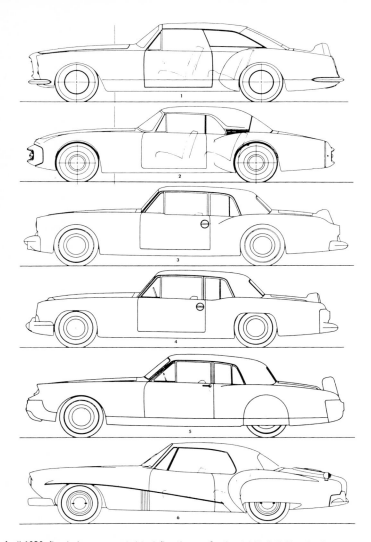
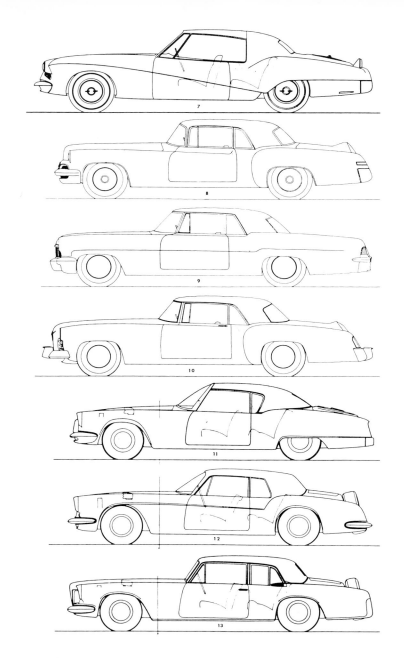

In April 1953, five designers competed to define the new Continental Mark II. Line drawings were prepared of front, rear and side views along with quarter renderings in color, all Honolulu blue, a favorite of William C. Ford. All the illustrations were matted identically. The designs were then viewed by the Ford Executive Committee, each member viewing alone and without consultation. The thirteen unsigned ideas are shown here and numbered only for purposes of identification now. 1, 2: Walter Buell Ford. 3, 4, 5: V. Gardner. 6, 7: R. Miller and A. Grisinger. 8, 9, 10: John Reinhart and the Special Products Group. 11, 12, 13: George W. Walker. The Executive Committee independently picked drawing number 9. A full-size clay was ready on June 25 and on July 7 final development of the Continental Mark II was approved.

The Eldorado Brougham was Cadillac's answer to the Continental Mark II. This splendid folly was introduced in December 1956. Never a commercial success, highest sales were 400 in 1957.

A clay model of the Continental Mark II prepared in late spring of 1953. Apart from hubcap design, the final form of the Mark II is virtually complete.

always to a remarkably clean and uncluttered philosophy. The spare-tire bulge in the trunk was still the most identifying styling echo of the original Continental though the tire underneath destroyed any pretense of great luggage space. The treatment of the interior was also tasteful, especially the handsome instrument panel consisting of four round gauge clusters which included a clock and tachometer. These instruments were carefully tested for accuracy.

All materials used were of the highest quality. Choice leather was very often fitted to a new seat pattern in which the bolster idea became dominant with inset panels of contrasting colors. The leather was from Bridge of Weir. Hide inspection was severe, resulting in a very high rejection rate for extremely minor flaws normally passed by other automotive users. The Matelasse material was also offered. Full foam cushions were used. Carpeting was ninety percent rayon and ten percent nylon. The electric switch panel in the driver's armrest controlled the windows, vents and the power seat. The doors were mounted on extra-heavy hinges with a safety latch, extra locking pin, and stops at forty-six or seventy degrees.

When it came to colors, the Continental offered thirty-nine interior trim options plus four new iridescent colors in addition to the numerous other normal paint tones. In all, there were 216 cataloged color combinations. If this failed to satisfy the buyers, dealers were encouraged to use a special order procedure which could and did produce a gray car with pink leather or lambswool carpets, kilometer

speedometers, foot tire pumps, heavy-duty springs, foreign language owners manuals, and just about anything within reason that a buyer might desire in color or equipment.

Though the running gear was virtually stock Lincoln components, all engines were partially disassembled after the dynamometer test for inspection and then reassembled and retested. Transmissions were road tested in a vehicle before installation. The finished car was again dynamometer tested, followed by a road test. Nuts and bolts were torqued to aircraft standards; wheel alignment was held to super-fine tolerances; and wheels, tires and drums were all balanced. No effort was spared to produce a perfect car.

Even after production got under way a novel quality control system was developed, called the 'hot spot eliminator' in which the ten most frequent quality faults were determined each day and a concentrated effort was made to eliminate them the *next day*.

The body panels, after fitting, were disassembled for simultaneous painting to insure a perfect color match. Interiors were trimmed from single bolts of cloth and matched hides. Undercoating was standard and plating was three times as durable as required by Society of Automotive

John Reinhart's mastery of line and form is everywhere evident in the superb balance of the Continental Mark III. It was the cleanest design from Detroit in the fifties. The absence of brightwork and decoration is remarkable. But the car was tremendously large and great bulk in the lower half of the body tended to give a 'squatty' look.

Engineers standards. The cars were finally shipped with a fleece-lined canvas and plastic cover to prevent any damage in delivery.

There was early planning for a convertible in addition to the coupe body style and Harley Copp designed an extra-heavy frame with some square-tube cross members between the cow-belly peripheral frame rails, a factor in the heavy weight of the car. The frame was good but unnecessarily strong because the convertible project never materialized, and one cross member was removed from 1957 production frames. The retractible hardtop design scheduled for the Continental was satisfactory but low production estimates made it prohibitive in cost, so the whole project was sent over to Ford where Reinhart later modified it

into the 1957 Skyliner Retractible Hardtop. The idea reappeared in soft-top form in the 1961 Continental.

One Mark II Continental convertible was built by Derham in Rosemont, Pennsylvania, to the design of Buehrig and Reinhart as a planning prototype which wound up in the William Clay Ford family. There were no quarter windows and the great expanse of canvas was reminiscent of the original Continental cabriolet. In particular, the top line was especially neat, both when up and folded. This car was sold to Paul Wagner, a vice president at Ford, and then passed into the open market. The projected price of the convertible was approximately $18,000 and production would undoubtedly have been minuscule. The absence of Lincoln quality control and the accompanying reluctance of the company to issue a warranty helped to decide against the project, despite the undoubted excellence of the Derham product.

74

The integration of the spare tire hump on the Continental Mark II was superb and the rear ensemble is unusually harmonious. The spare wheel hump broke up the vast rear deck expanse and gave a light feel to the rear of the car.

The Continental Mark II instrument panel and dashboard were elegant and quite simple when compared to competitors. Styling restraint was the keynote of the Mark II.

A second Mark II convertible was built in Palm Beach, Florida, apparently without factory authority. Though the top appeared to be slightly higher than the Derham car, the metal-covered boot was particularly attractive.

The pre-announcement build-up for the Continental Mark II was elaborate. Mark I Continentals were made available for television and movie use, beginning in 1954, and were used in the *Caine Mutiny*, *Magnificent Obsession* and *Dragnet* series. The Lincoln Continental Owners Club was given new assistance and encouragement and William Clay Ford was appointed honorary president. An unsuccessful attempt was made to find the first Continental for display at the Ford Museum. A 'whispering' campaign was begun, including speculative articles placed in major magazines and interviews with prominent executives suggesting a possible new Continental to be introduced in 1955. A public relations build-up of William Clay Ford compared him to Edsel in the creative relationship to the new car, and in October 1954 a formal announcement was made of the Mark II at the Lincoln Continental Owners Club meeting at Greenfield Village.

A national press meeting was held on October 5, 1955, preceding the October 21 introduction at Dearborn. The Mark II was first publicly displayed at the Paris Auto Show on October 6, 1955. Private showings were held in Detroit, New York, Houston, Chicago, San Francisco and Los Angeles between October 7 and 19, at which William Clay Ford

personally greeted some 400 to 700 carefully selected guests. Pianist George Feyer was on hand to provide music. Advertising crescendoed in both class and mass-audience magazines. A special television commercial was aired on the *Ed Sullivan Show*. Everything was made ready for the great opening moment.

And what did the public see? An undeniably handsome car, clean to the point of appearing spartan when compared to the jukebox mid-fifties styling of most cars. The restraint of the exterior design could not conceal the fact that the car was very big and the rather squared-off rocker panels, when compared to the Cadillac Eldorado Brougham, gave the Continental a 'squatty' look. Cadillac salesmen were quick to call the Mark II "overweight and undersexed." It may have been overweight but the sex part—or lack of it—was deliberate. The Mark II did not have the targeting of the original Continental. An owner profile constructed very early in pre-announcement sales analysis revealed that the typical buyer was a fifty-one-year-old businessman with a $30,000 annual income, three dependents, a $50,000 home and membership in the local country club. The rather bland styling of the Mark II coupled

Heavy hood insulation, a cast-aluminum rocker-arm cover and a small engine-compartment light were some of the nice touches on the Continental Mark II.

A row of Mark II Continentals, lovingly cherished by members of the Lincoln Continental Owners Club. Having survived the first 25 years, these cars will probably go on indefinitely under the watchful scrutiny of their owners.

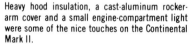

with the heavy emphasis on quality, especially in the splendid interiors, was right on target.

Sales took off briskly and *Business Week* reported the success on November 26, 1955, under the heading "Selling Like Hot Cakes." *Business Week* found buyers standing in line one month after introduction, most often waiting with cash in hand. At the production rate of thirteen per day in November, a line formed quickly. Dealers were choosy. One salesman said, "I won't sell this car to a man who doesn't belong to it, even if he has the money." He eschewed gangsters, racketeers and dope peddlers. Another dealer refused a sale because the buyer wanted to haggle over price. In Beverly Hills, a one-hundred-dollar cash bonus for a sale was offered by five customers.

Houston sold all of its original eight Continentals at $1,000 over list. Cleveland reported sixty-seven backorders. Early buyers included Mervin LeRoy, Stewart Granger, Arnold Kirkeby and A. L. Williams of Cleveland. Williams was considered a good buyer because he was a British naval officer in World War I, president of Clevite Research, and he moved in the better Cleveland clubs.

There is a certain comic opera atmosphere in *Business Week's* reports of Continental Mark II popularity because two months later the whole bubble had collapsed. In January 1956 demand for the Mark II had already slackened to the point where dealers were beginning to discount. This was fatal to the carefully prepared image and sales management took quick steps to counter the trend.

Of the 1,300 Lincoln dealers, some 650 had signed up for Continental distribution and an attempt was made to reduce the size of this dealer body. Remaining dealers were then categorized in three classes: The top group (X) was required to maintain a demonstrator, accept a monthly quota, and send a top salesman to an intensive sales training course in Dearborn. The second group (Y) was required to maintain a demonstrator, and the third group (Z) had no special requirement. These steps helped to reduce some of the bootlegging that had begun.

A direct-mail program was targeted to 50,000 people whose individual estimated net worth was over $100,000. Follow-up included coordination with the local dealer, invitations for viewing and feedback to the division. It was a good program but it did not work because "contacts were not being made with the right people; $100,000 of net worth apparently was no indicator of interest in the Mark II." What *was* the indicator of interest in the Mark II? This continued to be the crucial question and one that was never really answered by the Continental Division. Having built the 'perfect' modern classic, buyers should have been steady, enthusiastic, and in a volume to meet at least the break-even point of 2,500 cars per year.

Sales fell steadily during 1956. The initial production of 1,251 units in the closing months of 1955 was the best that the Continental could do. The total production for 1956 was 1,307 units and for the opening five months of 1957, only 442 cars were built.

What went wrong? Perhaps nothing went wrong. Reinhart's styling was restrained and beautiful, a tremendous contrast to the extremes of the time. The quality control was superb, probably the best in Detroit. The careful introduction and follow-through was a model for the industry. The Continental Division had three roving service engineers doing nothing but attending to customer complaints. Yet the car did not sell.

It was too expensive. In the last analysis, the motor industry remains a competitive industry, quite likely the most competitive industry in America. The Continental price was established not by cost studies but by image studies. In the image business there was no equal of Cadillac and here the Continental took its lumps. The Eldorado Brougham introduced in December 1956 was Cadillac's answer to the Continental. It was a splendid super-car, full of engineering novelties which were its eventual undoing. The Eldorado Brougham, with 163 electric motors, relays, switches, solenoids and light bulbs, was clearly a delicious folly. The original price was scheduled at $8,500, which escalated quickly to $13,000 over a four-year period. Brougham sales were terrible—only 400 units in 1957, 304 in 1958, 99 in 1959 and 101 in 1960. If Cadillac could not read, or reach, the market, how could Lincoln? The truth is that the Continental was easily the better car, but both Cadillac and the Continental Division were operating in a 'cloud cuckoo land' of hazy ideas no doubt generated in part by the astronomical success of the 1955 sales year.

One thing the Continental Mark II did was to escalate prices at the top of the luxury market. In 1957, 1958 and 1959 Cadillac raised the price of the 75 series approximately $1,000 per year. General Motors had no intention of being outflanked by Ford. The price of Eldorado

John Reinhart's retractible hardtop design for the Continental Mark II never reached production. Instead, it was diverted to the Ford Skyliner for 1957. Apart from a slightly bulky rear deck, it was a very neat design. Peugeot pioneered an electrically-powered retractible hardtop cabriolet in 1934 on their 201 series.

Broughams 'stabilized' at $13,074—a price as fictitious as the Continental's $10,000. Amid such madness, the normal restraints of profit are simply forgotten. So it was for both the Cadillac Eldorado and Continental. Of the two, Cadillac took the bigger bath. The estimated loss on each Eldorado Brougham was $3,500, while the Continental loss was $1,000 per car.

Furthermore, the Continental did not sell because the Thunderbird was closer to the target of the original Continental. The T-Bird success in both two-passenger and four-passenger form went from strength to strength. The price relationship of the T-Bird to the standard Ford was much more like that of the Continental Mark I to the Zephyr. The youthful if not zestful feel of the T-Bird more closely approximated the original Continental rather than the heavy, memorial lines of the Mark II.

The Mark II was discontinued on May 8, 1957. The Oakwood Boulevard plant was vacated to make way for the Edsel, in retrospect an ominous development.

CHAPTER 7

Misunderstood Giant—1958-60

BEN D. MILLS, vice president and general manager of the Lincoln Division, told John Najjar, the new chief stylist appointed by George Walker in 1955, that the forthcoming Lincoln in 1958 was to be "tasteful, smart and with dignity." Mills said that the car should clearly offer more interior space than the Cadillac and should have fresh individuality. What constituted 'fresh individuality'? The tail blades for the 1957 Lincoln, already adopted as planning began for the 1958 car, were not admired by Najjar, not only because they would distort the award-winning 1956 design but because the fin craze was everywhere and was a tacit imitation of Cadillac. The fin route offered no fresh individuality.

Virgil Exner's first new car for Chrysler was the 1955 model in which a hint of the wedge look appeared in the rear fender emphasis. The 1956 Chrysler design took another step toward the wedge, leading to the fully unified design of 1957. There was no fresh individuality in following the wedge line.

John Najjar had come to Ford in December 1936, beginning as an apprentice tool and die maker. E. T. Gregorie moved him shortly afterwards into the new styling department where Najjar learned his craft. Early Najjar credits included the 1949 Mercury grille, and Najjar's

appointment as Lincoln stylist was a tribute to his long, successful career in the Ford Motor Company.

The 1958 Lincoln had other design objectives beyond those of manager Mills. Earle MacPherson, with an eye on exceeding Cadillac's interior dimensions, realized at once that the new car should be very big. Furthermore, the new Wixom unit body plant, likely site for Lincoln production, argued for a frameless approach. That no one had built a frameless car of great bulk did not deter MacPherson.

Najjar and his studio analyzed the current Cadillac very carefully and characterized it as a car with a soft, round look, set off by the ubiquitous fins. Najjar could only have guessed that Cadillac was on the brink of the most bizarre period in its styling history, culminating with the 1959 car. It is to Najjar's credit that his first premise for the 1958 Lincoln was to move away from fins.

A more fruitful analysis was the identification of the Ford 'look' as basically rectilinear, begun by Walker's 1949 Ford, so sharply different from the Gregorie 1949 Mercury and Lincoln. The 1952 Walker cars were somewhat squared off and by 1955 angles were everywhere. The layout of the 1958 Lincoln reflected this linearity not only in the basic body structure but in the numerous distinctive details that Najjar

1958 Continental Mark III. The unity of line in profile was splendid, though one wonders if a conventional rear window might not have helped sales.

applied. The most noticeable feature was the canted blades, amplified from a theme on the 1957 Ford which provided a very pronounced cradling of the greenhouse. Angularity was further emphasized by the sculpturing of the side panels, an idea found in the 1957 Mercury rear fenders, though in the case of the Lincoln the front fenders were given dramatic hollows behind the wheel arches, an altogether novel treatment. The headlamps were set at the approximate angle of the canted blades, producing a curious and easily identifiable front appearance dubbed the 'Chinese look' by critics. There was no question that Najjar's design brought character to the Lincoln front end. At the base of the side panels there was flaring, which complemented the upper blades and gave a feeling of support to the whole car—an exciting and fresh idea. Another novelty was the reverse-angled window treatment, again emphasizing the rectilinear look. L. David Ash was the design executive responsible for exterior development while Bud Kaufman handled interiors.

Harley Copp was in charge of engineering for the new Lincoln. His success in developing the Mark II was not to be repeated with the 1958 car because MacPherson was adamant on the unitized body concept.

Copp had assumed that the 1958 car would be a natural progression from the 1955-57 car and early styling ideas confirmed this. MacPherson felt that 'all new' could mean a break-through in unit body techniques which would bring lower weight and other advantages. The questions of noise isolation, vibrations and torsional rigidity faded away before a clean slate of engineering opportunity.

The unit body had not been widely used apart from the small European cars such as the prewar Volkswagen and Lancia. In America, only the Zephyr, Chrysler Airflow and Hudson-Nash products showed unit construction of any bulk. Engineers were nearly unanimous in pointing out that unit construction advantages fall away with increasing size. No one knew quite what the critical size might be.

The decision for unit construction was not simply MacPherson's. The new four-passenger T-Bird to be built at Wixom was a unit body for reasons of low profile and deep footwells. By November 1955, the utilization of the Wixom plant entirely for T-Birds was increasingly

The front view of the 1958 Lincoln was hard to ignore. Canted headlamps and extraordinary bumper tips served to delineate the bulk of the car. No one could doubt that Najjar set out to design the biggest car on the road.

The side view of the 1958 Continental convertible accentuated the car's tremendous bulk. That long, flat deck and the neat cover over the folded top made all other cars seem compact.

suspect economically. The decision to build the new Lincoln at Wixom would neatly round out the production capacity and this decision came from Breech, McNamara and the Executive Committee. Copp continued to criticize this decision on the basis of excess weight, which he felt would be inevitable, but the program was now committed and with only two years of lead time, the pressure was on.

One further decision was now made, namely to exceed Cadillac not only in interior dimensions but in wheelbase. Cadillac wheelbases had been hovering around 130 inches, specifically 129 inches for the 1955 Model 62 and 133 inches for the 60 Special. The new Lincoln fell precisely in between at 131 inches, which Copp calculated would imply a 5,000-pound car.

Planning moved forward quickly and near-crisis timing prevailed. A prototype was ready by May 1956. Development revealed that the torsional rigidity simply was not present in a body that was essentially pillarless, and reinforcing was applied with monotonous regularity. On

test, the original prototype collapsed in the rear quarter panel when subjected to severe potholes.

A key problem was weld failure, as Copp reported it. The weld effectiveness did not come close to the work of Nash, so John Dykstra reorganized the whole welding operation and the sixty-five percent effectiveness was lifted to ninety percent. Further reinforcement was called for plus endless engineering revisions. Some were not so minor. The all-new coil spring suspension worked well but the rear coils flew right out under one severe bump. Planned airbags were discarded, probably with good reason as Cadillac was soon to discover the peril of such suspension novelty in the Eldorado Brougham.

With weight rising rapidly, the existing Lincoln engine was clearly inadequate so a new 430-cubic-inch engine was readied for the 1958 model. The engine delivered 375 bhp at 4800 rpm and 490 pounds-feet of torque at 3100 rpm. This thundering power plant was well able to cope with the new weight but gas mileage was bound to be terrible. A new, extra-low rear-end ratio of 2.87:1 was fitted but it did not lift gas mileage much above 10 mpg.

Particular attention was paid to the combustion chamber of the new engine. The wedge shape was clearly the way to go and the wedge was formed by angling the top of the block ten degrees. A flat head could thus be fitted and the piston was also flat except for a step at the narrowest end of the wedge, which increased turbulence by jetting the fuel-air mixture across the combustion chamber toward the spark plug. The increased size of the engine made quick heat build-up more

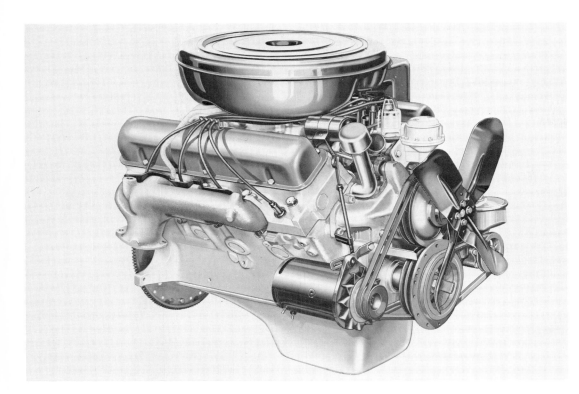

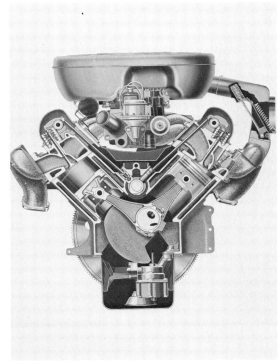

The 1958 engine was all-new and boasted 375 bhp from 430 cubic inches. It was a superb powerplant and hauled the 5,000-pound Lincoln from rest to 60 mph in about nine seconds. The top of this new engine was angled ten degrees, making possible a flat head. The tremendous compact strength of the engine is evident in cross section (right). It would be hard to improve the breathing through these very large ports.

important in the interest of economy and durability. Three thermostats were fitted which also helped interior heater performance.

The transmission was larger to handle the new torque and it retained the three-speed system. Wheel diameter fell from fifteen to fourteen inches and brake diameters shrank from twelve to eleven inches. Much wider drums were fitted, three and a half inches wide at both front and rear, and lining area was boosted from 207.5 to 293 square inches, a forty-three percent increase.

The end result was awesome. The Lincoln was 229 inches long — nineteen feet of automobile. No American car was as long except for the stretched limousines such as the Cadillac 75. Even the Rolls-Royce Phantom IV was shorter by an inch or two. The gargantuan Daimler limousines of the postwar period such as the DE-36 were a foot

shorter. In fact, no Rolls-Royce of any model exceeded this overall length until the Phantom V.

Najjar's styling had certainly emphasized the rectilinear aspect of the car—it was all corners and projections. The Cadillac was exceeded in every dimension. The great new engine was far beyond Cadillac whose 310 bhp looked positively puny. Lincoln performance matched the horsepower rating—0-60 in under nine seconds, a phenomenal achievement for a car over 5,000 pounds.

This Mark III four-door was styled by John Reinhart and continued all of the basic ideas of his splendid Mark II. It was a very big, striking car. The roofline was exceptionally flat. When it became obvious the Mark II wasn't a marketing success this idea was shelved. Reinhart's Mark III grille (right) was even simpler than the production Mark II. The very massive opening needed the vertical bars of 1957.

The Lincoln was offered in two series, the Capri and the deluxe Premiere. There were three body styles: the four-door sedan, the four-door hardtop and the two-door hardtop. The Lincoln grille was inset with thin horizontal bars and underneath it was a very massive bumper with unusual flared ends. Ornamentation was modest with a single chrome spear along the side of the car, a tasteful contrast to the lavish use of side chrome trim on the GM competitors. The Premiere was easily identified by a little eight-pointed star at the front of the spear.

The Lincoln had been flirting with an ever more ornamented rear deck treatment, beginning in 1956, and in 1958 the development had reached the point where it could honestly be called a grille.

The instrument panel was mounted on a very large near-vertical surface directly in front of the driver which press releases described as "aircraft type." A semi-circular speedometer dominated the instruments and controls. Lincoln was proud of the front-mounted air-conditioning system which ducted through the doors to the rear seat area and was controlled by a single knob. Two other knobs on the instrument panel provided "seasonal control in converting from summer cooling to winter heating."

All in all, the 1958 Lincoln was a tremendous car, a bold and innovative use of the unit body construction principle. The initial rationale for the unit body, namely low weight with great rigidity, had

somehow disappeared and the cars were very heavy; the Lincoln four-door hardtop weighed 4,810 pounds. This weight was slightly above that of Cadillac and Imperial but the new Lincoln engine was well able to bring about tremendous performance at the price of fuel economy, and owners were content with anything over 10 mpg.

Meanwhile the fate of the Continental had been decided. John Reinhart had begun work on a 1958 Continental in 1955 and clays had been prepared. The second-generation Continental Mark II, in a four-door presentation form, was clearly an evolvement. The car was lower, with a very flat roof panel, and the profile was unmistakably Mark II. However, the sudden fall-off in sales in early 1957 brought the whole project to a halt. A further effort was made by Reinhart to integrate a 1958 Continental with Najjar's new car. The results in clay form were not happy. Rear treatments showed experiments with fins and a touch of Virgil Exner's Chrysler wedge. On the scale of the new 229-inch car, the massiveness at the rear became grotesque. Clearly, Reinhart's efforts were leading nowhere and he left the company in 1958.

If the Continental name was to be preserved, it was painfully clear by early 1957 that the best that could be accomplished was to market the Continental as a top-of-the-line Lincoln. Ash and Najjar were ready and their Continental treatment offered a finely textured mesh-type front grille. At the rear, three taillights were set in a similar grille pattern. It was a shrewd decision because the Continental version of the new Lincoln out-sold both the Premiere and the Capri from 1958 to 1960, in Mark III, IV and V labels.

After the Mark III project was canceled, Reinhart attempted to work up a new Continental based on John Najjar's 1958 design. Najjar's greenhouse is untouched and the fender sculpture is unmistakable. The front bumper and fender development is Reinhart's, as is the new rear fender.

A full-size clay of Reinhart's Mark III Continental. The grille and over/under headlight arrangement did not survive but the general body outline was unchanged.

The Continental, dubbed the Mark III, was offered with the same three bodies plus a convertible. The instant styling identification was a reverse-slanted power rear window, a useful idea in snowy climates where the window would remain relatively clear. Even the convertible had this feature. The convertible was folded beneath metal decks which automatically opened when the top came down. The rear Continental spare tire hump was gone, for there was no sheet metal difference between the Lincoln and Continental series.

Interiors continued Lincoln's sumptuous traditions and featured Bridge of Weir leather. The Continental offered three all-cloth combinations, eight leather and nylon selections and six all-leather options plus an additional leather color in the convertible. Twenty-one exterior colors combined into 103 two-tone combinations. In all, with eleven fabrics plus leather and vinyl, there were 145 interior options. The stylists' imaginations knew few restraints and advertising copywriters may be pardoned for being caught up in the excitement when presidential black was described as an "exciting new color."

Announcements were made on October 25, 1957. Lincoln factory prices started at $5,113 for the Capri coupe and $5,874 for the Premiere four-door hardtop. The Continental two-door was $6,135, with the convertible and four-door hardtop at $6,593. The Cadillac 62 de Ville four-door was $5,817. Imperial prices peaked with the LeBaron line at $6,321 though the cheapest Southampton started at $5,124. All these luxury cars offered power steering and automatic transmission as standard but the list of extras was considerable.

The objectives of 1955 were clearly met and the new Lincoln no longer needed an apology from anyone as to inferior size, power and performance to the Cadillac. The 1958 Cadillac had sprouted very substantial new tail blades, although it had a slightly simplified grille treatment when compared to 1957's excesses. It was a low time for General Motors styling. The 1958 Buick was covered with chrome, and Oldsmobile and Pontiac were not far behind. The Chrysler line was given a minor facelift and looked positively conservative against the competition.

Sales and registrations for 1958 were down for all the luxury makes:

Cadillac	122,577	−13%
Lincoln	26,577	−28%
Imperial	16,102	−57%
Packard	2,599	−49%

The Lincoln survived the 1958 season better than most. The Imperial threat faded as fast as it had started. Packard was finished, with the sad Studebaker echoes finally over. Chrysler's wedge had a serious setback, while Cadillac's momentum carried it along. Of all the cars in the

John Najjar has the longest continuous service in Ford styling. He joined the firm in 1936 as an apprentice tool and die maker but was quickly moved into styling by E. T. Gregorie. After numerous credits, including the 1949 Mercury grille, Najjar was charged with the styling of the 1958 Lincolns and Continentals. His Continental Mark III is all angles and corners and conveys aggression coupled with tremendous bulk. The front fender sculpturing is remarkable—a design idea of tremendous novelty. The public had a hard time understanding the whole concept and sales were disappointing.

luxury class, only the Lincoln was all-new, no doubt the reason for its relatively good showing but a long way from a forward sales movement.

The 1958 Lincoln was yet another major image change and *Motor Trend* tested the Lincoln, Cadillac and Imperial, reporting the results in the September 1958 issue. The Imperial was the widest, the Lincoln the longest and quickest, the Cadillac the softest ride and most economical. The 1958 Lincoln was no longer the leading road car; Imperial was given honors here. Braking on these big cars was poor. Fading occurred after four or five 60-to-20 mph slowdowns and on the seventh stop the brakes were finished on all three cars.

Lincoln was faulted heavily for rattles, an ironic criticism for a unit-construction car. Body panels shook on rough roads and the noise was objectionable. The doors fitted too tightly and *Motor Trend* reported

the weatherstripping had torn away on the left rear. The windshield wipers operated poorly. Lincoln virtues included easy entry to the rear seat, good grouping of controls within the driver's reach and good instrument placement, albeit with nighttime reflection on the windshield. The car had a good driving seat position and was responsive in traffic, though one-half turn of free play was noted in the steering. Directional stability on the road was outstanding. Convenient interior lighting was noted along with fine leather.

Lincoln management pondered over the modest reception the new car had been given by the public. Now that Cadillac had been exceeded in nearly every way, there should have been a great surge of buyer interest. The 1958 model year was a disappointment for all the manufacturers, but Lincoln had hopes for a breakthrough on the assault against Cadillac. One problem might have been the reluctance of the public to accept another new image from Lincoln; it was only four years since the Mexican road race victories. The buyers of that type of hot car would not touch the new giant of 1958. It was obvious that Lincoln was now going after a new clientele—specifically a direct appeal to the Cadillac buyer.

Front-end experiments for a Mark III Continental based on Najjar's 1958 Lincoln.

This 1959 Continental boasts some slash-strip trim not seen on general production.

There were doubts about the car. *Motor Trend's* criticisms were what might be expected for a new car, built in a new plant, by new employees, under a rush program. But trouble with the unit body was persistent. The promised tight tolerances not only produced the occasional tight door but did not end the vibrations and noise. There was a steady effort to bring new silence and rigidity into the body design.

The reaction to the new Lincoln and Continental by the motoring press was generally very favorable, bordering on 'puffery' in some instances. It was soon clear, however, that criticism of the new style was widespread. The 1958 car was not a design that could be ignored and it had the virtue of being defiantly different, entirely apart from its very great size. Nothing could be done about the size, but the styling idiosyncrasies could be muted and Don DeLaRossa set out to do just that, following his appointment as Najjar's successor. Early reports of disappointing sales of the 1958 car confirmed DeLaRossa's previous decision to make the 1959 car more conventional and, presumably, more acceptable.

The most obvious Najjar touch, the strong concave sculpturing behind the front wheels, was eliminated, with only an echo of the old outline. The massiveness of the bumpers was reduced, the protruding angles softened and the overall length of the car shortened by two inches. A chrome accent panel was laid on the rear quarter of the Lincoln, a reminder of the Buick styling gimmickry which seemed to have engulfed General Motors styling. The new Lincoln and Continental were less 'squatty' and more unified, particularly in the front grille area.

When compared to the 1959 Cadillacs, the Lincolns were handsome. The rear fender blades of the Cadillac were now out of control—the

final exhaustion of themes begun in 1948. The Cadillac had become a grotesque caricature of its former grace and would take five more years to extricate itself from the last trace of this folly.

Chrysler design was also bizarre and the big rear fin theme was elaborated into maximum vulgarity. The Imperial was picking up chrome trim here and there and would continue on a downward styling course until the 1962 model. The rest of the line had rear fender fins, ending in lethal points, with appropriate chrome slatherings. Amid such tastelessness, DeLaRossa's 1959 restyling looked good. Lincoln engineering changes were minor. Engine compression was reduced to 10:1 and horsepower fell back to 350, though torque remained the same at 490 pounds-feet. The engineers were struggling with the noise problem in the unit body and much was made in the press releases about eliminating resonance points through applying various frequencies of an 'electro-mechanical exciter' to each metal body component. Sound deadeners were then applied including waffle felt, fiberglass, mastic and jute.

Two new bodies did appear in the Continental line and were important for they reintroduced the Lincoln Division into a traditional market. The new town car and limousine featured a padded roof and were similar in appearance. The limousine offered a divider window and front leather upholstery along with a rear-seat radio, smoking set, reading lights and hand grips. In the garish styling year of 1959, these two new formal sedans had an unusual dignity, perhaps one reason they were overlooked by buyers. Only forty-nine limousines and seventy-

The 1959 revisions of the Continental by Don DeLaRossa smoothed away the most obvious idiosyncrasies of the 1958 car. Front fender sculpturing was eliminated and only a raised molding remained. The front bumpers pulled back from the very sharp corners and the bullet-shaped bumper guards were eliminated.

Continental's 1960 styling revisions were minor, most noticeable of which was a conventional bumper that eliminated the corners entirely. Bullet bumper guards returned. The chrome trim in the front fender area added nothing. Light-colored cars looked especially big.

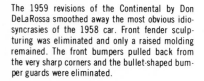

eight formal sedans were sold. The buyer of a true luxury seven-passenger limousine was still dependent upon the Cadillac 75 series, marketed in 1959 as a 67 series of which 1,400 were produced.

It was another disappointing year for the Lincoln Division. Total production fell to 26,906—a 9.3 percent drop. Imperial production rose slightly to 17,262, and Cadillac dwarfed all competition with production of 142,272, a 16.8 percent increase. Tasteless or not, the Cadillac with its extraordinary rear fender blades seemed to be well-tuned to the public's desires.

Subtle but tasteful changes occurred in the 1960 Lincoln and Continental. The Continental roof was shortened at the front to remove the little lip over the windshield. The grille was die cast and expanded into the headlight area, a welcome change since the front end had yet more unity. The hood over the Lincoln rear window was also removed, revealing a pleasing curvature at the top of the window. The Lincoln grille featured long, raised rectangular slots. The usual changes were made in trim and identifying features highlighted in the Lincoln by a full-length chrome spear or tapered molding along the side crease line.

The instrument panel was redesigned and featured four pods in which were set circular dials. The left pod contained fuel, temperature, generator and oil indicators; the second pod the speedometer; the third

the heating and ventilator indicators; and the fourth pod housed the clock. Reliability was increased with printed circuitry and the top of the pod assembly was easily removed for servicing. There were three warning lights for the electric door locks, trunk unlock device and the automatic Multi-Luber.

After two model years the coil springs at the rear were abandoned in favor of half-elliptic leaf springs. The coils had been a problem in the development of the 1958 car. Though these mounting problems were solved, the unit body was better served by a leaf spring which gave four points of support rather than two. Bigger shocks complemented the springs. The new rear suspension made possible an increase in the gasoline tank size from twenty-two to twenty-five gallons. The brake lining thickness was also increased.

Engine changes were aimed at increasing smoothness and economy. A two-barrel carburetor helped economy at the cost of reducing horsepower to 315 and torque to 460 pounds-feet. Engine mountings were improved and the air silencer was redesigned in the interest of quietness. A convenient improvement was the location of fuses and circuit breakers under a sturdy cover which was named the 'power box' and contributed to new neatness in the engine compartment.

Further simplification came with the mounting of the power-steering pump on the crankshaft thus eliminating belt slippage. A hot-idle compensating device appeared in the form of a bimetallic thermostat which increased air flow to the manifold under high temperature conditions. The mufflers were fully aluminized for long life and silence.

Rubber was used liberally in spring mountings, shock mounts, drive-shaft couplings, transmission damper strut mounts and elsewhere. Two hundred pounds of absorbers, deadeners, sealers and anti-rattlers were added to the cars, highlighted by a second sound barrier near the firewall consisting of felt and two-inch-thick fiberglass. The engineers

This 1960 Lincoln four-door landau profile has a completely redesigned roof. Also, more rear window glass area, restyled instrument panel and new Hotchkiss rear suspension. The rear window was restyled on the 1960 Lincoln into more conventional themes. The long molding strip helped unify the car. The sharp rear fender blade remained.

sprayed, applied, glued and sealed wherever they had a chance. The result was an impressive improvement in silence. It was a good training exercise for the cars to come.

The 1958-60 Lincolns and Continentals remain a puzzling interlude in the history of the Lincoln, in part because the image they projected was so very different from what came before and what would follow. They were very large yet the 1949 Cosmopolitan had probed the limits of sheer bulk, with far less success. The 1958 car was a radical styling break with all that had come before. It was a hard car for the public to embrace. The rectilinearity with the sharp corners and reverse angles was a very aggressive, nearly hostile design. It was not a car to 'love.' Yet here Lincoln was not much different from its contemporaries who were producing blades and fins and points absolutely outrageous in some of their expressions. It was a forceful time for the stylists, and their aggressions were unmuted. In truth, the Ford top management was still uncertain about what the Lincoln should be. The 1958 car proved that beating Cadillac on dimensions was not enough as a design objective, nor was it enough to be different. The dilemma of the Lincoln may be compared to that of the postwar Daimler, regularly producing cars in the DE-27 and DE-36 series reaching eighteen feet in length, longer than any Rolls-Royce of the period except the Phantom IV and V. The Daimlers were never even a remote threat to Rolls-Royce and sold in paltry numbers. Even royal patronage could not help.

The public, as always, had the final say. They did not understand the car and failed to grasp the luxury image implied in the great bulk. It was unfortunate that the Lincoln appeared at that very moment in the market when small cars were making their most dramatic advances. The lowly Rambler doubled sales in 1958 and 1959, while the imports led by Volkswagen and Renault broke all previous records.

In the fall of 1963, five years later, the 1958 Lincoln Premiere four-door had an average retail of $960 in the *Kelley Kar Blue Book*. The comparable Cadillac de Ville brought $1,635. Only a year later the Premiere was down to $525, not too far from junking value when any major repairs came along. The comparable de Ville was still over $1,000.

Production of the 1960 car was stopped earlier than usual to permit the major changes at Wixom for the 1961 model and to work off inventories. Only 13,734 Lincolns were produced and 11,086 Continentals, of which 170 were limousines and formal sedans. Imperial turned out 17,703 and Cadillac a phenomenal 142,184. The Lincoln Division looked ahead to better times.

The Continental Bullseye—1961-65

AS PRODUCTION COMMENCED on the 1958 cars, thoughts of both management and the stylists turned to 1961, the next normal major restyling year. There was considerable confusion in the minds of all about what to do. The industry as a whole was in a turbulent styling period. The Cadillacs for 1958 were offering new, higher rear fender blades of razor sharpness with ever more garish chrome slatherings here and there. The Cadillac styling team seemed quite without restraint and inside information on the 1959 cars pointed toward an even more bizarre tail treatment. The Imperial had come through a banner year in 1957 with tremendous sales of 33,017—triple the previous year's—and naturally stood pat on its design of proven merit. The sudden drop of Imperial sales in 1958 must have been puzzling to the Chrysler management, and may have stimulated the styling revisions of the early 1960's which gradually destroyed the dignity and cleanliness of the original design.

Ben Mills at Lincoln was understandably depressed by the modest reception of the 1958 cars. Something had to be done and design exercises began at once in the Lincoln studio now headed by Eugene

Bordinat. Bordinat had come up through the GM styling studio until 1947 when he moved to Ford and then to Lincoln in the early 1950's, where he worked on the restyling of the 1955 Lincoln and took part in the general development of Lincolns from that time forward. Bordinat had made a study of the Cadillac styling success and concluded that through the preceding ten-year period a key factor was the continuity of size and principal styling features. Two Cadillac styling qualities were obvious, namely the fin and the grille, which served to maintain the car's basic image despite various changes of chrome trim, bumper layout and even greenhouse revisions. It was Bordinat's view that Lincoln needed to develop such an image to properly counter Cadillac's status leadership in the luxury field.

Accordingly, the Lincoln studio's first efforts were to evolve the Najjar car into a possible 1961 model. The minor styling revisions for 1959 and 1960 were aimed at reducing the dramatic angularity of the 1958 car, which was both its identifying strength and its sales weakness. The 1960 Lincoln had been smoothed out considerably and Bordinat's first efforts moved forward from that point. The boxiness of the

The remarkable 1961 Lincoln Continental—a masterpiece in styling from any angle. The small greenhouse was the key to creating the impression of size on what remained a very compact chassis.

greenhouse was modified by introducing a slightly descending roofline from the windshield to break up the bulkiness of the 1958 car. It was a good effort, though the car remained gargantuan.

From 1955 to 1961 the vice president of styling was George Walker, a gifted veteran in the industry whose entry into the Ford organization was through his design of the 1949 Ford. Some of the staff of Walker's private industrial design firm came with him to Ford in 1955, including Elwood P. Engel, another product of the GM design school. Engel had been working in the Special Projects styling section with a team

consisting of Najjar, Robert Thomas—who had worked with Reinhart on the Continental Mark II—and Colin G. Neale.

In the summer of 1958 they had styled a new four-place Thunderbird for possible introduction in 1961. It was an exceptionally clean car with virtually no styling relationship to any Ford product—a true special project. In the cramped basement studio of the Ford design building, this Engel T-Bird was viewed by Robert McNamara, soon to be

The 1961 Cadillac with its sculptured sides, fins, curved windshield pillar and elaborate fender tips was suddenly old-fashioned with the appearance of the ultra-clean 1961 Lincoln Continental.

Following Kennedy's assassination, the 1961 presidential limousine was returned to Hess and Eisenhardt in Cincinnati and rebuilt to the form shown here. Rear security was beefed up with bullet-proof glass. Engineering was by John Krause.

corporate president in 1960. McNamara must have sensed the echoes of the original Mark II in the clean T-Bird design, for his thoughts turned at once to the possibility of a new Continental. He asked Engel if the T-Bird could be stretched into a Lincoln and Engel allowed as how a couple of weeks might be enough to do the job. A crash program ensued, and by early fall of 1958 the 1961 Continental was essentially styled.

It is not fair to say that Bordinat and DeLaRossa in the upstairs studio were simply out-designed by Engel. The wisdom of having an advanced design studio is that such a studio can work without the usual restraints of existing models and their implications. Bordinat was struggling with dimensions laid down by the 1958 car and the great bulk of that car blocked the evolution of new and more efficient packages. It would soon be obvious to everyone in the corporation that the Lincoln would make yet another image change before the stability that Bordinat desired could be attained.

The new Continental, as an evolution of a T-Bird, offered a production opportunity that was immediately grasped by management. The Wixom plant capacity far exceeded the T-Bird production needs

and it was essential that Lincoln production be maintained there for some time if the plant were to be economical. This meant that the unit body would be continued into the sixties since Wixom was committed to this method with the T-Bird. If the 1961 Continental could be sized more closely to the T-Bird, even greater economies might result—the most essential being the utilization of the same cowl structure in which the most complicated assembly procedures of the car were located. This very desirable situation was achieved despite the considerable difference in styling, wheelbases and specifications. It is one of the reasons why the Continental was kept under such stringent dimensional styling control, which turned out to be a great virtue.

The dimensional limits of the new Continental presented a challenge to the stylists and engineers. Heading the engineering team was Harold C. MacDonald, who had come to Ford in 1948 with Earle MacPherson and in the late fifties was assistant chief engineer at Ford. The new wheelbase was reduced from 131 to 123 inches and it was an important factor in enabling MacDonald to increase torsional rigidity. Cadillac, however, was still building cars on a 130-inch wheelbase with no shrinking in sight. The problem for the stylist was how to compete in the luxury field with a car that was now going to be clearly smaller, or, to put it another way, how could the new Lincoln project an image of mass without simply out-dimensioning the Cadillac as the 1958 car had done?

There were several styling answers. The first was the use of extremely flat body panels with neither the sculpturing of the 1958 car nor the roundness so desired by the sheet metal engineers to give the necessary strength. The result was the first of the 'new look' cars of the sixties, quite unlike any luxury competition and soon to be copied by all. The crispness of panels was exceptionally well-integrated. A second styling touch was the use of a nearly vertical side panel without the usual mid-point bulge. This one idea greatly enhanced the sense of mass of the car and was further strengthened by the use of a thin chrome strip at the top edge, running the length of the car. A quick look at the Chrysler and Cadillac for 1961 reveals at once the brilliance of the Lincoln treatment which Cadillac would emulate by 1963 and Chrysler a bit later. In one bold stroke the finny, sculptured look was made obsolete.

The stylists further helped the new Continental by the use of an extreme tumblehome angle in the greenhouse, which gave the impression of the passenger compartment being nestled comfortably between those broad, flat side panels. The angle was further enhanced by the use of curved window glass. From whatever point one viewed the car, the sense of control in the greenhouse line was obvious. The effect was elegant because one instinctively thought of the classic cars in which the passenger compartment was dwarfed by the general bulk of the chassis and body. The Continental thus achieved a large look by keeping the passenger compartment under the tightest control.

This masterpiece of styling was further helped by the discreet use of trim and accessories. The styling teams resisted all temptation to decorate the car. Najjar was quoted as saying that "the Continental should be like an elegant lady in a simple black dress, with her jewelry nothing more than an uncomplicated diamond necklace." It seems likely that not only Engel but Bordinat, DeLaRossa, Thomas, Neale and all the others were simply fatigued with the bizarre and flamboyant styling of the fifties and it is to their credit that the new car was indeed elegantly simple.

In profile an echo of the old Mark II showed in the taillight treatment and it worked beautifully. The grille, described by Colin Neale as the "Eversharp razor design," was not unlike that of the Mark II but without even the simple vertical bars the Mark II had used. Beyond these echoes, however, the new Continental had little indebtedness to the Mark II and was, if anything, even simpler and cleaner than the Reinhart car.

The interior design was commendably restrained when compared to the 'jukebox' interior of the Imperial and the rather heavy Cadillac dash. A novel touch was the concealment of the air-conditioning

The 1961 Continental had curved glass windows. The rear door opened rearward, a novelty that recalled the classics of the thirties. The doors were very thick.

controls and outlet behind a central dash panel that opened up when in use. Other layouts followed the usual corporate practices.

The superb styling of the Continental was a prelude to a comparable effort by Harold C. MacDonald and the engineers who came up with the finest car that the Ford Motor Company had ever produced. Preparation and planning were meticulous. About one hundred 1960 Lincolns were fitted with numerous 1961 mechanical parts to give a running test in the hands of owners under normal usage. Engineers closely followed these special cars to check on reliability and service problems. A change in idle carburetion air supply was thus monitored along with a new piston design and new exhaust valve rotators. The 1960 engine—430 cubic inches—was used, its reliability entirely proven although horsepower was dropped from 315 to 300 in a further quest for

No other word but 'grille' can describe the rear deck treatment of the 1961 Continental. Symmetry and cleanliness of every element is evident.

The Continental was not without technical novelty despite its conventional specifications. Hydraulic windshield wipers were driven from the power-steering pump. The rear doors on the convertible were hinged at the rear because of the absence of a structurally supportive B-pillar and, furthermore, had an interference fit of the rear windows which required each window to automatically lower six inches when the door latch was pressed.

Once the specifications were established and the engineering completed, an all-out effort was made to deliver perfection in both quality of items and assembly. No cost was spared in ordering the finest materials for every part of the interior. The leather and carpet quality stood out, even after years of use. One satisfied owner wrote that "after eleven years and 140,000 miles the beige leather appears factory fresh and not a stitch has let go." The chrome on this same car was one hundred percent original and perfect as was the paint "despite perpetual polishing."

The mechanical quality was equaled by premium specifications for all components. Galvanized steel was used for underside parts exposed to saltwater spray. The window-lift motors used stainless steel shafts and were sealed in liquid rubber. The shock absorber shafts were chrome-plated.

Car assembly was carefully monitored. One car per day was pulled for examination against the master jig to insure that all fits were within the very close tolerances specified. One car per week was torn apart by inspectors for yet more detailed analysis. One car in ten on the line was removed for on-the-spot checks of door openings and other key areas. Most components received similar testing. Every engine received three hours of testing culminating with 3500-rpm running, after which it was torn down, inspected and reassembled. The automatic transmission was given a thirty-minute test. The generator was given a running test. Even the radio was tuned and played before and after installation.

Once the car was assembled it was given a twelve-mile road test which lasted for an hour though no tester was hurried. Nearly 200 items were checked off. In addition to the road test, the car was given a three-minute water spray for a leak check. Then the car was returned to the 'slick-up' line where a further unhurried inspection was made.

So confident was the Lincoln Division about this quality control that on October 31, 1960, Henry Ford announced that the new Continental would carry a twenty-four-month, 24,000-mile warranty. This was double the warranty on the remainder of the 1961 Ford product line and far in excess of the usual ninety-day, 4,000-mile warranty of the industry.

smoothness and silence. The 1960 transmission was also used but the drive line presented special problems with the new low profile of the car. By tilting the engine at seven degrees, a very low universal joint was achieved and the resultant sharp connecting angle of the universal was solved by making it a double Cardan joint, the work of D. R. Veazey. The drive shaft itself, now subject to increased fore and aft motion, was made of a double steel tube separated by a compressed rubber bushing. A complicated transmission slip joint of roller bearings inside splines and a spring-steel transmission support completed a sophisticated drive-line system.

The enemy of unit body construction is noise, and the engineers worked overtime to insulate all machinery motion from the body. Special attention was given to spring mountings, with heavy rubber bushings at the front and a rubber-lined metal box at the rear. Rubber bushings were also used in the front suspension and shock absorbers. Sound deadening and insulation were applied liberally.

The four-door convertible was a new body style for the year and was the first such body offered in the industry since the Frazer Manhattan of 1951. The torsional rigidity of the Continental was 10,000 pounds-feet per degree, an exceptionally good figure and some sixty-seven percent above the 1960 car. The convertible body needed only 300 pounds of additional strengthening, of which one hundred pounds were in harmonic balancing weights at the end of the bumpers. The top mechanism was a complex array of eleven relays, motors and actuating switchwork which produced a completely disappearing top covered by a flush deck. The design was lifted from the 1957 Ford Skyliner. The convertible was simply splendid.

Ben Mills announced the prices on November 1 with the f.o.b. list of $5,565 on the sedan and $6,166 on the convertible. The cars went on sale the same day.

The new Lincoln was greeted with enthusiastic reviews. *Car Life* magazine gave it an award for engineering excellence. The Industrial Design Institute gave the 1961 car a bronze medal.

Testers were impressed with the ride, though one journalist thought that the soft ride caused part of the tendency to have a floating feeling at high speeds. Cornering at speed produced wallow—despite efforts to improve the suspension with a front drag strut and bigger rear shackle bushings, all of which allowed fore and aft movement of the wheels. One got the impression that the wheels were moving here and there and

Instrument panel for the 1961 Lincoln Continental was neat and functional. Deep, recessed areas at the glovebox door and instruments helped the sense of spaciousness in a very tight interior. The primary air-conditioning duct (right) was housed behind a central panel which opened as shown.

Eleven relays, motors and actuating switchwork were required to operate the Lincoln Continental convertible. The vulnerability of this mechanism to rear-end damage can be imagined.

to and fro, all in the interest of a smooth ride. The chassis engineering philosophy behind the 1952 road car was a distant memory.

Meanwhile, Cadillac was trying to extricate itself from the 1959 extreme fin styling, a fact noted by *Motor Trend* when commenting on the 1961 car which no longer needed to use "startling gimmicks or garish ornamentation to make the car different." Alas, though the gimmicky fins were shrinking, side sculpturing appeared in the manner

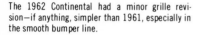

The 1962 Continental had a minor grille revision—if anything, simpler than 1961, especially in the smooth bumper line.

The 1962 Imperial was a good effort to pull back from the extremes of 1961. Continental influence could already be felt in the newly squared-off rear window outline and rear fender. But it was still a long way from the Continental's superb simplicity.

of Najjar's 1958 Lincoln design. The Cadillac remained garish and lacked the simple good taste of the Lincoln. The Imperial received minor restyling for 1961 and remained bold, finny and heavily molded—in short, everything that the Lincoln was not. The Imperial was huge, the biggest of the luxury three, and the four-door version outweighed Lincoln and Cadillac. It had a forty-eight-foot turning circle and, with a high hood line, was a handful to maneuver. The Imperial's instrument panel was unusually garish with a cavernous set of dials flanked by the pushbuttons of transmission and climate-control systems.

Against this competition, the Lincoln was wonderfully fresh and should have taken off with heavy sales. However, production for the 1961 model totaled 25,164 units of which 2,857 were convertibles, only 344 above the 1960 model. One reason was certainly the slow production startup, caused by the exacting and time-consuming testing procedures. This was one new car that appeared with virtually all the bugs worked out and the public may have been too slow to perceive the extraordinarily high standards of quality control. The public may be

forgiven for not discovering how good the new Lincoln was at first, because showroom traffic was not exactly brisk at the end of the 1958-60 period.

There was another factor which worked against the new Lincoln and was misunderstood by the public, and that was price. The f.o.b. figure settled at $6,067 for the four-door hardtop, a $600 increase over the cheapest 1960 Lincoln. The Cadillac Model 62 had a base price of $5,058 and the Imperial Southampton $5,109. This difference was substantial though deceptive because the Lincoln was delivered with unusually full equipment, the principal option being air conditioning. The delivered prices of the luxury cars were very similar when equally equipped but the public saw initially only that $1,000 premium that Lincoln required.

Lincoln had a sales gain for 1961—modest, but a gain. Cadillac production fell 3,850 units and Imperial had a bad year with production diving from 17,703 to 12,249.

In March 1961, a new presidential limousine was delivered to the White House. It was engineered by John Krause of the Hess and Eisenhardt firm in Cincinnati. The wheelbase was lengthened to 156 inches, slightly under the old Sunshine Special's 160 inches but longer than the 1950 bubble-top's 145 inches. Much strengthening was applied to the undercarriage. A hydraulically lifted rear seat was fitted. The assortment of tops included a bubble, a black cover for the bubble, a stainless top for the forward section and a formal rear top, all of which were removable for parades. Mouton carpets, lap robes with the presidential seal and the usual array of accessories were fitted. The car was in navy blue and weighed about 9,000 pounds. A specially picked and assembled stock engine was fitted and the suspension and all components were strengthened.

Following the Kennedy assassination, this car was returned to Hess and Eisenhardt for refitting. A new bubble was prepared in bulletproof glass, not in plastic. It served as the presidential parade car for eight years and logged over 50,000 driving miles and one million miles in the air. The car remained in service performing lesser chores until 1978, at which time it was returned to Dearborn for display in the Henry Ford Museum.

A regular Lincoln Continental was also fitted with a bubble top for Jacqueline Kennedy in 1961. Hess and Eisenhardt continued to supply special coachwork on the Continental chassis, principally in customizing the standard body.

Eugene Bordinat's desire for a continuing image along with management's general pleasure with the new car meant few changes for 1962. Since sales climbed steadily until the mid-sixties, his faith was justified. The grille was given a slight revision and the center bar was removed. Bumper changes were minor and, if anything, even cleaner than 1961. Body insulation was increased and weight went up about forty-five pounds. Lincoln advertising stressed weight as a proof of strength and stability, noting that the Lincoln weighed more than 400 pounds over the Cadillac de Ville, perhaps an answer to any criticism of the new smaller size of the Continental. Little refinements included power-vent windows, automatic headlight dimmer, remote-control deck release and a rear electric antenna. A padded sun visor and right vanity mirror suggested that the stylists were gilding the lily.

The Cadillac for 1962 offered few styling changes since the 1961 car had had a new body shell. The Imperial, however, was given a speedy restyling and Virgil Exner was ordered, against his judgment, to reduce the tail fins. Exner, a fin enthusiast, likened the '62 Chrysler line to "picked chickens" but the public found them pleasing and sales improved for the Imperial. *Motor Trend* did road tests on the three comparably equipped luxury cars in May 1962. The principal results follow:

	Lincoln Continental Four-Door	Cadillac 60 Special	Imperial LeBaron
Basic price	$6,074	$6,366	$6,422
Price tested	$6,797	$7,773	$7,940
0-60 (sec.)	12.4	10.8	11.0
Stop from 60 (ft.)	205	152	185
Weight (lbs.)	5,132	4,710	4,805
Overall length (in.)	213	222	227

Some interesting conclusions may be readily drawn from these statistics. Lincoln was paying a heavy weight penalty for the unit frame in a car that was dimensionally much smaller than the competition. That weight showed up dramatically in the acceleration and braking figures, inferior to both Cadillac's and Imperial's. On price the Continental was competitive against the 60 Special and Imperial LeBaron, although it must be remembered that cheaper models were offered by both Cadillac and Imperial. Despite the weight penalty, *Motor Trend* testers found that the Continental was the only one of the trio that would 'burn rubber' on full-throttle acceleration.

Even though the Lincoln had the biggest engine and heaviest weight, it put up the best fuel economy—from ten to fifteen miles per gallon. Cadillac followed with nine to thirteen and the Imperial was last with eight to twelve. The two-barrel carburetor on the big Lincoln engine was clearly helping.

Perhaps symbolic of Lincoln's quest for quality was the report of absolutely no speedometer error up to 80 mph, while the Cadillac and Imperial both showed about a six-percent increase at eighty.

Other impressions of the three cars were subjective. In summary, the Lincoln Continental seemed to score as a splendid success after only one year of production, the Cadillac excelled in endless refinements, and the Imperial seemed to elicit the most common word—luxury.

Imperial production totals for 1962 were 14,337. Cadillac broke all records with 160,840, while Lincoln produced 31,061, of which 3,212 were convertibles.

A twenty-three percent increase in sales for 1962 was certainly satisfying for Lincoln management but it was still a very long way from a challenge to Cadillac. The sales were the best since 1957, with a product sharply targeted in the luxury market.

The 1963 Lincoln Continental was characterized by the motoring press as a car with "subtle refinements," a euphemism for little progress in some cars but for Lincoln a truthful expression of continued engineering achievement. The most conspicuous styling change was the slightly raised rear deck, squared-off to diminish the blade feeling though the blades were already tastefully done when compared to the competition. The new deck suggested solidness and added a little more luggage space.

The engineers did well. Horsepower moved from 300 to 320, though still below Cadillac's 325 and Imperial's 340. The horsepower race continued in full swing and 300 hp was no longer distinctive; the top-of-the-line Mercury offered the same output from a 390-cubic-inch engine. The whole question of horsepower would soon be completely detached from the luxury field as the muscle cars appeared. In mid-1963 the

There was a lot of the new Continental in the 1963 Cadillac. The sides were smooth, window outlines more angular and front posts straight and clean. But the fins continued and the grille was still busy.

Mercury Marauder was introduced with a 427-cubic-inch engine developing as much as 425 hp. The horsepower race would last through the sixties, Cadillac eventually coming up with a 500-cubic-inch engine of 400 bhp in the 1970 Eldorado and Imperial peaking at 350 bhp from 440 cubic inches also in 1970, while Lincoln would reach 365 from 460 cubic inches. As federal regulations grew in the seventies, the bhp ratings fell back dramatically and perhaps saved the luxury cars from further folly. Lincoln's increase in horsepower was principally through a new four-barrel carburetor in which two secondary barrels were used only intermittently for maximum performance. The engineers were still eager to preserve some economy and theorized that the two-barrel primaries would likely be in use ninety percent of the time, so the primaries were centered over the manifold. The piston faces were redesigned for more squish and quench.

A welcome new item was the alternator, although Chrysler had led the way on this innovation. New power-vent windows, a six-way power seat and a front-mounted antenna with a new AM-FM radio all reflected a general technical refinement in the industry. The exhaust also received improvements including increased use of stainless steel and free-flow design. Universal joints were enlarged with a 30,000-mile service interval to handle new torque and to reflect the growing trend of the Ford Motor Company toward low-maintenance designs.

Weight remained steady for 1963 though Lincoln continued to make advertising copy noting that the Continental was one of the heaviest cars in the industry—nearly 400 pounds heavier than the Cadillac de Ville sedan. Henry Ford senior would not have understood.

Aluminum front brake drums were now fitted to the sedan, as previously used on the convertible. The elaborate testing procedure was continued in 1963. Engines were given a fifteen-minute run-in at the equivalent of 35 mph in high gear followed by a half hour at 60 and two and a quarter hours at 90 mph. Following an inspection, rod and main bearing bolts were retorqued and the engine was then mounted in the car for the twelve-mile road test. Transmissions were given a thirty-minute test. These procedures continued to set Lincoln apart from all other domestic manufacturers.

Zero-to-sixty time was 10.9 seconds, very good for a car of around 5,400 pounds and reflecting the 465 pounds-feet of torque of the largest engine in the industry.

Motor Trend's road test said that the car was "solid and free from vibrations as any car on the road, bar none." New piloted wheel hubs eliminated the necessity for the lug nuts to effect alignment, a factor in high-speed smoothness. Slight understeering was decreased with a raise in tire pressure from twenty-four to twenty-eight pounds. Braking with the new front aluminum drums on the sedan was improved though not fade-free. Fuel consumption dropped off one mpg from the ten-to-fifteen range to nine-to-fourteen. Timed top speed was 108 but the tester felt that 110 or 112 was possible.

For the spring 1963 New York Automobile Show, the Lincoln-Mercury Division prepared a special Continental called the Lido which featured a black vinyl top with a Persian Sand exterior color, and individual front seats between which was a console with a small snack bar. Metallic-finished Persian Sand leather with bolsters in diamond-luster crinkle-grain leather and mouton carpeting completed the interior ensemble. Small vertical louver trim strips on the rear door were much like the old Cadillac 60 Special and the 1958 Eldorado Seville. The car was not properly a styling exercise but really became a trimming experiment, and the vinyl roof and mouton carpeting ideas would be found in the forthcoming Lehmann-Peterson limousines.

In May 1963, the first announcement of the Lehmann-Peterson limousines appeared. George Lehmann and Robert Peterson formed a partnership with headquarters on Sawyer Avenue in Chicago. A Lincoln Continental was sectioned and the wheelbase extended to 160 inches. Two rear-facing seats were placed behind the division. A beverage compartment, television set and secretary's desk were optional equipment.

Gene Bordinat received his early training at GM styling and moved to Ford in 1947. After various assignments, Bordinat became vice president of design in 1961, a position he continues to hold making him the senior styling director in the industry. The 1963 Continental convertible—a design of magnificent simplicity and fine balance. Few cars have been so quickly recognized as having timeless beauty.

At the time of the announcement, one limousine had been completed. The key to success for the new firm lay in the blessing of the Ford Motor Company. Though the May announcement included a statement that the normal two-year or 24,000-mile warranty applied, the actual testing was done on a 1964 limousine prepared in November 1963. A 4,000-mile test took place at the proving grounds in Dearborn. The car passed, and the usual warranty was then given to Lehmann-Peterson production.

The announced price was $13,400 plus optional equipment. Unlike so many custom projects that fade almost at once following announcement, the Lehmann-Peterson limousine went into production and quickly found a market for an outstandingly good-looking big limousine. The basic Continental lines extended well, and the sheer length of the car at once set it apart from the Cadillac 75.

As production evolved and the small firm settled down, the limousine was steadily improved and by 1968 a truly dazzling array of luxury options were available. The basic price had risen to $15,104. An elaborate communication system costing $500 allowed total control of an intercom by the passenger. The divider glass could be ordered either fully powered ($350) or manually sliding ($250). The television set was a

nine-inch model ($295) using the standard Lincoln antenna. The beverage service ($200) consisted of four silver-plated tumblers, three flasks, three shot measures and an insulated ice bucket.

Ordinary items included mouton carpeting, signal-seeking radio or stereo tape player, rear clock, rear courtesy lights and an escort umbrella stowed below the front seat, to name a partial list. With air conditioning and divider glass the total weight of the limousine was over 6,100 pounds.

The Lincoln Division soon recognized the value of the Lehmann-Peterson limousine as a useful and prestigious addition to the regular Continental line. Arrangements were quickly made to take orders for the limousine through regular Lincoln dealers. Cars would then be shipped from Wixom to Chicago where the customizing would take place. By October 1965, over one hundred units had been delivered. The firm survived into the early seventies.

The 1964 Imperial was Elwood Engel's copy of Elwood Engel's 1961 Lincoln Continental.

This 1964 town brougham was built on a 131-inch wheelbase and featured lavish interior equipment. The car was strictly for show and was not road-worthy. The clean Lincoln Continental design was especially attractive in this formal form.

After three years, the Lincoln Continental would normally receive a major restyling but Bordinat's objective of a stable luxury image with some highlighting identifying features precluded the sort of innovations that had marked the decade of the fifties. The compact luxury theme had been sold enthusiastically and the car's success was a tribute to a brilliant body design on a 123-inch wheelbase. The fact remained that the norm for the luxury market was a wheelbase between 129 and 130 inches as used by Cadillac and Imperial. The time seemed ripe for a modest expansion of the Lincoln wheelbase to 126 inches, for at least three reasons: 1) the Lincoln image could be brought subtly closer to its competitors with lengthening, no matter what the virtues of compact luxury; 2) greater interior room; and 3) the Lincoln wheelbase served as a limit to Mercury and Ford expansions, the difference between the big Ford and the Lincoln in 1963 being but four inches. In particular the expansion of the Mercury was an important step in Ford product development. In 1965, the Mercury would be moved up to the old Lincoln Continental wheelbase of 123 inches.

The additional three inches on the 1964 Lincoln were used directly in the rear seating dimensions, the most cramped part of the car. The

rear door was extended three inches and legroom was upped a like amount. The very tight knee dimensions of only 5.4 inches went up to 7.7 inches. The interior designers further emphasized the change by moving the front seat forward approximately two inches so that five additional inches separated the front and rear seat backs. A dash redesign minimized the tighter front seat dimensions though legroom dropped three inches. The net effect was to bring the Lincoln's interior feel much closer to both Cadillac and Imperial. Continental customers could no longer react negatively to the Lincoln's compact rear seating arrangement.

Refinements continued in 1964, including a low-fuel warning light, automatic parking brake release, map light and other consumer-oriented touches. The new vertically adjustable steering wheel was a useful technical gadget.

The 1964 Lincoln was well received and production moved up to 36,297—the best year since 1957.

It was in 1964 and 1965 that a stunning show car appeared, the Lincoln Continental town brougham. The brougham body style, originated by an order from Henry Peter, first Baron of Brougham and Vaux in 1837, was a small, closed, two-seat carriage with sharply angular lines. The motor brougham was a razor-edged, paneled formal town car, the chauffeur entirely exposed with but minimum weather protection in the form of a small leather extension buttoned between the windshield and roof.

The Lincoln Continental's crisp styling made it an ideal subject for the brougham treatment. The wheelbase of the Continental was

lengthened to 131 inches, providing new room for the open chauffeur compartment. Turning lights were mounted on the side of the front fenders and courtesy lights on the posts between front and rear compartments. The roof was covered in black vinyl and the rear window was small in the formal style. Walnut was used on the moldings and deep pile carpeting and broadcloth upholstery completed the interior specifications. Equipment included a magazine rack, mobile telephone set, radio and intercom.

The car was well received and it was updated in exterior appearance for 1965. The color remained Plaza Blue Pearl but was renamed simply Dark Blue Pearl. A double rocker-panel bright molding was installed, landau bars appeared and a simulated pull-out roof for the chauffeur was added. There were plans for a royalty light to be placed on top of the windshield but this does not appear on early press release programs.

The town brougham was never roadworthy and the Lincoln Division warned handlers that the car was 'cobbled,' and should not be driven. When absolutely necessary, the car was to do as little as possible and then at very low speeds with utmost care. In fact, the car was meant for static viewing and the instruments, rear door windows, radio, intercom and mobile phone were inoperable.

The town brougham was not put in production, the economics of such a low-volume model complicated by the need for the elongated-wheelbase chassis which, without front roof support, posed serious rigidity problems. Even elongating the convertible chassis to 131 inches would have required a major engineering effort. It is a pity because the car remained one of the most handsome and successful of the styling exercises of the sixties.

The 1964 Continental grille had vertical bars like the Mark II. Flat window glass allowed for an enlarged greenhouse.

In 1964 the Continental side windows became flat—certainly cheaper to produce but also a reflection of increased greenhouse size.

In 1964, Lincoln was paid the compliment of imitation as Elwood Engel, who had joined Chrysler in 1961, produced a completely new Imperial which bore more than a casual resemblance to the Continental. The rear deck was squared-off and a Continental rear tire bulge appeared. The Lincoln influence was seen in the molding highlight along the top of the smooth, slab sides and the front bumper inset into the fender. It must have been right because Imperial sales shot up sixty-five percent to 23,285—the second best year since 1955.

Clearly Lincoln was gaining nicely with the Engel design, and the flattery of the Imperial copy was not unnoticed by the industry. Yet another year of the successful formula seemed in order, though the grille change for 1965 was the most radical so far. The Lincoln

The splendid papal limousine was used by Pope Paul VI on his visit to New York in October 1965. The alterations were performed in less than ten days by Lehmann-Peterson in Chicago. A single throne-type seat was mounted in the rear compartment.

Continental grille had always presented a center horizontal crease with a low hoodline set off by the very pronounced front fender prow. For 1965, the crease disappeared and a much more massive vertical grille replaced it along with a more massive hood.

It was in 1965 that the sheer bulk and weight of the Continental became an issue in both road tests and the comments of auto journalists. The convertible weighed in at 5,720 pounds, making it heavier than even the Cadillac Fleetwood limousines. Performance was merely adequate and the 430-cubic-inch engine was working hard to produce a 0-60 mph time of 12.9 seconds. Understeer was pronounced, the result of up-front weight. Handling was clearly not the strong point of these very heavy cars but ride and comfort were unexcelled. The convertible's trunk was nearly useless with the top down and extremely awkward for loading with the top up. Side loading over the fenders was difficult with luggage and it was nearly impossible to reach the spare tire. Rigidity had suffered a bit on the convertible, perhaps in part due to the lengthening of the wheelbase.

Front disc brakes were fitted of 11.87-inch diameter with four hydraulic pistons closing the calipers. Power brakes were naturally included, with sixty per cent of the power to the front wheels. The power brakes were vastly superior to the drums; in fact Lincoln braking led the way in the luxury field.

Fuel economy ran from nine to twelve miles per gallon of premium fuel, but with a twenty-four-gallon fuel tank a 240-mile range seemed reasonable.

The testers concluded that they would prefer a sedan but the convertible remained unique in American automotive offerings. Apart from disc brakes—a very welcome advance—and a transistorized ignition system, there was very little else to talk about in the new car. But it was enough for the moment and production again increased to 40,180—nearly equal to the 1953 success with the Pan-American road race cars. Paul F. Lorenz, the new manager of the division, was justifiably pleased with the record.

There was still one other special car prepared in this period, for the visit of Pope Paul VI on October 4, 1965. The car chosen was one of the original two limousines prepared in November 1963 for the 40,000-mile tests by Ford engineers. In August 1964, this car was returned to

Lehmann-Peterson for a new engine and in December the top was removed for experiments in bubble-top conversions. The side and roof rails were retained for structural purposes and to permit roll-up windows. The car was intended for parade work in the Chicago area.

On September 22, 1965, this car was ordered to be converted into a special parade car and work progressed day and night until September 30. Forty craftsmen worked on the job with as many as eight on the car at one time.

The body was strengthened for a projected passenger load of five in the rear compartment, two in the driver's compartment, six police on the running boards fitted to the sides and rear, plus 300 pounds of extra equipment. The pope's special seat had armrests and a high back and could be raised seven inches by a crank. The seats were in pleated black vinyl with mouton carpeting.

A separate electrical circuit powered a loudspeaker system which was supplied by four 12-volt batteries mounted in the trunk and charged externally. The amplifier was of 75 watts and fed four five-inch speakers. Two flourescent lamps illuminated the pope and two others were placed at the front of the car to light three flags—the United States, United Nations and papal.

The rear passenger roof was detachable and was made of transparent heavy-duty vinyl. A windscreen of plexiglass was mounted on the open section to protect the pope whether seated or standing. The car weighed about 6,000 pounds, with a tire size of 9.15x15 inches. Following Pope Paul VI's visit, the car was returned to Chicago. In February 1966, the roof of the Lehmann-Peterson factory collapsed under the weight of a heavy snowfall and the papal interior of the limousine was destroyed and removed and the car was refitted for normal parade work in Chicago.

In the summer of 1968 this same car was again refitted as a papal limousine, this time with rear air-conditioning and other refinements, at a cost of $3,000. The car was delivered on July 25 and was shipped to Bogotá aboard the Grace Lines S.S. *Santa Mariana* for the Eucharistic Conference in August. It was accompanied by engineer R. E. Peterson.

The 1965 Lincoln Continental had a new massive vertical grille which, in profile, slightly lengthened the front fender line.

Of all of the specials, the pope's limousine remains one of the most attractive, the plexiglass windshield providing a decidedly nautical effect. It was truly a papal land cruiser.

The successful elongation of the Continental into the presidential and papal cars is a tribute to the basic excellence of the design. However good a design, though, five years is a long time to remain both esthetically and commercially viable. There was little doubt that the Lincoln Continental dominated the first half of the sixties in sheer elegance and quite likely in quality. Yet Cadillac, with ever-growing sales, seemed as unreachable as ever in the dominance it exerted in the luxury field. It was time for a major evaluation and planning.

CHAPTER 9

New Triumph For Mark III—1966-68

FRESH LINCOLN MARKETING evaluation had begun as early as 1963 when William Clay Ford, now vice president of Product Planning and Styling, along with Ben D. Mills, general manager of Lincoln-Mercury Division, initiated merchandising studies in the luxury field. An important analysis issued in 1966 reviewed the proposals. Uppermost in the minds of everyone connected with the Lincoln Continental was the desire to build the "reputational image of the car by creating an atmosphere of quality, exclusivity and prestige." A second merchandising goal was to stimulate dealer attitude toward the cars so that significant improvements would be made in the areas of selling effort, merchandising practices, point-of-sales condition and service. In other words, the house had to be put in order.

Beginning in 1961 the Lincoln marketing efforts had been as follows: 1) restrict production to meet retail demand and avoid 'distress' merchandising practices; 2) control dealer appointments, particularly in multiple-point markets in order to enhance franchise value and encourage dealer investment in their Lincoln business; and 3) continue to improve engineering and assembly quality levels to the highest possible degree. This third item undoubtedly may have limited sales in the 1961 startup but by 1963 production capacity was well able to cope

with more sales. The production problem, however, was unusual. In the years 1963 to 1965, two thirds of the annual model production took place between the fall introduction and January. Retail deliveries in this same fall period for 1963 were fifty-four percent of annual sales; in 1964, fifty-six percent; and in 1965, fifty-seven percent. Cadillac had a much steadier sales rate, the comparable figures being 1963, thirty-eight percent; 1964, thirty-nine percent; and 1965, thirty-two percent. This concentration of sales in the fall period was neither an efficient way to produce automobiles nor a successful way to sell them. Once the initial fall sales program passed, the rest of the year was difficult for Lincoln dealers.

The sales department might well have added a fourth factor which was novel in the Lincoln program, namely that the building of a car with very minor styling changes reduced the tendency for the annual trade-in on the new model. The 30,000 annual sales rate of the Lincoln Continental thus contained more first-time Lincoln buyers, or conquest sales as the merchandising group termed it.

This thesis was tested in two ways. In the 1961-63 period, conquest sales were fifty-three percent, of which seventeen percent were from Cadillac. In the 1964-65 period conquest sales fell to forty-one percent

The 1966 Lincoln Continental was the first major restyling of the 1961 car. The break or hump in the horizontal line at the rear door was combined with a break line on the slab side, creating a new look. Marketing experts worried that the change was too radical. They need not have—sales were up.

as Lincoln owners began to trade in their cars after three years of use.

Another way of testing owner loyalty was to measure how many Lincoln owners retained their cars after one year of service:

1958-60	64%
1961	73%
1962	81%
1963	80%
1964	90%

Lincoln loyalty was increasing rapidly. Another study in the 1966 marketing analysis demonstrated that the new Lincoln loyalty was primarily responsible for sales progress after 1963. Owners liked their Lincolns and were trading them in for new ones. The quality control people were understandably pleased about this but the marketing people were more interested in the conquest sales against Cadillac which hovered at seventeen percent of Lincoln's volume from 1961 to 1965. Lincoln conquest sales were good indeed against lower-priced competitors—a positive sign of the car's new reputation.

The new Lincoln owner loyalty surpassed Cadillac owner loyalty in the after-three-year period beginning in 1964, an exceptionally happy statistic because it demonstrated that Lincoln quality was neither ephemeral nor unperceived.

Success does not come overnight, nor does image-building. One way of testing such success is to measure wholesale used-car prices at a fixed point in the depreciation curve, usually May, one year after the model year. The following chart tells the story:

Model	Lincoln	Cadillac de Ville	Difference
1958-60 avg.	$3,110	$3,853	-$743
1961	3,888	3,895	- 7
1962	3,631	3,784	- 153
1963	3,647	3,809	- 162
1964	3,571	3,874	- 303

The implications of this chart are subtle, but especially useful because there was nearly absolute new-price stability in the Cadillac de Ville from 1961 to 1964. Cadillac resale seemed to hold rock-steady.

Heavily hooded instrument panel of the 1966 Lincoln Continental. Controls and instruments were clear, minimal and handsome.

Lincoln sales experts were not certain about the reception of this new 1966 two-door hardtop. A 1963 study suggested that 4,500 might be "anticipated." But this handsome new car was well received with 15,766 units produced. The two-door helped Lincoln compete evenly with Cadillac.

declines of the late fifties. Yet even while sales were climbing, the penetration of the luxury market was modest because of Cadillac's great production increases. Whereas from 1958 to 1960 the penetration of the Lincoln Continental was 15.3 percent, by 1964 it had risen to but 16.3 percent.

The bottom line was profit, and average dealer profit doubled from the 1958-60 period to the 1964-65 period because unit profits went from $469 to $606 and sales nearly doubled. Lincoln dealers finally had something to sell and were obviously enthusiastic. The Lincoln Division lost sixty million dollars in the 1958-60 cycle, but from 1961 to 1965 managed to recover twenty million, with profitability each year.

The overall results of the merchandising study were both hopeful and somewhat discouraging. The negative side, according to the 1966 report, was that the 1961-65 "Lincoln Continental had not achieved prestige parity with Cadillac in the eyes of the general public and, specifically, luxury car buyers." On the positive side, there was no question that the car was making steady progress and owner attitudes and loyalty had "been building a sound platform from which to launch a more direct offensive when the proper opportunity presents itself."

That opportunity seemed to be 1966. A market survey made in January 1964 suggested that there was a significant and perhaps growing number of Cadillac owners "who in varying degrees were dissatisfied with their car, both in terms of product and prestige." Follow-up studies suggested that dissatisfaction was increasing, and in

Lincoln resale started very strong in 1961, reflecting the novelty and public acceptance of the new model. Thereafter, the resale picture weakened slowly, an especially distressing fact since Lincoln prices were raised about $200 in 1963. The direct dollar comparisons between Lincoln and Cadillac were misleading because f.o.b. base prices for the Lincoln included lavish factory equipment. Lincoln merchandisers were consoled by the tremendous improvement in the resale value of the 1961 car over its immediate predecessor.

On the brighter side, however, sales volume had a steady upward trend throughout the life of the new Lincoln Continental, reversing the

the second quarter of 1965, Cadillac constituted over twenty percent of Lincoln conquest trades. It may well have been that Cadillac's very success and high-volume production had begun to undermine the prestige based in some measure upon exclusiveness. Lincoln planners hoped that the 1966 car could capitalize on this trend.

Yet another factor was being considered by Lincoln management. The basic two-body offering of the Lincoln was weak against Cadillac's two-door hardtops in both the Calais and de Ville models, not to mention the Eldorado convertible, the prestige leader of the line. It was clear that at least a two-door coupe was essential in opening up buyer options. A 1963 study suggested that sales of 4,500 two-door hardtops "might be anticipated," which, in that year, would have meant about fourteen percent of production. In the same year, twenty-seven percent of Mercury production was in two-door coupes of various configurations. Cadillac two-door production hovered at thirty percent in 1963. This excessively conservative prediction was refuted by the 1966 production of 15,766 Lincoln two-doors, about twenty-nine percent of total volume and quite close to Cadillac percentages. Perhaps the market analysts were confused by the Ford corporate product mix in which the Thunderbird functioned nicely as a two-door, high-quality vehicle with more than a passing relationship to the Lincoln. The fact that the 1961 car emerged from a Thunderbird design had not been forgotten. Both the T-Bird and the Lincoln continued to be built at Wixom and both used unit body construction. A Lincoln two-door could easily have impinged on the T-Bird market. In fact, this very confusion would soon appear in the development of the Mark III, often seen by the public as a variation on the T-Bird's basic design.

The 1966 cars were given a major restyling, which presented a fresh opportunity to develop a distinctive two-door version. The new car was instantly recognized by a break in the horizontal line at the top of the slab sides. There was not only a subtle break and down-flow at the rear but the slab sides themselves were given a break line. The grille was facelifted, and the massive, square, vertical feeling was strengthened. Some of the marketing experts were worried that the styling was too radical a departure from the past and would be rejected by Lincoln Continental owners and the general public. And indeed, initial public reaction in a *Wall Street Journal* sketch was not altogether favorable.

A detailed analysis was undertaken of Lincoln pricing policy. The fully equipped Continental was priced substantially above the Cadillac Calais and de Ville. The cheapest Cadillac Calais two-door had a wholesale price of $3,781—almost $1,000 under the Lincoln's $4,717. The truth was that the Continental was going head-to-head against the 60 Special at $4,838, while the Lincoln convertible at $5,207 (wholesale)

was above the Eldorado at $5,053. Burdened with this method of pricing, the sales advances of the Continental must be seen as all the more remarkable.

It was the Lincoln Division's long-range program to bring the "Lincoln car line in a position directly competitive in price and product with the Cadillac car line." The addition of the two-door body was a step in that direction. The problem of direct price competition was more difficult because it suggested substantial reduction in the Lincoln price, which might seriously undermine the "reputational values" that the car had enjoyed since 1961.

What was needed was a showroom sticker price closer to Cadillac's so that the comparison shopper would not instantly dismiss the Lincoln. The answer was to reduce the lavish equipment level of the Lincoln, thus avoiding a direct price cut and still achieving an image of price parity with Cadillac. The adjustment of Lincoln's standard equipment to the de Ville level reduced the wholesale price by $345 and by $455 retail. The items now optional included power vent windows, power door locks, six-way power seat, radio, and white sidewall tires. Though the Continental had been merchandised as a fully equipped car, the steady addition of options over the years had begun to dilute that image, and the marketing experts hoped that little further damage would be done.

Furthermore, Lincoln option prices were brought into line with comparable Cadillac items. For example, the leather trim option price was raised while the air-conditioner price was lowered. Also, the two-door Lincoln was priced $189 wholesale below the four-door, similar to the de Ville. The end result of these changes was to bring Lincoln's lowest-priced 1966 model $534 under the price of the wholesale delivered 1965 car, with a retail reduction of $704 on the four-door sedan sticker price.

The retail price gap between the new two-door and the four-door was $265, a number finely tuned by the merchandisers. Too narrow a gap might have hurt the introduction of the new body, while too wide a gap might have damaged the Continental image.

The major engineering change was the entirely new 462-cubic-inch engine, a monstrous 750-pound unit, the largest in the industry. It was far more than a boring and stroking of the old engine and included changes to accommodate a larger bell housing, new cylinder heads, and intake manifold. Water passages around the exhaust valves and plugs were nearly doubled in size. Intake valve diameter was slightly increased and valve lift went up from .40 inch to .44 inch along with six more degrees of duration. The 340 bhp represented .73 per cubic inch, not unusually high and far less than the 425-horsepower engines used in

Under construction is the 1966 Allegheny-Ludlum Lincoln Continental convertible. Three were reputedly built and finished in brushed stainless, the only way to counter the scratch problems of stainless steel.

One of the Allegheny-Ludlum stainless steel 1936 Fords. The lights have become sealed beams and the hood has the usual 1936 fitting problems at the leading edge. The stainless steel bodies, however, showed little deterioration over the years.

the muscle cars then available from the Big Three. The torque figure of 485 pounds-feet was impressive. It was exceeded only by the 490 pounds-feet of the big 426-cubic-inch Chrysler, but the Lincoln torque peak came at 2800 rpm while the Chrysler peaked at 4000. The new Lincoln engine was ready to work without fussing revs. The drive line was strengthened to handle the new engine and the very low 2.8:1 rear end had a 9 3/8-inch ring gear.

The big engine retained most of the engineering ideas used before, including the symmetrical placement of primary carburetor barrels — continuing the theory that all four barrels would be used only about ten percent of the time. The fuel pump was given a thermostatically controlled bypass valve so that when above 120 degrees, fuel would circulate back to the tank, reducing vapor lock and clearing bubbles.

The usual three-hour break-in continued on these engines, followed by a pan drop, inspection, tightening and adjustment as needed. Following mating with the transmission, an additional twenty-seven-

minute test program was done to check the shifting points and any further matters. The twelve-mile road test continued.

A large console faced the driver with numerous warning lights to signal open doors and trunk, low oil and battery level, and unbuckled seatbelts.

The seats were very comfortable and were available with a new super-soft nylon tricot which Hermann Brunn described as a flat stretch-knit material that draped well and clung to the hand. Additional comfort was provided by a fully-automatic air conditioner with a temperature-control dial on a par with the best in the industry.

The 1966 car was very fast, the new engine producing a 0-60 time of under eleven seconds and a top speed of approximately 125 mph. These times were recorded with the two-door at a curb weight of 5,380 pounds. The sedan weighed one hundred pounds more and the convertible 500 more, so the coupe's performance may be considered optimal. The disc brakes were satisfactory, though heavy use with a 6,000-pound loaded convertible continued to be an exercise in faith.

The Lehmann-Peterson limousine was offered again in 1966, the third year, and adopted all of the new features of the model year. For 1966 sales went up forty-five percent, and General Sales Manager Frank

E. Zimmerman of the Lincoln-Mercury Division was especially pleased with the rental and livery use of the limousine, as it served to introduce people to Lincoln luxury.

A much more novel experimental car appeared in 1966, yet another effort by Allegheny-Ludlum Steel Corporation in Pittsburgh. In 1936 the firm had cooperated with the Ford Motor Company in Detroit by constructing six Ford V-8 sedans with stainless steel bodies. These cars had a remarkable history and survival and had been used for sales purposes by the steel company. The feat was repeated in 1966 to celebrate the completion of the fifty thousandth car in the model year, a record since the introduction of the new Lincoln Continental in the fall of 1960. The fifty thousandth car, a convertible, was built in stainless steel supplied by Allegheny-Ludlum. Two additional replicas were built for the steel company. Though the unit body presented fresh problems in stainless steel, the results were striking.

The 1966 Cadillac was given another minor facelift, the car now exceptionally smooth in appearance. The principal technical change was the variable-ratio power steering. The Imperial continued Engel's clean look with the Continental spare tire now gone.

When the shouting was over and the sales meetings had ended, it had been a good year for Lincoln with production at 54,755, the best since the extra-long production year of the 1949 model which had begun in mid-1948. On a calendar-year basis, sales of 49,234 were the best since the war. The new formula for pricing, the new two-door car with solid sales of 15,766, and the effort to smooth out the sales year

107

Time was running out for the four-door convertible when this 1967 Lincoln Continental was photographed on the proving grounds. Only 2,276 were produced and in 1968 it was no longer offered.

The Lincoln Continental Coronation Coupe II was first shown at the Chicago Auto Show on February 25. The gold pearlescent finish was matched by a gold padded vinyl roof. Strictly a show car, it was never put into production.

had all worked. Edgar F. Laux, new vice president and general manager of the Lincoln-Mercury Division, could well be pleased.

Imperial production fell back to a disappointing 13,743 though Chrysler as a whole did well. Cadillac had a record production year of 196,675.

The 1967 model year for Lincoln Continental was a waiting year, as the energies of the division were by then focused on the forthcoming Mark III. The Continental received very minor changes, principally a horsepower increase to 340. Slim vertical bars set off the grille, now slightly recessed. The superb reception of the 1966 cars carried forward to 1967 though production fell back to 45,667 — the first retreat since 1960. The four-door convertible was terminated with a final year production of 2,276, well below the usual 3,000-plus production. The car was widely admired but the sales volume simply was not there.

Sales Manager Zimmerman continued to push the Lehmann-Peterson executive limousines. He noted that on a recent business trip to New York he saw three custom-built Lincolns at a Park Avenue intersection at the same time, one going through and two waiting for the traffic signal to change. Zimmerman noted that "while the Lincoln Continental executive limousine is recognized as the ultimate in prestige and luxury motoring around the world, most of all we wanted to earn the 'Park

Avenue Seal of Approval'—and it has." Basic price of the limousine was then about $15,000 and when fully loaded with all accessories could touch $20,000.

The 1968 Lincoln Continental was offered in but two body styles, the two-door coupe and the sedan. The coupe was given a new roofline or greenhouse, similar to the Mark III in the quarter-window cut-out. The grille received minor revision though the parking lights were removed to the leading edges of the front fenders. The Continental star, a victim of new federal safety regulations, was removed from the crown of the hood and placed flush against its front face.

A new and ominous note appeared in the first reference to federal emission controls; carburetion refinements were required to burn fuel more completely and reduce exhaust emissions. The goal was toward leaner fuel-air mixture and it was met by a new dual-diaphragm distributor. Bizarre options included an automatic ride leveler with inflatable rear shock absorbers complete with air pressure tank and the usual sensing devices. The automatic headlamp dimmer which had been troubled from ignition interference was relocated in the left front fender.

Throughout the sixties the Lincoln Continental had been steadily improved and perfected. The fundamental excellence of the design was

On October 23, 1967, two of these Lincoln Continental convertibles were delivered to the U.S. Secret Service. The rear platform and hand-hold bar retracted neatly. The window frames were also sturdy hand-holds for agents standing on the running boards.

This picture, dated November 10, 1967, shows the 1968 Lehmann-Peterson limousine, unusually well proportioned for such a large car and similar to the big Mercedes 600 limousines.

more than vindicated and the engineers and stylists examined and reexamined every aspect of the car in the search for perfection. New technologies helped, such as the transistors used in the headlight dimmers in the 1968 car in place of vacuum tubes. Combined stereo tape decks with FM were changing radios into 'sound systems.' Dual-chamber whitewall tires appeared in 1967 for extra blowout protection. The Turbo-Drive transmission was recalibrated for 1968 and a flexible coupling isolated the steering gear from the steering column shaft.

Lincoln interior design continued to lead the industry. Walnut wood grain appliqué was used on both dash and door trim. A new Limoges fabric offered a nylon seating surface with great durability. Seat cushion trim styles included diamond, parallel pleat, or all-pleat patterns. The usual dazzling array of color combinations in cloths and leathers was continued.

Two new Lincoln Continental convertibles were delivered to the U.S. Secret Service in October 1967, to be used as security vehicles in official functions and parades. Eleven-inch running boards and rear platforms allowed ample standing room. The rear door was split and a fifteen-inch walk-through was thus made possible by opening one half of the door. The latest electronic gear was fitted along with sirens, red emergency lights and a PA system.

Prices took a jump as war-fueled inflation began. The f.o.b. base price for a four-door was $6,634, the two-door $6,400. The Cadillac de Ville was $6,463 and the Imperial Crown four-door hardtop was $6,774.

Cadillac came up with a new 472-cubic-inch engine with 375 bhp and 525 pounds-feet of torque but with a low engine weight of 600

pounds. Grille changes were minor. Production zoomed to 230,003. The Imperial, also with minor styling changes, had a production total of 15,361, down slightly from 1967. Lincoln totals for the year were 39,134—good, but lower than the 1967 numbers.

The value of Lincoln marketing research was highlighted by a conclusion drawn in the summer of 1968, namely that the Cadillac Calais, the cheapest of the line, had gradually declined from thirty-six percent of luxury volume in 1962 to eight percent. It was in 1968 that the Eldorado coupe outsold the two-body Calais line, and though the line would live through 1976, the consumer preference in the luxury class would hardly settle for anything less than the best. This confirmed the pricing policy of the Continental which had challenged the de Ville line. However, a high price alone was not enough to maintain public buyer esteem of the Imperial, which in the LeBaron form had never been outpriced by either Lincoln or the Cadillac de Ville.

Important news for 1968 was the introduction of the front-wheel-drive Cadillac Eldorado, a new personal car which shared much with the Oldsmobile Toronado, introduced the previous year. The Eldorado had a long gestation period going back to 1959. The front-wheel drive was settled in mid-1963 and the final production prototype was completed in May 1964. Rumors of Cadillac's new Eldorado had been

The 1968 Lincoln Continental coupe with a new roofline similar to the Mark III. The Continental star was now mounted on the crown of the hood to meet federal safety regulations. The parking lamps were moved into the front fender edge, again like the Mark III.

The short, high rear deck was David Ash's brilliant innovation. It made the Mark III appear compact and allowed for a smooth integration of the Continental spare.

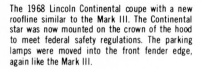

circulating for years and Ben Mills, Henry Ford and Lee Iacocca could hardly have been unaware of a possible challenge.

Iacocca was fresh from his success with the Mustang whose sales were sensational in 1965. It was natural that his thoughts should turn to the possibility of a personal car in the luxury field, initially more as an extension of the Mustang idea rather than as a response to the new Eldorado.

It was Iacocca who assigned the initial work on the Mark III to the Special Design Office, a group headed by L. David Ash. This group had been formed about 1960 and would be disbanded at the end of the decade. With the Advanced Design Office and the regular house design office, it formed what Iacocca liked to call the chocolate, strawberry and vanilla triangle of design teams.

Ash was a veteran at the Ford Motor Company, having begun in November 1947. He was to be cast as an interior design man and was the director of the Interior Design Office from 1971 until his retirement in 1977. Yet he had played an important role in developing the external surfaces of the 1958 Najjar car. Ash had as his second-in-command Arthur Querfeld; Ralph Peters was the product planner who would report to General Manager Lorenz and look after budget and timing matters.

Design work began in September 1965, under the code name Lancelot. The base for the new car was the 117-inch-long perimeter-frame four-door T-Bird, which would be introduced in 1967. The use of the T-Bird cowl section would again reduce production costs. However, Iacocca was firm in laying down some key ideas that would set the Mark III apart from the T-Bird. It was Iacocca who ordered the Continental spare tire look, the squared-off quasi-Rolls-Royce radiator grille and a hood six feet long—longer even than the Mark II.

A key styling innovation was the raising of the upper back panel two inches above that of the T-Bird, an idea of Ash's which at once changed the whole appearance of the car. (The upper back panel is that piece of sheet metal between the trunk lid and the rear window.) The effect was to 'swallow up' the roof and give the car a hunched look. The peak of the rear fender was raised to accommodate the two-inch rise of the deck lid. The result was a greater percentage of the height of the car in the side panels, a return to a styling idea of the late twenties in which window heights became extremely limited. The T-Bird roof panel was used along with the A-pillar and the side glass but the rest of the Mark III was new.

On the short 117-inch wheelbase the new Mark III body was another superb demonstration of the compact luxury that had marked the 1961 Continental. The rest of the car's design was equally creative. Hermann C. Brunn talked about the new interiors: "The seats have wrinkles. We put them in deliberately because we think they denote comfort and luxury. The quality control people thought the wrinkles shouldn't be there and the stylists had to convince them that this is what was wanted." The standard interior trim was the nylon tricot cloth with vinyl in a choice of six colors. Leather with vinyl trim was frequently chosen by buyers and was offered in nine colors. Attractive diamond patterns were used in the seats with the bolsters now shaped by foam and hung like independent cushions. The front seat was of a split-bench design, individually adjusted with two-way power mechanisms. Six-way power systems plus adjustable headrests were offered at extra cost.

The superb upholstery offerings were complemented by wood grain appliqués on the instrument panel and doors in East India rosewood or English oak, each keyed to the various colors of the interior. Deep-cut pile carpeting was also color-keyed to complete the ensemble.

The instrument panel was designed around five dial pods containing a full range of instruments though a tachometer was not among them. The Select-Shift three-speed Turbo-Drive transmission suggested that over-revving would not be a problem even for enthusiastic drivers. Elaborate radio and air-conditioning systems were in keeping with the general luxury of the Mark III. Auxiliary lighting included reading lights in the rear-quarter pillars, courtesy lights in the door armrests, ashtray light, glovebox light, map light, luggage compartment light, side marker lights, back-up lights, emergency flasher lights and warning lights for closed headlamp doors, car door ajar, open trunk lid and unfastened seatbelts.

The 55-ampere alternator had its work to do, especially with a battery of eighty-five ampere-hours capacity. Modern technology no longer required the high-amp-capacity batteries required by low-charging generators.

Twenty-two exterior colors were offered and were keyed to the nine interior colors. In addition, three vinyl roof colors were available. Eight accent stripes were available in any combination. Mixing all of these options produced a theoretical total of 4,752 color combinations. Few could criticize.

The running gear and engine were drawn from the well-proven Lincoln specifications. The 460-cubic-inch engine was rated at 365 horsepower with 500 pounds-feet of torque. This power plant, mated with a 2.8:1 rear axle, produced exceptional performance in the Mark III because the Mark III's weight was 4,738 pounds as compared to the Continental's 5,093 pounds. Zero-to-sixty time was a remarkable 8.3 seconds. Overall length at 216 inches was five inches shorter than the Continental.

The Mark III was clearly a brilliant new car but Ford executives were cautious. Eugene Bordinat was candid in his hopes for the car: "We have put things on the Mark III that make it evident that this is an expensive car." The initial press release of February 13, 1968, coyly described the new grille as "reminiscent of some current and past luxury motorcars." The use of the Anglicized term 'motorcar' suggests the obvious copy of the Rolls-Royce grille, beautifully adapted to the

The target car for the new Mark III was this 1967 Cadillac Fleetwood Eldorado (foreground). It was much bigger than the Mark III, and in the long competition ahead, the Eldorado would lose.

Mark III with a flattened top angle and a slight vee shape. Very elaborate plating techniques insured durability.

Bordinat reflected upon the Mark III's bold new ideas: "We tried to be a little controversial. We did not design to offend anybody . . . but when they see it, people will be divided into two camps. Some will respond to this sort of thing and will decide they have to have it. Others wouldn't touch it with a ten-foot pole." Bordinat then added a prophetic statement: "The buffs may not like it but the people with money will." As it eventually turned out, Bordinat's appraisal was much too modest—both the monied and the buffs found the car enchanting.

There was unusual care in analyzing the future market for the Mark III, in recognition, perhaps, of past errors with both the Edsel and the

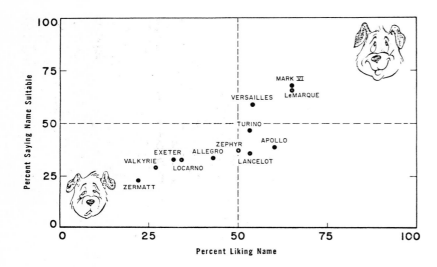

Visual results of the Lincoln-Mercury Division's name research project of October 1966. The curiously anglicized 'Turino' was correctly spelled in 1970 for the Ford Torino. For 1978 'Zephyr' did indeed seem a happier choice than 'Zermatt.'

Most distinctive feature of the new Mark III was the sharply defined grille which would evolve in the seventies to become the identifying feature of the whole Lincoln line. There are distant echoes of both Rolls-Royce and Mercedes in the design but the development and detail are quite fresh. First shown at the Chicago Auto Show on February 24, 1968, press releases suggested the design translated themes of the Mark II, but the Mark III was closer to the 1961 Lincoln Continental.

Mark II. Ford market research had come a long way in the ten years since the Edsel debacle and, once the Mark III design was fixed, many studies were undertaken.

In September 1966, a name study was initiated, with personal interviews with 296 owners of 1963, or newer, luxury cars and top-series, medium-priced cars. Respondents were shown pictures of the forthcoming Mark III and the Eldorado, the latter not yet introduced either. Twelve names were evaluated and the results appeared in an accompanying chart. The Mark III, IV and V names had been used from 1958 to 1960 without much success, yet Mark VI rated highest, with LeMarque second and Versailles third. In any event, Mark III was chosen despite its having been used before.

In August 1967, another study of 298 owners of 1964, or newer, luxury and top-series medium-priced cars was made by Oxtoby-Smith to compare Continental, Mark III and Eldorado from an image standpoint. Mark III scored high with the descriptive terms "expensive," "a lot of prestige" and "luxurious." The Mark III was "sportier" than the Continental. A similar test from respondents drawn entirely from GM and Chrysler owners produced similar results. On the negative side, the Mark III was perceived to have low resale value and was uneconomical to operate, issues which were not, perhaps, too critical in the luxury market.

About the same time, Kenyon and Eckhardt did a similar study of 631 owners in which the image ratings were based on preview advertising layouts without copy. The Mark III was rated about equal to Eldorado overall, apart from the resale value.

From April to June, Rogers National Research did a study called a "Luxury Convertible Clinic" in which the Lincoln line was compared to the Cadillac line. The Mark III profile was considered to have unique appearance but again the resale value was thought to be too low.

The summary of these surveys gave Lincoln marketing people general encouragement, though the road seemed long toward establishing the Mark III as a high-resale-value car. The styling was clearly different and brought strong opinion, both positive and negative. A particularly hopeful result was the discovery that the same proportion of Cadillac owners showed interest in the Mark III as Continental owners showed in the Cadillac, the much larger body of Cadillac owners suggesting that this was a good trade-off.

The elaborate marketing studies were matched by a very careful promotional campaign which began after the final basic design was approved in February 1966. Though hints of a new car were heard in 1966, the first presentation of the new car was made to the Lincoln Continental Owners Club in June 1967. The target date for announcement was February 12, 1968, but a Ford strike delayed production so that on Lincoln's birthday 1968, the announcement of the new car was made only at Dearborn. Press kits were available in December to make possible national magazine news releases in February. A splendid presentation at the Ford Rotunda marked the unveiling of the Mark III with the major speech by E. F. 'Gar' Laux. Few, if any, cars were available from normal production on February 12. Production for March totaled only 626 units and dealer announcement was on April 5, with perhaps half of the dealers still unsupplied with a show car. However, the introduction of the Mark III in the spring was another effort in smoothing out the production cycles at the Wixom plant.

The price of the new Mark III was set at $6,585, slightly under the Eldorado. The mistakes of the Mark II pricing were not to be repeated. Lincoln management hoped for a sale of 20,000 units in the first production year, March 1968 to late 1969, admittedly a 'long' year. This ruled out symbolic, image-making prices.

The soul-searching of Lincoln management and the caution of the marketing people were all unnecessary. The sales of the Mark III took off at once and belied the studied indifference of the Cadillac marketing men. Production for the opening ten months in 1968

The 1968 Cadillac still had heavy sculpturing and brightwork at the bottom edge of the car which pulled one's eyes downward. A giant 472-cubic-inch engine was needed. Cadillac sales of 230,003 were five times those of Lincoln.

totaled 7,770 and climbed steadily in 1969, nicely ahead of sales projections.

The Mark III was given no model year identification initially, in part because of the intent of the division to market it without change at least through 1969, and in the hopeful words of General Manager Edgar Laux, "There will be no vintage on this car." The strategy certainly did not hurt production which zoomed to 23,088 in 1969, only fractionally short of the Eldorado's total of 23,333. Initial press criticism faded before the terrific public response. Whereas in 1968 Bill Sanders was disappointed by the lack of luxury features, he gamely acknowledged that the waiting lists for the new car were as long as "army chow lines" in mid-1969. The explanation may have been that the Mark III was turning out to be a very personal, superb-driving automobile, in contrast to the more bulky and sedate Eldorado. In short, the car was a sensation.

CHAPTER 10

King Of The Hill—1969-73

THE REVISIONS FOR the 1969 Continental were carried out by the 'house' styling divison headed by corporate Vice President Eugene Bordinat. Iacocca might have termed it the 'vanilla' group but Bordinat's taste and direction were proving to be anything but bland. His crisp, sharp styling ideas found fresh expression on the Continental in a new grille of fine rectangular bars set off by bolder bars at intervals somewhat reminiscent of Mercedes' styling.

This grille change was the principal visual revision and the advance product information release is filled with phrases like "will not sacrifice premium quality for the sake of innovation . . . proven evolutionary refinement, not mere change . . continuity . . . retain the highly successful characteristic . . . continue to assure the competitive edge . . . again . . . as usual." Perhaps the marketing people overdid the theme because few doubted the excellence of the Continental.

A new town car interior option was offered, declared to be "big news" by the copywriters. New soft leather seat inserts with hidden threads, napped nylon headlining, deeper pile carpeting and a vinyl padded appliqué completed the decor group. Lincoln stylists and engineers were straining to come up with refinements. Detail changes included a double-jet windshield washer nozzle and a molded rubber

tap added to the underside of the brake pedal to help keep the driver's toe from slipping under the pedal when moving it over from the accelerator.

Brake horsepower was raised to 365, matching the Mark III. It turned out to be the peak for Lincoln as federal emission controls gradually choked off outputs.

The Lincoln compared favorably with the competition in 1969. Though the sedan weighed 5,208 pounds, about four hundred pounds heavier than both the comparable Imperial and Cadillac, the Lincoln's performance was the best with a 0-60 time of nine seconds. Gasoline mileage was the lowest, however, with a range of 8.6 to 10 mpg. The brakes were exceptional and a 110-foot stopping distance from 60 mph compared very favorably to Cadillac's 150 feet for the same speed. The Lincoln was an awesome engineering achievement.

On the all-important question of quality, Lincoln evidenced closer attention to construction detail and had the quietest ride. Both Imperial and Cadillac showed quality declines in assembly and increased use of plastic and flimsy material.

The Continental base price for a four-door sedan was $6,063, about $300 higher than the Imperial LeBaron and the Cadillac Coupe de Ville.

This 1969 Lincoln town sedan was a custom show car, with smooth Mark III headlamp covers. Strictly a one-off design exercise, it was not unlike the 1964 town brougham.

The accessory list was long and few buyers got out the door for under $7,000.

Lincoln production totaled 38,290—barely off from 1968 but exceptionally strong when considered with the sales of the Mark III which must have siphoned off many normal Continental customers. The Imperial did better in 1969 with 22,077 units, a tribute to Engel's very clean look, complete with the raised rear deck and hip-high rear fender line borrowed from the Continental. Cadillac sales totaled 223,237. The Lincoln Division's total production was 27.4 percent of Cadillac's, a great improvement from 1968.

A new presidential limousine was delivered in October 1968. Lehmann-Peterson extended the wheelbase to their normal 160 inches and in cooperation with the Secret Service and the Pittsburgh Plate Glass Company produced a remarkable new vehicle to replace the 1961 parade car still in service. The 1969 car had separate heating and air conditioning units for front and rear compartments, twin two-way communication systems, a glass roof with detachable vinyl cover, a

The 1969 presidential limousine was delivered on October 14, 1968. The center glass section of the roof opened to allow standing during parades, as shown here. Secret Service men could stand on the rear platform. Interior of the limousine (right) was finished in silver-gray pinstripe cloth with carpet in silver mouton.

public address system, a sound system to transmit outside sound to the interior, a rear fold-down platform bumper for Secret Service agents and a hydraulic adjustable rear handrail. The center section of the roof could be opened to permit the occupants to stand during a parade. A reflective aluminum fabric cover could be placed over the glass panels to prevent heat build-up when parked.

Silver-gray pinstripe cloth was used in the interior, as in the Mark III. Theater-type rear-facing seats were added to the rear compartment. A 40-watt fluorescent interior light was installed in the rear compartment so that the passengers could be seen at night. Because of the large glass area the rear air-conditioning system was exceptionally powerful with six registers, an extra condenser and a two-speed compressor. The presidential flag, when mounted on the left front fender, was illuminated by three miniature spotlights as was the American flag on the opposite fender.

The Wixom unit body construction had continued on the Lincoln Continental since 1961 and excellent torsional rigidity had been achieved. However, the Lincoln was about to be stretched and Fred Bloom, chief engineer for Lincoln, concluded that a return to body-frame construction was needed. There was also an additional benefit in cost reduction as greater interchangeability of underbody and chassis components would be permitted with all other Ford products. The perimeter frame was adopted, used with success by the Mark III. The wheelbase was extended one inch to 127 inches with overall length now at 225 inches. The Mercury line had grown a great deal, and in 1969 the Marquis was fractionally longer than the Lincoln. Compact luxury was a great theme but this was too much; in 1970 the Lincoln was 0.7 inch longer than the Marquis.

The tread base at the front was widened almost two inches and at the rear 3.3 inches. Thus a substantially larger car was dictated, with interior dimensions improved in almost all categories. Despite these expansions, the weight of the 1970 car was down nearly three hundred pounds because of the abandonment of unit construction.

The Lincoln was new in many ways, yet the basic line of 1969 was retained, again in conformity with Bordinat's dictates on consistent

The 1969 Lincoln grille used themes reminiscent of Mercedes. It was a handsome design. This sedan weighed 5,208 pounds, some four hundred pounds heavier than a comparable Cadillac or Imperial. Despite the weight, 0-60 mph time was nine seconds, an astonishing figure.

The 1970 Mark III was hardly changed from 1969 and there was little need after the brilliant beginning. The hubcaps were given enlarged centers, a step away from the wire wheel effect of 1969.

Cadillac and Lincoln would look more and more alike in the seventies, but it was now Cadillac picking up Lincoln ideas. No better illustration of this could be found than the 1969 Cadillac grille, a very sharp break from 1968 styling and now quite similar to Lincoln. Cadillac gradually reduced side sculpturing, again a subtle compliment to Lincoln's superb styling.

image-building. The front headlamps were fully concealed. Very strong horizontal bar motifs characterized the grille which was gradually becoming more sharply defined in the center (like an old-style proper radiator) in the manner of the Mark III. Windwings were abandoned in recognition of the vast improvements in ventilation. A major change was the hinging of the rear doors on the B-pillar, an answer to frequent objections from Cadillac 'conquest' prospects. The new rear doors were 4.5 inches wider, the front doors six inches wider. The car was much 'hippier' in the rear with a new larger trunk as the major gain.

The rear suspension was completely changed, coil springs now serving as the primary cushioning agent. A system of links handling driving force, torque reaction and lateral motion was provided to stabilize the whole setup.

The twelve-mile road test was abandoned in favor of a road-test simulator which overcame the disadvantages of bad weather, tester bias and imprecise gauging. Although not advertised, the new simulator also reduced costs.

Federal regulation of the car industry was growing rapidly and a non-tamperable odometer was fitted. California cars were equipped with an evaporative emission control system which collected, filtered and stored vapors while the car was standing and then purged them through the carburetor when the engine was started.

Engine horsepower was advertised, as in 1969, with 500 pounds-feet of torque. Performance was strong with a 0-60 time at the 8.6-second level with the standard 2.8:1 rear end, and it was a tenth of a second better with the optional 3.0 rear end.

 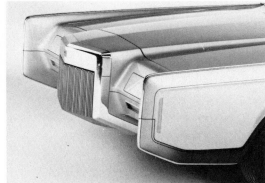

This 1970 Dual Cowl Phaeton Mark III was presented at the Chicago Auto Show on February 21. Though it was neither a phaeton nor did it have dual cowls, the topless coupe with dual windshields was an attractive and racy show car. At right, the Dual Cowl's stylish grille that extends beneath the car.

The very high quality level in Lincoln interiors was given yet another design critique by Stu Frey of the body engineering office and David Ash of the interior design team. Among other changes, latex foam replaced urethane as the seat padding. The body frame construction at once provided new opportunities for sound insulation and the car was more silent than ever.

The instrument panel took on some of the Mark III flavor with gauges appearing in individual cutouts. The vinyl wood grain and shag carpeting was in the best tradition of the times.

The new feature list for 1970 is impressive. The Sure-Track brake system was applied to the rear wheels by cycling brake application up to four times per second to avoid lock-up. The stardust paint used bronze instead of aluminum particles to give a gold metallic effect to four of the color choices. An electric rear window defroster was available with a ten-minute automatic shutoff. A ten-second windshield wiper interval option prevented dry-wiping and streaking. The windshield wipers parked in a concealed position, and electric operation replaced hydraulic. The map light was given a time-delay switch. In fact, forty new features were touted for the 1970 cars.

Handling was improved and the typical luxury car wallow, common to both Cadillac and Lincoln in 1969, was much reduced. Numerous testers remarked on the better cornering, flatter ride and heightened controllability.

The 1970 Mark III, though basically unchanged, received the detailing improvements of the Continental including the stardust paint, concealed windshield wipers and the computerized simulated road-test. Michelin 225R15 radial tires improved handling and answered the problem of short tire life. Genuine walnut wood trim replaced the appliqués used previously. The steering wheel, like that of the Continental, was a modified oval design with three spokes and a rim horn-blow.

Total Lincoln production was 59,127, down very slightly from 1969. The exciting competition was between the Mark III and the Eldorado, the Eldorado production totaling 23,842 against the Mark III's 21,432, a very fair fight.

This rivalry prompted *Motor Trend* to begin a new series of comparison studies between the two cars entitled "King of the Hill." The Mark III scored over Cadillac on seat configuration, leather quality, sheer plushness of the interior and an "intimacy" from a "strictly posh, luxury standpoint." Cadillac scored over the Mark III on headroom, general organization of the driving compartment and readability of instruments. *Motor Trend* concluded that the edge went to the Mark III.

Reaction was thunderous. *Motor Trend* noted a large number of neatly typed critiques on business letterheads with legible signatures. There was also a large volume of vituperative correspondence in which the owners of Chevrolets or Fords expressed their biases toward the Eldorado or Mark III as an extension of their ownership of a modest car in the same corporate family.

A charming Mark III special was prepared for the Chicago Automobile Show on February 21, 1970, called the 'dual cowl phaeton.' It was neither a phaeton nor had it dual cowls, but the car featured two windshields fitted to a topless coupe, the rear windshield being cleverly split to fold forward with the split front seat back. The car was never seriously considered for production.

A golden anniversary was in store for Lincoln in 1971 and it was a good time to celebrate. The division could boast an uninterrupted history of quality production with sales volumes and profits through the late sixties of gratifying proportions. The Bordinat image-rebuilding of the sixties, beginning with Lincoln Continental, had been entirely successful in reestablishing the car as a top luxury product and worthy rival to Cadillac. Though sales were up, Cadillac leadership was not yet threatened except in the personal car area where the Mark III was a brilliant success against the Eldorado.

Changes for 1971 were modest in light of the substantial revision in 1970. The grille was die cast with horizontal bars, a restyling of 1970 themes. Lincoln grille design had alternated between the small rectangular grid pattern of the original 1961 Continental and the horizontal bars that had first appeared in 1965. The Mark III grille, vertical bars within a massive chrome shell, remained virtually stable and would be continued into the Mark IV series. Such stability again confirmed Bordinat's goal of continuity and inevitably overwhelmed the Continental's changing frontal appearance so that in 1977 both cars were essentially using the Mark grille.

The 1971 trim changes included a new headlamp door design and front-end ornament. New paint options included two metallic colors with aluminum dust, termed moondust, a color series added in mid-1970. The 1970 stardust line of colors, which had emphasized bronze dust, was eliminated though the dark paint shades continued to use bronze.

The 1970 Lincoln Continental coupe was smooth and continued the elegant restraint that marked the series since 1961. The parking lamps were removed from the front fender tips. The longer wheelbase of the perimeter frame helped the flow of the line.

Lincoln Continental sedan for 1971—a handsome car that carried the final statement of the hump over the rear wheels introduced in 1966.

Air conditioning was now fitted to every car along with tinted window glass. The success of the radial-ply tires on the 1970 Mark III prompted the use of 225R15 Michelins on the Continental.

A much more serious problem was the rising level of emission controls now required by both federal and California law. The 1970 California evaporative device became standard for the rest of the states while California cars were fitted with a new nitrous oxide control system. The basic change was in distributor timing which provided retarded ignition under certain low-speed conditions. A speed sensor connected to the speedometer cable, a solenoid vacuum switch and an ambient temperature switch all added up to future complications. Performance was affected because distributor advance was blocked below 28 mph on acceleration. Horsepower and torque ratings were unchanged.

The Mark III changes included a standard 3.00:1 rear axle, perhaps in recognition of the new performance handicap caused by emission controls. A traction-lock differential, speed control, bigger hinged seats and the splendid power-operated sunroof of 1970 were among the options.

Production continued to climb for the Mark III to 27,091, far better than the Eldorado coupe total of 20,568. But the Eldorado was offered

The 1971 Lincoln Continental received minor styling revisions. The horizontal bar theme was never as appealing as the small rectangle-grid pattern.

The 1972 Lincoln Continental was freshly styled, the most noticeable feature being the straightening of the upper edge of the rear door panel in the sedans. The grille was rich and the star ornament returned to the prow of the hood. Production jumped to 45,969 units.

in convertible form in 1971 with production of 6,800, for a total of 27,368.

The Eldorado had grown in 1971 with the 120-inch wheelbase extended to 126.3 inches. Fresh styling in the Eldorado to take advantage of the new wheelbase was matched with extensive front-end revisions on the standard cars. Production for Cadillac totaled 188,537 while gross production for the Lincoln Division was 62,642—quite certainly the best percentage Lincoln had yet achieved in the luxury segment of the market. The Imperial, now part of the Chrysler line again, had production of 11,558, practically unchanged from 1970.

John Lamm wrote the "King of the Hill" piece for *Motor Trend* in 1971. It was the Eldorado that offered the changes for that year and Lamm reacted to the "more cluttered design that involves extra bulges, a big chrome 'scoop' on the side and that rear quarter window." Mark III styling remained "smooth, clean, though boxy." A particularly telling criticism of the Eldorado was finish, well down from the Mark III on such items as the padded top, and in areas of visibly shoddy assembly.

Eldorado interiors were better arranged than the Mark III. Eldorado instrument layout continued superior to Mark III, yet Lamm believed it was "stark." The bright fabrics of the Eldorado compared unfavorably

to the leather of the Mark III. The comparisons really boiled down to a question of style and grace. "The Mark III still comes off like the family that has lived gracefully for years with its money, while the Eldorado feels like 'nouveau riche' trying so hard to tell the world it's wealthy." Lamm's words must have given Cadillac executives apoplexy.

Mark III braking was slightly inferior. The new Cadillac engine at 8.5:1 compression was able to handle lead-free gasoline while the Mark III's 10.0:1 compression, down 0.5, was still on premium. Performance was comparable but the Eldorado base price was $1,000 below the Mark III, though equipment options tended to equalize the price. *Motor Trend's* final conclusion was that the Mark III was still "King of the Hill"—the top prestige automobile.

The Lincoln-Mercury Division was ready for 1972 with a line of cars that broke all production records. Though the Mercury side of the partnership produced over 460,000 units, the senior marque had explosive gains also, which for the first time posed the serious possibility of absolute leadership in the luxury field.

The 1972 Continental deserved the success because the styling refinements were beautifully handled. The most noticeable feature was a straightening of the upper edge of the rear door panel on the sedans, doing away with the hump effect. A new bright rocker panel and a bright fender peak molding recalled the original 1961 car and gave the '72 a lighter appearance.

The die-cast mesh grille, again similar to the Mercedes theme, was beautifully done and certainly looked richer than the heavy horizontal bars. A neat touch was the return of the Continental star to the prow of the bow which at once softened the rather blunt nose of the 1971 face. An unusual idea was the creation of a mini-vent, in essence a double front door window that lowered separately rather than pivoting as in the old 'no-draft' system.

There were eighteen standard colors, ten of which were metallics. In addition, there were four moondust metallics. Five vinyl roof colors were offered. Interior upholstery was knitted tricot or woven brocade. A new fabric called 'lamont' was offered on the twin Comfort Lounge seats. Glove-soft leather was available on all interiors and was heavily ordered.

Lincoln had always been deeply concerned about quietness, and promotional copy now talked readily about the silencing qualities of a "slightly flexible" box-rail perimeter frame with a very strong, rigid body as opposed to the old unitized construction. Weight was still just under 5,000 pounds for the Continental, another benefit of the perimeter frame layout.

Attention to weight was important because emission control measures were now very serious. Low-lead gasoline forced a reduction of compression to 8.5:1 and gross horsepower was abandoned in favor of net horsepower which plummeted to 212. How much of the old 365 bhp of 1971 was mere press puffery is conjectural, but it was evident that the horsepower race was absolutely finished. Cadillac bhp for the year was 220 with the Eldorado at 235. Lincoln torque dropped to 342 pounds-feet.

Performance fell off slightly, but not as much as might be expected with such a hefty horsepower and torque drop. The 1972 Mark IV time from 0-60 mph was only 0.3 seconds longer, and this with an increase in curb weight of over 200 pounds. Since the horsepower drop was forty-two percent one must conclude that the 1971 rating was in brake Shetland pony power.

A new body style was created for 1972, the town car, in essence a trim option which used a sharp delineating line across the body at the B-pillar. With the rear half of the roof padded and the addition of an opera light at the B-pillar, there was an unmistakable recall of a classic town car. The chauffeur's section, however, was anything but utilitarian.

The brilliant Continental was overshadowed by the new Mark IV, quite certainly the greatest sales triumph yet for Lincoln. Wes Dahlberg was to take charge of the Mark IV and it was a formidable assignment. Dave Ash's Mark III had done well against the Eldorado and was the finest commercial success in the luxury field for the Lincoln-Mercury Division to date. Eugene Bordinat's axiom of continuity had proven its worth and Dahlberg recognized at once that the Mark IV would be a

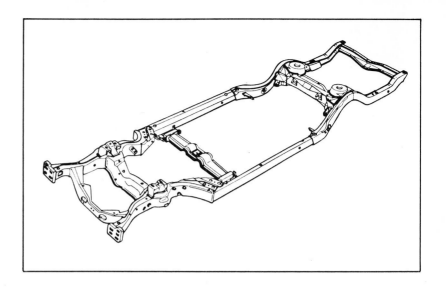

The 1972 Mark IV perimeter frame—typical of Lincoln practice in the seventies.

refinement of the Mark III. Nevertheless, the new car had to have sufficient novelty to generate a fresh sales impetus. Few stylists could forget 1953, when the Chrysler Corporation restyled their cars and nobody noticed.

The wheelbase for the Mark IV was the first major change, with an extension of 3.2 inches to 120.4 inches, giving Dahlberg more freedom. The Eldorado was on a 126.3-inch wheelbase and it is a tribute to Ash that he was able to convey so much of the luxury feel on the shorter 117.2-inch wheelbase of the Mark III. The particular advantage of the new wheelbase showed in increased legroom, especially in the rear compartment which was increased two inches. The tread was spread another inch to sixty-three inches in front and 63.1 in the rear.

Dahlberg's handling of the Mark IV revision was brilliant. Following a general dictum of Bordinat, the styling moved toward crisper surfaces and edges. The grille, now nicely 'frozen,' was little changed but the best styling revisions were in the rear quarter window area. The rear fender hump was removed and a nicely sculptured 'elbow' set the quarter light. The beltline setback was removed entirely which, at the

The splendid new Mark IV for 1972 was built on a 120.4-inch wheelbase, 3.2 inches longer than the Mark III. Stylist Wes Dahlberg used the increased length to advantage. The Mark IV was exceptionally smooth and a sales sensation, trouncing the Eldorado.

rear, heightened the fender peak and retained the Mark III's bulky look but with greater subtlety. The whole design was exquisite and, with the added length, the car's balance was flawless.

The most noticeable single feature of the Mark IV was the oval opera window which Bordinat wisely recognized as a styling gimmick of great value. It would appear elsewhere in the Lincoln line. The Lincoln Continental star was well placed at the top of the radiator shell. Dahlberg did not forget the details. Part of the success of the new design were very thin A-pillars. The door handles were recessed. The taillights were removed from the rear quarter panels to the bumpers,

though impact standards later forced the lamps back into the fixed sheel metal. A nice interior refinement was the locking plunger, which after being depressed to lock the door could be further depressed to lock the opposite door.

The technical specifications were similar to the Continental but, unlike the Eldorado, the bhp rating for the Mark IV was given no premium over the Continental line. New, however, was the coil spring rear suspension which utilized four control arms plus a torsion bar. The instrument panel now offered some crash protection, windshield wipers were given an intermittent cycle and steel rails were added to the doors for increased side-impact protection, evidence of growing federal pressure.

The Mark IV price was up $100 but the Continental price for the four-door sedan was reduced $130. The Cadillac de Ville was still some $200 cheaper in sedan form but again the accessory lists were different and obscured the true nature of the comparisons. *Motor Trend,* in their annual "King of the Hill" test, came up with a total price of $10,926 for the Eldorado, and $9,910.50 for the Mark IV. The truth was that as each car came along with the various options, the price could vary over a thousand dollars. Few chose less, more chose 'the lot.'

The comparison of the Mark IV with the Eldorado was deeper than price. It was obvious to top executives at both Ford and General Motors that the two cars were ideally matched for major combat and corporate image was at stake in the rivalry. Unseen on the horizon was the challenge of Mercedes, which entered the super-luxury market with the 6.3 sedan in 1969. It was the first big postwar passenger V-8 engine for Daimler-Benz and boasted astonishing performance, though the externals of the car were barely distinguishable from the contemporary 280 series. But the price in 1969 was double that of the Eldorado and the new car seemed hardly any threat despite impeccable finish and superior road manners.

In 1971 the 3.5 liter V-8 appeared in the Mercedes lineup to be followed in 1973 by the 4.5-liter engine, both cars developing much-expanded sales despite prices that continued to be nearly double those of the Eldorado. The threat was not in sheer sales volume but in the creation of a prestige image that would nibble away at the upper end of the luxury market for both Cadillac and Lincoln. What was definitely ignored by Lincoln and Cadillac in the early seventies was the challenge to the concept of size as the hallmark of luxury. The significance of the Mercedes market penetration—with a car of no more than 113-inch wheelbase and styling that could aptly be called non-styling—was dismissed; particularly since the California market was supplying the principal buying volume for Mercedes and all other foreign cars. As one Detroit executive put it, "California is a foreign country."

The demise of Cadillac's supreme status symbol image thus took place first in California, perhaps more a victim of its own success than the challenge of Mercedes. Lincoln profited from the Cadillac image deterioration as buyers sought something 'different.' The new Mark IV provided a brilliant option in 1972.

The *Motor Trend* test of the two cars was unusually thorough. Eldorado front-wheel drive scored on straight-line stability while the Mark IV seemed to sway a bit, the new rear suspension perhaps requiring firmer shocks. Both personal cars were faulted for their seating, with a tendency to give the testers lower back aches, a most unexpected appraisal of what looked to be divanesque comfort. Here again, Mercedes offered the astonishing alternative of the super-hard

The Mercedes-Benz 300 SEL 3.5 first appeared in the U.S. in 1971 at almost twice the price of the Lincoln Continental. It defied almost all of Detroit's assumptions about luxury specifications. A used 1971 Mercedes 3.5 was worth three times the comparable Lincoln on the used-car market in 1975. It was hard for Detroit to understand.

seat, which was a concept so novel for the American luxury market as to literally put off potential buyers.

The Mark IV acceleration was slightly slower than the Cadillac but the braking distances were practically identical—153 feet for a panic stop from sixty miles per hour. The Eldorado suffered from severe brake fade while the Mark IV had rear-wheel hop and a pronounced brake pull to the left. Testers preferred the Eldorado over the Mark IV for long-distance driving though both the Mercedes 280 SE and the Jaguar XJ-6 had superior road manners and were top choices. The eleven miles-per-gallon fuel consumption was the same for both domestic cars.

A new comparison was repair frequency and both cars scored equally, Lincoln quality no longer in doubt. In fact, there was some quiet criticism of Cadillac quality having fallen in 1971 and 1972. Another telling comparison was the retention of resale value. The *Kelley Kar Blue Book* for May-June 1972 revealed that the Mark III was doing better than the Eldorado in this all-important measurement of consumer opinion. Lincoln executives could well have cheered over this victory even though it may have been due in part to the changing public perception of the Cadillac rather than sheer Lincoln superiority. The *Motor Trend* staff was nearly unanimous in voting the Mark IV a better-looking car than the Eldorado. The Cadillac personal car had become so big as to appear swollen and the drivers reacted unfavorably to its sheer bulk.

The criticism of leather used only on sitting and leaning surfaces of the interior, a practice long used by Jaguar, could only be seen in reference to the big Mercedes where 'leather' meant leather *everywhere*. Some wary buyers even refused to believe that Lincoln leather was genuine leather, again a case of superior image-building by Mercedes which was shortly to threaten the market. Mercedes leather "smelled" right.

Motor Trend's final decision was to award the Eldorado the 1972 title of "King of the Hill," principally because of road and track performance. But the Mark IV won on styling and general luxury appeal and *Motor Trend* acknowledged that "Perhaps that makes the Mark IV the grass roots winner."

The grass roots seemed to think so, as some 48,591 Mark IV's were produced in the opening model year, a commercial triumph rivaling the Mustang's 1964-65 season. The Eldorado coupe totaled only 32,099 units with the convertible adding another 7,975. The Lincoln Continental production totaled 45,969 for gross Lincoln Division production of 94,560 against Cadillac gross production of 267,787. It was easily the best year in Lincoln history.

Chrysler Imperial production was 15,794, a good increase over 1971 but now clearly out of the running. The Lincoln had captured thirty-three percent of the domestic luxury sales. Still unnoticed was the Mercedes sales of 41,000 units in 1972, seventy-five percent of which were over $9,300-per-car base price.

The great changes for 1972 plus the mighty sales results forecast few changes in 1973 and this was openly admitted in the advance data book. The successful Continental styling was passed down to the Mercury and helped set new sales records. For the Lincoln line, it was gilding the lily. A new town coupe extended the town sedan trim options which included cavalry twill vinyl roof, owners initials on a front door plaque, silver-plated keys and corduroy velour interiors among other features.

The twenty-three standard colors and the four moondust color options were continued. Interior options totaled thirty-four on the sedan, twenty-eight on the coupe and six on the town coupe and town sedan.

Detail refinements included yet more sound insulation, prompting Jim Brokaw in a test report in *Motor Trend* to observe that he could

hear himself breathe. The radial tire size was increased to 230x15 or LR78x15. Front disc brakes were improved with new caliper rigidity, lower line pressures by using larger pistons and extra-hard lining which reduced pedal travel.

Tightening emission standards were met by the closed crankcase ventilation system, a fuel vapor emission control system and exhaust emission controls. As for the exhaust standards, the hydrocarbons and carbon monoxide were controlled by changed fuel-air ratios and ignition timing. The nitrous oxide standard was met by an exhaust gas recirculation system which diluted the incoming fuel-air charge and reduced combustion temperatures. It all looked good on paper but it was the beginning of deteriorating performance as the carburetor no longer dealt with 'pure' elements. Despite this new hobbling of the engine, the Lincoln bhp was rated at 219, with torque up to 360 pounds-feet.

The other federal regulation required a 5-mph and a 2½-mph impact-absorbing bumper at the front and rear respectively. The meeting of this standard added 130 pounds to the Lincoln and extended the bumper three inches. All the skills of Bordinat and his stylists could not conceal the protruding bumper mass which gave the Continental and the Mark IV a front-heavy look. The bumper was heavier and extended across the base of the grille, losing the beautiful depth of the original 1972 design.

A new side-terminal battery was fitted with the amperage rating falling from eighty-five to seventy-five while the alternator rating moved up from fifty-five to sixty-five. The only real requirement for the battery was to have sufficient power for starting. The alternator carried the load during almost all other running conditions.

The Mark IV shared all of these technical specifications with the Continental. The Mark IV rear suspension was more closely controlled and the shocks were now mounted at fifty degrees from vertical instead of thirty-six to counter the swaying noted in the road tests. The shocks contained a freon-filled bag that resisted foaming under high-velocity shock motions, a tacit admission that under heavy use rear-end control was breaking down. The shock valving was also improved to increase damping effectiveness.

The rear brake drums were widened one quarter inch with an eleven-percent improvement in drum-swept area, a needed change in the light of 1972 brake testing reports.

Mark IV styling, apart from the bumper and very minor trim and grille touches, was unchanged and continued to convey the superior sense of luxury over the more 'house designed' Eldorado. And since the cars were so similar to the 1972 models, *Motor Trend* awarded the

After a spectacular opening year, the 1973 Continental Mark IV was little changed. The grille was a die-cast revision of the 1972 theme, hardly noticed by the casual viewer. Sales zoomed.

On June 18, 1973, this Lincoln Continental town car was presented to Leonid I. Brezhnev, general secretary of the Communist Party of the Soviet Union, during his visit to an eight-day summit conference in Washington, D.C. Continental changes were few for 1973. Block lettering above the grille, a small script medallion above the left headlamp, and revised front bumper with standard guards were among minor styling changes.

"King of the Hill" title again to the Eldorado. But Mark IV production set another new record with 69,437 units, far beyond Eldorado. Gross production for the Lincoln Division was 128,083.

The fuel shortage appeared in 1973 as a further challenge to luxury cars. The success of Mercedes raised the question as to whether or not America's great luxury cars might not conceivably grow smaller. William Benton, new general manager of the Lincoln-Mercury Division, was firm in his conviction that downsizing the Continental was out of the question. The success of the Mercedes was not because of its size but because of its appeal as an imported car. The reasoning continued that if Lincoln were to build a downsized luxury car it would be a commercial disaster. The merchandising assumption here was that the successful, upwardly mobile American buyer saw a great luxury car as the end of the rainbow—with power, comfort, weight and size the principal rewards. Benton perfectly expressed Detroit's general philosophy of the early seventies, which would carry the Lincoln Division successfully to the end of the decade. Yet there was a tiny glimmer of something new ahead as Benton suggested that there might be an evolution that could shrink the luxury size in the '80's. The prophetic accuracy of what may have been an offhand remark can hardly be overemphasized as the Lincoln Division would present the new Mark VI for 1980 as a downsized car.

Robert Lund at Cadillac was more concerned about the Mercedes threat, with the honest recognition that any car that can sell 40,000

units in the luxury market deserves the closest inspection. Lund was well aware of the changed Cadillac image and the fact that Mercedes buyers were generally younger, always a bad sign for the marketing future. The typical Cadillac buyer remained an aging executive who had long since found the Holy Grail. Lund was pleased that Cadillac was the 1973 Indianapolis pace car, a move toward appealing to younger buyers who supposedly might identify with Indy, though the 500-mile race itself had a peculiar geriatric overtone in comparison to Grand Prix racing. What Lund could not say was that the development work on the new small Cadillac, with a wheelbase of only 114.3 inches, was well under way as 1973 came to a close, and was a direct response to the Mercedes challenge.

CHAPTER
11

Final Big-Car Fling—1974-77

GASOLINE PRICES WERE edging up sharply in 1974 and several motoring journalists were predicting the end of the big luxury car. Jim Brokaw summed up the time with his usual wit: "Crippled by the fuel flap and sniggered at lewdly by those smug Mercedes owners, today it seems these great mastodons are dismissed as symbols of an ancient aristocracy." Though 1974 saw some substantial retrenchment in luxury sales, the dirge was premature. The Imperial was all-new and excellent, and both Cadillac and Lincoln reached new heights of sheer luxury.

The Continental for 1974 was given a minor facelift, the grille now showing vertical bars, a step toward the Mark IV image. The effect was pleasant but redesigned bumpers were more bulky than ever, the rear now also having to meet the 5-mph impact standard. A swinging pendulum test was also applied to bumpers in 1974, a reason for their growing bulk. Roof crush strength was also increased to meet a federal standard that required the roof to resist a flat block pressed on the forward edge with a force one and one half times the curb weight of the vehicle, i.e., about 7,500 pounds. Meeting this test required reinforced roof pillars, increased sheet metal thickness and some revised structural members.

California emission control standards required the fitting of a belt-driven air pump to inject air into the engine exhaust to mix with unburned hydrocarbons and carbon monoxide. The equipment included check valves, anti-backfire valves, rubber hoses and an air distribution manifold for each cylinder bank, and injectors in the exhaust ports. Most irritating of the new federal regulations was the starter interlock system which required that first the driver must be seated and then the lap belt had to be pulled out (same for the passenger if that seat was occupied). If there was an attempt to defeat the system by permanently pulling out the belts or buckling them on the seat, the engine would still not start. Also, simply pulling out and releasing did not bypass the system either. If the driver failed to follow the correct sequence, a warning light and buzzer came on when the ignition key was inserted. The whole system was wondrously complex and relentlessly infuriating to the driver. The systems were mechanically disabled by the thousands and public furor forced a reconsideration of the concept of federal intervention in safety measures.

The cost of all this intervention was in both dollars and weight. The Continental was up 168 pounds to 5,384 for the four-door sedan. An equipped Lincoln was over 5,400 pounds, slightly heavier than the

The 1974 Lincoln Continental sports a new grille with vertical bars similar to the Mark IV. Its impact-absorbing bumpers protrude awkwardly.

Cadillac brougham and nearly 500 pounds over the Imperial LeBaron despite the latter's unitized construction.

The extraordinary preoccupation with growing federal standards tended to deflect the traditional Lincoln emphasis on luxury and quality. Nevertheless, there was no retreat from the goal of providing the finest in luxury cars. A good example is the AM/FM/MPX stereo radio with stereo tape player. Car radio technology had moved ahead very fast in the sixties and each year Lincoln had responded with fresh inventiveness. In 1973 the four-speaker sound system allowed AM, FM, FM stereo and eight-track stereo reproduction. In 1974 the five pushbuttons offered five AM and five FM choices whereas in 1973 only five stations FM or AM could be selected. The sliding-bar switch for AM/FM selection was replaced with two pushbuttons. The seek-and-

scan unit was controllable for selectivity by a town-and-country selector. Furthermore, the FM portion of the scan could be programed to stop at only stereo stations. (Of such refinements are new sales catalogs produced.) A novel option was a ski rack, which would certainly have destroyed whatever styling unity was present in the Lincoln automobile.

The biggest technical improvement on the '74 was a new power brake system that drew power from the hydraulic pump of the power steering system. A reservoir stored hydraulic fluid under pressure, allowing a limited number of power brake applications when the engine was not running. Front disc area was increased ten square inches.

These improvements were much needed because Lincoln braking was not leading the luxury pack. For 1974, the Imperial came out with four-wheel discs which produced a clean, straight-line panic stop within 130 feet at 60 mph. Lincoln managed 154 feet and Cadillac was a poor third with 183.

Engine horsepower, now quite irrelevant in the sales race, hovered just over the 200 bhp figure with Cadillac at 205, Lincoln at 215 and the Imperial at 230. Gasoline mileage for the Cadillac and Lincoln was in the 10.5 range while the Chrysler Imperial did a bit better at around fourteen.

Lincoln seating was superb in 1974, better than the over-soft, non-supporting Imperial, and ahead of Cadillac's Medici velour-covered cushions. Imperial had the most controllable and tautly-suspended chassis; perhaps those super-soft seats had a posterior purpose. The Continental's ride was the softest and perhaps best suited to the sort of work these super luxury cars would normally have to do.

The state of the art in the luxury field had reached such heights that critical comparisons produced only personal opinions as to location of controls, trim design and color schemes. From another standpoint, the three luxury cars had come to resemble each other so closely that buyer preference was now more regulated by capricious factors—which gave the advertising staffs a heavy responsibility.

The Lincoln-Mercury Division fitted solid state ignition to the 460-cubic-inch engine used in the Lincoln and some Mercurys and to the 400-cubic-inch engine offered in the Mercury Monterey and as a Cougar option. The purpose was more precise timing control, essential in the new emission-sensitive regulatory environment. Advantages were the elimination of breaker points and all related maintenance. Timing was no longer affected by wear of the contact breaker point's rubbing block so that timing changes over a long life were eliminated. Dwell angle was unchanged over a long service life. In California, solid state ignition was used on all Lincoln-Mercury Division engines over 200-cubic-inch displacement.

The 1974 Mark IV continued along proven lines. Sound insulation was further enhanced. A nice personal feature was the illuminated vanity mirror located in the visor (also available in the Continental) which had as a final touch a two-position switch controlling high- or low-intensity lighting. A sealed, maintenance-free battery was a welcome technical advance.

The fuel filler cap, previously behind the rear license plate, was moved to the side of the left quarter panel behind a hinged door. It fed a 26.5-gallon tank, up four gallons.

The fuel crisis had a sharp effect on Continental production, causing it to plummet to 36,669, a drop of thirty-seven percent. The de Ville production fell to 172,620, a twenty percent drop. The Mark IV showed better resistance to the sales decline with production of 57,316, a seventeen percent drop. Once again the Mark IV sales were far ahead of the Eldorado whose production for 1974 in both coupe and convertible models totaled 40,412. Total Cadillac production was 242,330. Chrysler Imperial LeBaron production totaled 14,426, not bad for a year in which the gasoline shortage caused a major downturn in sales.

Two big problems hit the auto industry in 1975. The first was the cumulative effect of the energy shortage which raised gasoline prices to undreamed of levels. Whereas a 1972 Lincoln buyer could count on gasoline for around thirty-five cents per gallon, by 1975 prices had been driven into the fifty-to-sixty cents area. The rush toward small cars was on. The second savage problem was inflation. The price increase of the basic Lincoln Continental four-door, f.o.b. Detroit, illustrated the problem. Equipment option changes had some effect but the trend was clear:

	Base	Difference
1971	$7,332	
1972	7,302	$-30
1973	7,474	172
1974	8,309	835
1975	9,214	905
1976	9,293	79
1977	9,636	343

It will be seen at once that the 1975 increases following on the 1974 increases were very heavy.

The effect was to force the manufacturers into rebate programs, led by Chrysler whose inventory at the beginning of 1975 was 300,000 cars. The Imperial suffered badly in the new climate because the price increase from 1974 to 1975 was $1,245 on the base retail LeBaron four-door at Detroit, and this on top of a $496 increase in 1974. Sales plummeted and for 1975 only 8,830 Imperials were produced, the lowest ever since its introduction in 1955.

The Lincoln-Mercury Division faced 1975 with the new Mercury Monarch, "an all-new smaller luxury sedan," significant because it was to become the base for the Lincoln Versailles two years later. The same chassis was used for the Ford Granada and that was, in turn, an outgrowth of the 1972 Ford Maverick, the first to use the 109.9-inch chassis. The 1972 Maverick chassis was related to the 1971 Mustang of 109 inches, which grew from the 108 inches of the original Mustang, which in turn goes back to the original Falcon—109.5 inches in 1960. The story might be how the Falcon became the Versailles.

A catalytic muffler appeared on the Lincolns for sale in California in 1975. Between fifty and sixty percent of the cars sold in the other forty-nine states were similarly equipped. The catalytic agent was platinum, designed for a 50,000-mile service life. California cars had a higher rear axle ratio of 3:1 and a slightly bigger tire size of 235x15.

Lincoln marketing was now veering away from the offering of excessive combinations of color, fabric and trim which had reached ludicrous proportions. The average buyer needed clearer choices and the idea of 'luxury groups' had taken hold. A luxury group meant simply that colors and options were coordinated into a limited number of choices. In 1975 there were five luxury groups: diamond blue, saddle white, silver, gold, and lipstick and white. The groups were extra-cost options, thus solving the problem of complex color orders and at the same time providing higher profit margins. It was a brilliant idea, soon to be augmented by the designer series.

Lincoln, like other manufacturers, was forced to tailor its offerings to fit growing state regulations. California emission laws were well known but California also had a noise regulation which mandated dual exhaust systems. New York demanded special rear window defrosting. The cost of building an automobile was rising to meet the state and federal demands.

The Lincoln Continental for 1975 was given a substantial restyling, especially in the greenhouse area, which was called the colonnade style. The B-pillar in the sedan was widened and an optional coach lamp was made available. The abandonment of an upper door molding and use of the door outline itself to define the roof goes back to an idea first used in the 1938 Cadillac 60 Special. Lincoln further enhanced the new '1938' look by using the oval quarter window of the Mark IV. The result was a beautifully refined, new look of great elegance and formality. The grille and front end received only minor styling changes in the form of accent vertical bars on the 1974 grille outline.

The coupe was restyled along similar lines—the fixed quarter window cut-out was offset with the optional carriage lamp. The appearances of the Lincoln coupe and Cadillac Coupe de Ville were now very similar.

Cadillac's new sales emphasis for 1975 was an attempt to change its image. Consider: "Efficient as it is elegant, rugged as it is rewarding." John Lamm, in *Motor Trend,* rightly suggested that these ideas had nothing to do with the sort of status image with which Cadillac had lived for decades. The truth was that that image no longer was automatically conveyed by Cadillac ownership. Prestige buyers,

Five luxury groups brought to the 1975 Mark IV a new coordination of color choices and options, which made life a little less complicated for the prospective buyer. Four-wheel disc brakes were new and welcome. Not so welcome were the increasing emissions equipment. Mark IV production totaled 47,145.

especially in the posh areas of the East and West Coasts, opted for Mercedes in record numbers at prices far higher than Cadillac. It was as though all of Detroit's assumptions about the goals of the luxury buyers, namely infinite refinement, silence, fabrics, gadgets, automated accessories and size were suddenly unimportant. And what did Mercedes offer? Obvious quality and finish; an unabashed acceptance of the automobile as a machine complete with heightened feedback of suspension, engine and transmission action; a Teutonic approach to trim, seat hardness and non-gadgetry; plus handling, braking and race-bred engineering superiority. The Mercedes instantly conveyed that it was a car for drivers—the Cadillac a car for riders.

When it came to chassis technology, brake development and sheer power-output efficiency, Cadillac was not in the running. The problem was that for the first time wealthy American buyers were seeking out car qualities that had been largely ignored by domestic builders. Cadillac reacted with advertising copy about efficiency and ruggedness—quite correct in terms of Cadillac's impressive technical history. But the design objectives of Cadillac and Mercedes were utterly disparate and no amount of advertising could change that fact.

Insofar as Lincoln was copying Cadillac (the 1975 coupe demonstrated how that was true), the Lincoln would be a victim of the

The 1975 Lincoln coupe was restyled and sported a new wider B-pillar. The 'Collonade style' was closer to the Cadillac though the Lincoln was perhaps more refined. In the town coupe version a coach lamp was always fitted. This car had a curb weight of 5,435 pounds.

same sort of buyer preference. The Lincoln, however, had the virtue of being slightly more exclusive because of smaller sales volume, and also because of the tremendous success of the Mark IV, clearly the most accepted personal car ever built in the luxury field. Insulated from California buying patterns and the unique New York market, Detroit designs continued to hold strong appeal for heartland America. Lincoln was targeted on this market with unusual precision. In essence, Detroit was building cars for Detroit. The question was whether or not California buying preferences, historically a tremendously important barometer of U.S. tastes, would eventually force Detroit to change.

The 1975 Lincoln Continental coupe was a masterpiece of Detroit design idioms in every way. The car had a curb weight of 5,435 pounds, almost 1,400 pounds more than the Mercedes 450 SL, which at once suggests the profound differences between the two cars. The 460-cubic-inch engine of the Lincoln produced 206 strangled federal horsepower while the 275-cubic-inch Mercedes engine produced 180 bhp, again a commentary on the great difference in design objectives. The big, lazy American engines of endless durability and tranquil temperament began to seem truly anachronistic against European designs which had focused for years on fuel efficiency. In 1975 Lincoln's 12 mpg seemed for the first time an indictment. It made no difference that a Mercedes

buyer, paying over double the price for a Mercedes 450, could hardly argue that fuel savings were important as a cost factor. The big Lincoln, 232 inches long, was able to go from 0-60 in 10.5 seconds, better than Cadillac by over a second—a tribute to Lincoln engineering which could produce performance even while forcing the great engine to pump, churn and haul numerous servo devices.

The quietness of Lincoln was superior to all challengers, a superiority matched in the opulent interiors. The magnificently soft Lincoln seating with six-way front power seats was superb except that testers, after four days of use, still talked about aching backs. Was there something in that Mercedes firmness? Volvo's talk of lumbar support had not yet penetrated mass-market thinking.

On freeways, the Lincoln was supreme. With a ride control that even had an effect on the rate of acceleration and deceleration, the car offered uncanny automation, enough so that one tester wanted to know if a button could not be supplied to provide hands-off-the-steering-wheel control.

The Lincoln Continental was a wonderful car, built to the highest standards of American refinement. With fresh new styling the sales were up, despite forebodings of fuel shortages and future sacrifices. Production in that troubled year of 1975 was excellent for both the Mark IV and the Lincoln. The Mark IV totaled 47,145 while the Lincoln chalked up 54,698 of which 21,185 were coupes, ample response to the correctness of restyling.

Mark IV mechanical changes included new four-wheel disc brakes coupled with the hydro-boost power system. The tilting steering wheel was now standard along with power door-locks, speed control and remote-control deck release. In recognition of California emission standards, the rear axle ratio for California cars was 3:1 while for the other forty-nine states it was 2.75:1. Cadillac fortunes for 1975 turned out to be linked to the introduction of the new compact Seville, since production levels of all other models remained virtually the same. The calendar year production for Cadillac was a very low 170,197 as inventories were worked off.

The Seville was offered on a 114.3-inch wheelbase with a weight of just over 4,200 pounds, half a ton below the Cadillac 60 Special brougham. The weight was comparable to a 450 SEL Mercedes on a 116-inch wheelbase. A fuel-injected 350-cubic-inch engine produced a 0-60 time of 13.3 seconds and a maximum of 109 mph.

The Seville had crisp styling with knife edges everywhere and a near-vertical rear window. As *Road & Track* put it: "It was a very good Cadillac!"

Cadillac's truly inspired marketing approach was to price the Seville above the de Ville and brougham series, a frontal attack on the long-held idea that bigger is more expensive. It was the first signal from mighty General Motors that the next generation of cars would be downsized. The important question was whether or not the public would buy a smaller Cadillac at a higher price and the answer quickly became evident. Though introduced in May 1975, the car was dubbed a 1976 model. Early 1975 production totaled 16,355 while the 1976 production was 43,772 for a grand total of 60,127 Sevilles in the first fifteen-month model year. This was a tremendously strong start and accounted for nearly all of the overall Cadillac sales gains. It was the first time the American public had a chance to buy a compact luxury car that might be compared to the Jaguar and Mercedes and at a price that was greatly beneath the Mercedes.

The lesson was not lost on Lincoln management even though there was a very strong reluctance to downsize the Continental or the Mark IV. The objectives of the division for the past decade had been to meet or exceed Cadillac in dimensions and styling. The Mark IV had been brilliantly successful while the Continental was doing very well. For Cadillac to now change the game plan was disturbing, especially as sales volume developed for the Seville, revealing the presence of a new market. Accordingly, work was begun to provide a suitable answer to the Seville, a car that would eventually be introduced in March 1977. The rather tardy response to the Seville allowed Cadillac to gain a very strong hold in the compact luxury field, which would cause future concern at Lincoln.

The 1976 Continental Mark IV was available in the new designer series. Shown is the Hubert de Givenchy version.

Meanwhile, thoughts turned to the 1976 line and Lincoln was ready with announcements of the Continental on September 7, 1975, and the Mark IV a week later. There were few mechanical changes and the sheet metal was virtually unchanged. But 1976 brought a fresh approach to styling in the announcement of the new designer series for the Mark IV, four new optional trim designs by Emilio Pucci, Cartier, Hubert de Givenchy and Bill Blass. These designers each prepared a color-coordinated version of the Mark IV with the following specifications:

Blass: Dark blue metallic paint, cream landau vinyl roof, cream premium bodyside molding, cream and gold hood, opera window with Bill Blass script, blue Versailles-styled majestic cloth or blue leather seating surfaces and color-coordinated luggage compartment carpeting.

Cartier: Dove gray as a key color with red and white hood, and Cartier script on the opera window.

Givenchy: Aqua blue Diamond Fire paint, white landau vinyl roof, white premium bodyside molding, black and white hood, Givenchy opera window script, aqua blue interior and luggage compartment carpeting.

The 1976 Cadillac Seville was introduced very early on May 1, 1975, and 16,355 were produced. 1976 production zoomed to 43,772. Seville was a trend setter and the first American answer to the Mercedes. Lincoln's Versailles did not appear until spring 1977.

The brightwork highlights on this 1976 Mark IV are enhanced by a nice camera filter. This mid-year new introduction sports the Black Diamond Fire paint which contained metallic flake, producing a dark charcoal appearance with sparkle. A second mid-year introduction was the Desert Sand luxury group.

The 1976 Lincoln Continental coupe now looked very much like the Cadillac coupe, though the Lincoln quarter window was better integrated into the whole greenhouse design. Shown is the town coupe version.

Pucci: Dark red moondust paint, silver vinyl landau roof, silver premium bodyside molding, silver and lipstick-red hood, Pucci opera window script, dark red interior and trunk carpeting.

For salespersons the designer series helped 'close' confused customers by focusing on fewer offerings compared to the complex choices of the Lincoln color line.

The luxury groups continued in 1976, the final year. There were eight, as follows: blue diamond, saddle white, lipstick and white, gold and cream, red and rose, dark and light jade, jade and white and the Versailles option which was a soft, down-filled appearance in crushed majestic cloth. Mark IV buyers indifferent to these superb coordinated color options could continue to pick and choose from the rainbow color array of exteriors and interiors.

The sliding moonroof panel was also offered in five tints: silver, gold, brown, light jade or rose. It was a great year for color in the Mark IV.

The Lincoln line did not share this extraordinary series of design options for 1976 and offered only the town car with deeper carpet, a fancier new-style bench seat in leather, vinyl roof, coach lamps and the town car identification trim.

Lincoln management's confidence was well placed as sales moved forward. The Continental totaled 68,646 of which 24,663 were two-doors and 43,983 were four-doors—a postwar record exceeded only by the exceptionally long production of the 1949 car. Mark IV production continued strong with 56,110 units completed.

The 1977 Continental Mark V, another master-piece. The very sharp angularity was well handled by stylist Don DeLaRossa. A phenomenal 80,321 were produced.

The downsized 1977 Cadillac Sedan de Ville, 900 pounds lighter than 1976. Lincoln went ahead with big cars.

Over at Cadillac an all-time record was established with gross production of 309,139 of which 182,159 were de Villes, the Continental's primary marketing target. Against this target Lincoln sold nearly thirty-eight percent of Cadillac de Ville production, the best record of the decade. Yet the Seville, with its 43,772 production for 1976, tended to subdue rejoicing at Lincoln. Was the de Ville series entering a decline? Would the old rivalries suddenly no longer be valid?

For 1977, Lincoln was ready with a brand-new Mark V and restyled Continental. It was clear from the opening news releases of the Public Relations Department that Lincoln management had made a decision about marketing strategy: "Our standard cars are full-sized in every sense of the term as are our luxury offerings." It was a shrewd decision since the Cadillac de Ville was completely redesigned on a new 121.5-inch chassis with a smaller 425-cubic-inch engine to match. The General Motors downsizing was serious and Ford corporate management had opted to provide the bigger sizings for the traditional luxury-car buyer. It was a conservative yet hazardous course because of the new Corporate Average Fuel Economy (CAFE) standards which dictated rising miles-per-gallon fuel averages for the total product mix of any major automobile producer. Ford was well able to cope with these demands initially because of great success with the Pinto and its derivatives which provided balance at the economy end of the corporate fuel consumption range.

Thus the new Continental retained the general size of the 1976 cars. The new grille outline was straight from the Mark IV, a bold and clean shape which paid Rolls-Royce a sincere compliment. The usual stylist's variations and colors were offered. A fresh recognition of growing environmental problems indicated the fitting of the 400-cubic-inch engine on the California cars as a standard and required offering, a measure designed to meet the more stringent smog regulations of that state. California hydrocarbon requirements were 0.4 gram per mile as compared to 1.5 grams for the forty-nine-state federal requirement. The carbon monoxide requirement for California was approximately one half that of federal limits and the nitrous oxide limits were seventy-five percent of federal regulations. To meet these and growing federal demands, the catalytic converter was greatly enlarged with fifty percent more cell density. The same special California demands were met with the new Duraspark Ignition system, a refinement of the breakerless system. Likewise, carburetion was tailored to meet smog regulations. An optional high-altitude carburetor was fitted to the Denver-area cars. Life was growing more complicated for the engineers.

A very useful feature in the 1977 Lincolns was additional corrosion protection that used precoated steel fitted to the quarter panels, outer door panels, front fenders, doors and quarter lock pillars. Lincoln

The 1977 Lincoln Continental adopted the Mark V grille and a very successful adaptation it was. This four-door sold a sensational 68,160.

Two new spring color combinations were offered on the 1977 Mark V based on dark blue metallic and dove gray. The gray had been used in the Cartier designer series but not with the sharp blue contrasts in roof color and moldings. Lincoln was always the master in offering the loose pillow effect on interior seating.

continued to use phosphate primer, color coating and corrosion inhibitors, and sealers throughout the body. The relentless winter abuse of cars caused by salted roads was a continuing problem for U.S. manufacturers who lead the way in preventative construction methods to fight these troubles.

The Lincoln-Mercury Division's triumph for 1977 was the new Mark V, designed by Don DeLaRossa who headed a consortium including George Haldeman. The traditional grille, the spare tire bulge and the oval window remained. New were three hood louvers behind the front wheel, sharper window cutouts and increased angularity through the whole sheet metal layout. The car was very, very 'sharp' in its styling impact.

The luxurious interior options were further developed by a continuation of the designer series models. All designer series cars included a personalized twenty-two-karat gold-finish instrument panel nameplate, four turbine-spoke cast aluminum wheels, right- and left-

hand illuminated visor vanity mirrors, six-way passenger seat, dome and dual-beam map light and gray cut-pile luggage compartment carpeting. Each designer's logo was lettered in the opera windows. The individual designer combinations were specified as follows:

Bill Blass: Midnight blue paint, chamois-color vinyl roof and leather.

Cartier: Dove gray paint, vinyl roof, leather.

Hubert de Givenchy: Dark jade metallic paint, chamois pigskin-grain forward vinyl half-roof, dark jade leather, chamois-color hood.

Emilio Pucci: Black Diamond Fire paint, white cayman-grain vinyl roof, white leather.

The public was enchanted with the Mark V and sales began briskly. When the 1977 model year was finished, a phenomenal 80,321 Mark V's had been produced. The Eldorado coupe, hardly changed from 1976, showed a final production total of only 47,344. Clearly the Mark V was a smash hit.

The Continental production for 1977 was a stunning 95,600 of which 68,160 were four-doors and 27,440 were hardtops. The Cadillac de Ville figures totaled 155,549, of which, curiously, the coupe total was 93,925 and the sedan total 61,624; the proportion a reverse of Lincoln production. The Mark V had so penetrated the two-door luxury market as to syphon off the two-door Continental production.

The grand totals were instructive—Lincoln production was 175,921 and Cadillac's, excluding Seville and limousines, was 309,515. On a head-to-head model basis Lincoln had its best year ever, a sales triumph that, for the first time since the thirties, suggested Lincoln was not only competitive but a direct threat to Cadillac sales supremacy. Yet the Seville factor needed to be considered; it had a production total of 45,060 in 1977. The Seville was the principal reason Cadillac gross production was driven to an all-time high of 358,487.

No matter what Lincoln management thought about the downsized car in the past, it was clear that time was growing short for entry into the new market as revealed by the Seville.

CHAPTER 12

Versailles And Reducing Pains—1978-80

ON JANUARY 20, 1977, the Lincoln Mercury Division sent out advance material on a new small luxury car with a press release of March 28. The name that was selected was Versailles—the highly rated name of the earlier marketing study of 1966. The new car was designed to "appeal to a growing segment of automobile buyers interested in smaller luxury sedans," said the press release. "This group traditionally has had to choose from a few relatively high-priced European nameplates." No word here of Seville.

The Versailles, based on the 1975 Mercury Monarch, offered little technical novelty and in truth neither did the Seville. Stress was laid on quality control, fit and finish. Technical specifications were identical to the Mercury Monarch— 109.9-inch wheelbase, headroom 38.2 inches, shoulder room 55.8, rear-compartment headroom 37.6, hip room 51.2 inches. Fuel capacity was 19.2 gallons. The same engines were fitted as in the Monarch, the 351-cubic-inch V-8 for forty-nine states and the 302-cubic-inch unit for California. The Versailles weight was 3,916 pounds compared to 3,404 pounds for the Monarch and so the Versailles was given a 2.75:1 rear axle ratio compared to a 2.47:1 for the Monarch. The weight differential was caused by the luxurious fittings and insulation on the Versailles.

One minor sheet metal change distinguished the Versailles from the Monarch: the Continental spare tire hump in the rear deck. The problem for Lincoln marketing experts was to convince the buying public that the Versailles was worth more than twice the Monarch's base price, which explains the emphasis on quality in the press releases. One might recall the Vanden Plas Princess editions of the old B.M.C. basic Austins.

Alas, the buyers did not understand. What they saw was a very high-quality Monarch, a fact that Cadillac salepersons never tired of telling prospective Seville customers. Lacking distinctive sheet metal (apart from the Continental spare tire bulge), the new Versailles fooled few.

Lincoln marketing experts made a crucial decision in pricing. Well aware of the Versailles' Monarch antecedents, they priced the car some $2,000 below the Seville, that is, on a par with the Mark V. Given the choice of the brilliant Mark V or the highly deluxe Monarch, the buyers opted easily for the Mark V. The bold move of the Cadillac marketing experts to put the Seville well above the big cars simply could not carry along to the Versailles.

Sales confirmed all of the above conclusions. The first year, admittedly a short production year, showed 15,434 units produced, not

Lincoln's Versailles was introduced in the spring of 1977 and this 1978 model is virtually unchanged. The Lincoln grille works well with the basic Mercury Monarch body. Early sales in 1977 were good but demand fell off drastically in 1978.

The stunning 1978 Continental Mark V enjoyed thundering sales and 72,602 were produced, including 5,159 of this Diamond Jubilee edition which featured new landau vinyl roof, color-keyed vertical grille bars and beveled-glass opera windows with a simulated diamond chip laminated into each. The 1979 Mark V was little different though sales would be slower after the Iranian revolution threatened gasoline supplies.

The 1978 Lincoln Continental had more open rear fender cut-outs and lost a brightwork strip on the body side. Lincoln was now going against GM's downsizing. A lot of people wanted the big sedan and 67,110 were produced.

bad when compared to Seville. But the following year sales fell off drastically as opposed to the burgeoning growth of the Seville. Lincoln management's basic distrust of the small luxury car was confirmed. The decision to remain with the big car concept for 1978 seemed prudent to Lincoln management after the splendid success of the 1977 model. The ever-growing CAFE demands (18 mpg for 1978) posed serious questions, but the Ford Motor Company was still in a position to continue on what was a successful course. The new smaller Cadillacs were continued in all models from 1977 except the Eldorado which would enjoy one last year in its former dimensions, a fact not overlooked by buyers. Cadillac advertising had just an edge of defensiveness in reference to the new small size with phrases like "overall design that's right for today's world" and "proportioned for the times." Lincoln, by comparison, used phrases such as "full-sized luxury" and "reinforces the Lincoln tradition of full-sized luxury."

Yet even Lincoln management was well aware of the need to reduce weight; plastics, high-strength low-alloy steel, aluminum, and thin glass were examined and applied where possible. The smaller 400-cubic-inch 'California' engine was now standard, with the bigger 450-cubic-inch unit available as a forty-nine-state option. But whereas the 400-cubic-inch 1977 engine was fitted with a four-barrel carburetor, the 1978 engine standardized a two-barrel model and power dropped again. Axle ratio was now 2.75:1 even with the Traction-Lok differential which had been mated to a 3:1 ratio in 1977. In the Versailles the engine displacement dropped to 302 inches, same as the 1977 California standard engine. The smog control noose was tightening.

The new smaller engines were equipped with new and more drastic evaporative emission controls. In the case of the 302-cubic-inch Versailles engine, the system was even more sophisticated, involving an electronic engine control which monitored the system through various sensors of crankshaft position, throttle position, coolant temperature, inlet air temperature, manifold absolute pressure, barometric pressure and exhaust gas recirculation valve position. The results of these measurements were used by the electronic module to regulate the spark advance and the exhaust gas recirculator valve actuator. It was a hard challenge for local dealers' mechanics and ruled out the home tinkerer for good.

One result of all of these refinements was a gross reduction in weight of the four-door sedan of 207 pounds. The Mark V lost ninety-eight pounds while the Versailles lost twenty pounds (it is natural that the most recently designed and lightest car would lose the least weight).

Another approach to helping fuel economy was fresh attention to aerodynamics. The coast-down tests revealed both aerodynamic and rolling resistance which in turn was translated into one of the factors in the federal mileage-measurement tests. Frontal area for 1978 Lincolns was virtually unchanged since the basic body shells were untouched. The only factor allowing for improvement was the air-flow pattern which received detailed study. Unfortunately, there was virtually no visible external change of any type on the 1978 Lincolns and Mark V's. Little could be achieved for the model year in this area though other product lines of the division were altered by deflectors, spoilers and sheet metal contours.

The end result of these efforts was to lift the average EPA mileage for the Lincoln from 12 mpg for 1977 to 13-15 for 1978, with a remarkable 20 mpg highway rating. The Cadillac de Ville, by comparison, rated 14 mpg in 1977 and 13-14 in 1978.

Technical improvements continued and included a new electronic solid state voltage regulator and an automatic temperature control which, perversely, returned to the driver the previously automated control of fan speed.

A novel option on the Mark V was a miles-to-empty indicator in which an electronic calculator sensed speed and fuel level, producing an instant reading of miles still available. The readout was available on call by pressing a button. Below fifty miles the reading was continuous, thus serving as a fuel warning gauge. The calculating period in time was approximately one minute, so that fluctuations caused by momentary acceleration or idling would be averaged out.

A CB transreceiver was offered, bringing possible radio options up to nine.

The exterior treatment of the whole line was hardly changed. The Versailles offered a new dark red metallic paint. The Continental rear wheel arch was opened. However, the oval quarter windows disappeared. The Mark V, so successful in 1977, was given the most subtle of trim changes, hubcap designs and color options. The designer series was altered as the four artists moved to new color schemes. Bill Blass went from Midnight blue to cordovan with matching interiors. Pucci went from black Diamond Fire paint to silver metallic with dark red and dove gray interior leather. Givenchy moved from dark jade metallic to Midnight jade, retaining the chamois and jade matching interiors. Cartier abandoned dove gray for light Champagne with matching interiors.

Don DeLaRossa (left) has been a central figure in Ford's corporate design team. He was executive stylist in the Lincoln-Mercury studio in the late fifties and reworked the 1958 Lincoln. He played an important role in the Mustang project and was the chief stylist for the Mark V. Walter J. Oben (right) is the current general manager of the Lincoln-Mercury Division and a vice president of FoMoCo.

There was yet another limited production Mark V for 1978, the Diamond Jubilee edition which included as standard most of the Mark V options. Two paint options, Diamond blue metallic or Jubilee gold were matched to blue or gold six-way bucket seats. Production totaled 5,159.

Prices moved up rapidly; the f.o.b. base prices near the close of the production year were as follows:

Continental four-door	$10,166
Continental two-door	9,974
Mark V coupe	12,099
Designer series	13,899
Diamond Jubilee coupe	20,529
Versailles	12,529

The Carriage Roof option was offered in 1978 on the Mark V and became standard on the Bill Blass designer series. A white vinyl top embossed with a canvas weave enhanced the strong resemblance to a true convertible. Oval interior mirrors replaced the opera windows.

the $20,000-and-up category. These prices were dwarfed by Mercedes whose utilitarian four-cylinder sedan had a base of $16,647. The popular 450 V-8 sedan had crossed the $30,000 barrier and the 6.9 sedan was $45,000.

These extraordinary prices for imports posed some marketing questions for Lincoln planners. Snob values or driving rewards might explain the purchase of a Mercedes 450 at double the price of a Mark V designer coupe, the domestic car awash with marvelous luxury features and gadgets not to mention superb air-conditioning and sound systems. And only the most rabid foreign car enthusiast would challenge the robust longevity inherent in American engine and chassis design. But how was one to explain the very strong sales, for example, of the Mercedes four-cylinder diesel, a car of no appreciable performance, considerable noise and an image of sober utilitarianism yet at a price above virtually everything offered by both Lincoln and Cadillac? General Motors' response was to offer the diesel engine in both the Cadillac and Oldsmobile lines with great success as fuel shortages appeared and fuel prices soared.

Even as late as 1978 the invasion of the highest-priced imports, though disturbing, hardly posed a serious economic threat to both Lincoln and Cadillac. The production summaries for 1977 and 1978 reveal the tremendous volume of both firms.

Lincoln production:

	1977	1978
Versailles	15,434	8,931
four-door	68,160	67,110
two-door	27,440	20,977
Mark V	80,321	72,602
	191,355	169,620

The relative appeal of the various designer series and Diamond Jubilee cars is revealed in the 1978 sales figures:

Cartier	8,520
Blass	3,975
Pucci	3,125
Givenchy	917
Diamond Jubilee	5,159
	21,696

Cadillac production:

	1977	1978
Fleetwood sedan	28,000	36,800
De Ville coupe	138,750	117,750
De Ville sedan	95,421	88,951
75's and commercials	3,912	2,382
Eldorado	47,344	46,816
Seville	45,060	56,985
	358,487	349,684

These prices could be exceeded by several thousand dollars at showroom delivery sticker prices, depending on equipment and handling charges.

By way of comparison the Cadillac base f.o.b. prices are instructive:

De Ville four-door	$10,668
Eldorado two-door	11,921
Coupe Biarritz	13,786
Brougham	12,292
Seville	14,267
Seville Elegante	16,867

Cadillac pricing was thus nearly head-to-head with the comparative Lincoln models, but for the Seville which was very much higher than both the Versailles and all other models of both companies except the Diamond Jubilee Mark V which was posting a runaway price that had no comparable Cadillac rival.

The Chrysler line had abandoned all pretense at the upper luxury market and offered nothing in the Lincoln-Cadillac range. But the cheapest BMW 530 ci sedan had a base of $14,940 while the 633 CSi coupe was an astronomical $24,970. Jaguars were likewise ranging in

An analysis of these figures reveals at once the strength of the Mark V as the premier luxury offering of the Lincoln-Mercury Division. The next most popular car was the four-door Continental, its large size having the greatest advantage in the four-door competition. The failure of the Versailles to take hold against the Seville, whose sales continued to rise, was the principal problem of the Lincoln Division. This result fit in with the sales assumptions made two years earlier when Lincoln decided not to downsize until absolutely necessary. Lincoln dealers could be pardoned for their inability or perhaps disinterest in selling a product that directly challenged the basic sales pitch of the marque.

The question, then, was how to address the changing market, implicit in the sales figures for 1977 and 1978. The growing success of the Seville and the failure of the Versailles to be competitive was crucial. Since the whole Lincoln line was to be downsized for 1980, a decision made inevitable by CAFE requirements, the Versailles 'experiment' was taking on added importance. All those Lincoln buyers who were lining up for the last full-sized luxury car in 1979 would have to be wooed eventually to something smaller. If the first 'smaller' Lincoln was a failure, it meant trouble ahead for the marketing image that Lincoln would soon be forced to embrace. Thus, heavy attention was paid to the Versailles by both designers and engineers.

The first and most critical problem for 1979 was to disassociate the Versailles body outline from the Monarch-Granada. This was achieved by lengthening the roof some eight inches and then introducing a new, more vertical rear window. The effect was enhanced by padding the rear half of the roof forward to a sharp lateral band, a return to the town car look complete with an inset coachlamp in the B-pillar. The effect was new and fresh and brought the Versailles a distinctive and identifiable style. Though the new rear roofline was more like the Seville, the whole rear of the Versailles had more bulk in the Lincoln Mark V tradition. Furthermore, the Versailles offered more front overhang than the Seville, again a restatement of Mark V ideas. An added touch was a padded insert on the rear Continental spare wheel outline. Bordinat and his staff could be justly pleased with the transformation. Versailles interiors again achieved a level of sheer luxury and elegance unsurpassed by Seville, that quality of extra Lincoln plushness which testers had noted in the early 1970's on the Mark III and Mark IV when compared to the Eldorado.

The equipment on the Versailles was lavish and, in fact, a virtual test bed for everything that the Lincoln-Mercury Division offered. The completeness of the equipment is put into focus by the nature of the very few equipment options available such as *heated* left-hand remote-

The roof of the 1979 Versailles was extended eight inches and given a more vertical rear window. Town car roof padding and coachlamps completed the new look. Sales improved immediately.

control mirror, an integral electric garage door opener, forty-channel CB radio and an illuminated outside thermometer.

Illumination was very important on the Versailles. Consider the following partial lamp list: cornering lamps, coachlamps, backup lights, luggage compartment light, glovebox light, instrument panel courtesy light, ashtray light, engine compartment light, dual-beam dome light, rear-door courtesy light, rear-seat reading lamps, left- and right-hand illuminated vanity mirrors, illuminated entry system and the first U.S. use of halogen headlamps.

The Versailles wheelbase of 109.9 inches was substantially shorter than the Seville's 114.3 inches and the Mercedes 450 SEL's 116.7 inches. The success of the design on such a tight wheelbase was another tribute to the Bordinat team. At 3,848 pounds, the Versailles was sixty pounds lighter than the Mercedes and 330 pounds under the Seville, still rather heavy but indicative of the tremendous amount of servo equipment on board.

The compactness of the Versailles meant relatively tight rear interior dimensions, with legroom six inches less than that of the Continental four-door. Trunk space of 14.6 cubic feet was made possible only with

Last full-size Lincoln, the 1979 Continental four-door. It was a bold gamble in the light of growing fears of gasoline shortages. Dealers had a hard time clearing the last of their stock in the fall.

an inflatable spare tire, the penalty of conventional engine-axle layout. In comparison, the next-generation front-wheel-drive cars such as the Volkswagen Rabbit offered fifteen cubic feet behind the rear seat, with a ready-to-go spare tire. However, luggage space was hardly a criterion of the Versailles shopper. The Versailles was a superb example of American design in which the passenger was given nearly total isolation from the road. Isolation from road shock was total, too, with a steering ratio of 21.3:1 assisted by a fine power system — not the choice of a Mercedes owner, perhaps, but ideally tuned to American expectations. Sales of the new Versailles picked up at once and by mid-year it was increasingly evident that the new car was meeting with dealer and public approval.

The Continental was in its last year in the grand style and the most was made of its numerous virtues. Though little technical change was introduced, the model array was dazzling. The line started with the Continental four-door and two-door, plain only by comparison with what awaited the upward-striving buyer. The town car, in both coupe and sedan versions, increased the luxury level and was readily

identifiable by the oval rear window on the four-door and the transverse band at the B-pillar complete with integral coachlamp. The Williamsburg edition of the town car featured subtle two-tone exteriors and velour interiors. At the top of the line was the limited-edition collector series, so named in recognition of the final year of production of the 'big' Continental, and featuring a Midnight blue or white exterior and Midnight blue interiors. The oval window in the sedan was missing but the town car trim remained.

As the final statement of a great tradition, the 1979 Continental presented a lavish display of luxury, especially in the voluptuous interiors, with such abandon as to gladden the heart of the most skeptical sybarite. The 450 SEL Mercedes, though superbly finished, was practically spartan by comparison. Even the Cadillac Fleetwood brougham had an interior of Dante knit cloth which seemed downright utilitarian when compared with Lincoln's imaginative interiors.

Weight reduction continued and the Lincoln Continental curb weight was now under 5,000 pounds (4,843 pounds), down some 400 pounds from 1967. The 400-cubic-inch engine was able to handle a low 2.47:1 rear axle ratio in standard trim though in California the 2.75 axle was fitted. Laden with evaporative emission controls, the California version recorded no more than 10 mpg, as an EPA fuel estimate. The Mark V received parallel development in styling and interiors for 1979. Again a succession of luxury levels was offered and the 'standard' Mark V was only so described when related to the models offered above it.

The designer series continued with the Cartier edition using the basic Champagne color highlighted with dark red trim and accents. Bill Blass offered the mock convertible top in white with the car sides in Midnight blue metallic, the interior reflecting these sharp color contrasts with white leather and deep blue trim. The Pucci edition used turquoise exteriors and white interiors with Midnight blue accents; while the Givenchy was also in a blue, somewhat darker, with dark leather interiors and a distinctive Givenchy broadlace trim.

Prices went up, the collector series now nearing $25,000 West Coast delivered. Even the garden-variety Continental was $18,000. At these prices the question of fuel economy recalled the J. P. Morgan response to concerns about the cost of operating his giant yacht, yet the 10 mpg of the Mark V (California) was at the bottom of American cars. By the late fall of 1978 it was already clear that good sales of the final Lincoln grand statement had brought the Ford corporation's average fuel economy dangerously close to the 19 mpg minimum required for 1979 models. The corporate penalty for failure to meet the averaged mileage requirements was severe—five dollars for each one tenth of a mile per gallon below the requirement for each car produced. By December 1978 the Ford corporate average was so close to going under 19 mpg that prices were revised to make the Lincoln line more costly while the economy end of the Ford line was untouched.

It was a hard decision to make in the face of a GM sales blitz for the 1979 models which had forced both Ford and Chrysler on the defensive. The two-year lead that GM had established in the downsizing was finally paying off. General Motors' intensive advertising attacked, by implication, the Lincoln as the remaining big car. Buyers were still ready to have one last fling with the big Lincoln despite all that GM might advertise and sales were good in the fall. This was the reason for the CAFE problem, but to have to add on to the sticker price to discourage sales was a difficult pill for Lincoln marketing people to swallow.

There was a certain irony in the fuel problem because the 1978 figure for the big Lincoln was 14 mpg, equal to the de Ville and well ahead of Eldorado's 11 mpg. The penalty of meeting ever-increasing emission standards showed up principally in Lincoln's lowered fuel economy for 1979, especially since the car received the most minor of mechanical changes.

The sudden fuel crisis in February 1979 caused by the Iranian revolution brought new questions to the automobile market. Sales of big cars suffered throughout the industry but the Lincoln line showed remarkable resistance to declines. Though sales dipped a bit here and there, which gave some relief to the CAFE problem, the Lincoln sales projections were very nearly matched by the good results for the first few months of the year. In a sense the timing seemed perfect, the last of the big luxury cars phasing out amid unprecedented fuel-cost increases and general uncertainty about the future.

Things got much worse on the fuel front in late spring as lines formed at the gasoline stations. Sales of the heavy luxury cars nearly stopped and even the Lincoln, the last of the holdouts for sheer size, had hard moments. By late summer 1979, dealers were struggling to unload stocks in the face of massive buyer indifference. The crisis for Chrysler was nearly fatal and even GM could not offer a product mix that matched the fuel-starved times. Lincoln Continental production closed on June 8.

The 1980 cars came none too soon and were introduced amid confusion about fuel and the general future of Detroit's products. New car sales in the fall of 1979 were disappointing apart from the new General Motors 'X' cars and the small lines of the domestic manufacturers.

The whole Lincoln line was drastically downsized and was built on three new wheelbases: 117.4 inches for the Continental Mark VI four-door and the Lincoln Continental two-door and four-door; 114.4 inches

The Lincoln Continental coupe offered useful styling differences from the Mark VI coupe, in part because the long wheelbase allowed the development of a large rear seat area. This town coupe has Comfort-Lounge seats.

for the Mark VI two-door; and 109.9 inches for the Versailles. By offering the Mark VI in four-door form the implication was that the Mark series would now be a more deluxe trimmed Continental. There was some truth in this though the Mark VI coupe was shorter than the Continental coupe, a reversal of Lincoln marketing philosophy as regards size. The Mercury Marquis was also built on the 114.4-inch wheelbase (though listed as 114.3) while the Monarch appeared on the Versailles' 109.9-inch wheelbase. Product rationalization meant production economies.

The overall length of the Continental was reduced 13.8 inches and one might expect that the 1980 cars would be substantially smaller inside. Bordinat and the stylists came up with an unusually crisp body line with knife edges everywhere which provided maximum interior space. The extraordinary result was that interior dimensions were increased in most instances. Rear seat legroom went from 42 to 43.3 inches, and even luggage capacity in the new car was up from 21.2 to 22.4 cubic feet.

The Continental was provided in two series, the regular and town car versions. The usual array of Lincoln equipment was augmented in the town car with six-way power seats, a manual seat-back recliner, deluxe trim everywhere, and more luxurious seat designs. Nine colors

The brand new four-door Mark VI shared the 117.4-inch wheelbase of the Lincoln Continental. The traditional spare tire hump was set against a slanting rear deck surface. This 1980 Signature Series was offered in dark red metallic or silver metallic and was the prestige leader for the Mark VI.

plus seven optional moondust colors were available which, when combined with eight interior colors and five white-trim combinations, produced Lincoln's typical rainbow of choices. Downsizing was made as painless as possible.

The Mark VI offered the same number of colors but with variations from the Continental list. Those who were not content with the standard lavish offerings could begin to move upward by ordering the basic luxury group defined principally by the six-way power seat and deluxe trim options. The designer series continued with Cartier using pewter colors, Blass in blue, Pucci in fawn, and Givenchy in fawn and bittersweet (a copper tone). The signature series provided yet a further luxury option for Mark VI shoppers and was offered in dark red metallic and silver metallic. Equipment was lavish including garage door opener, removable and rechargeable glovebox light which could function as a

flashlight, and a keyless entry system. A close inspection of the new Mark VI cars, in whatever series or luxury option, conveyed the impression that very little had been given up in the downsizing and that the new cars were, if anything, full of fresh novelty and creature comforts.

The Versailles was caught somewhat in the downsizing and could hardly be shrunk further without losing the luxury image. Dimensions and interior styling were unchanged though colors and trim combinations were juggled. The mechanical specifications with the 302-cubic-inch engine and the 2.47:1 rear end ratio continued and were virtually identical to 1979.

On the technical side both the Continental and the Mark VI continued to use the perimeter frame but the Versailles pursued the unitized body construction.

The weight drop was substantial as the following table shows:

	1979	1980
Mark VI two-door	4,779 lbs	4,004 lbs
Mark VI four-door		4,099
Lincoln Continental two-door	4,841	3,962
Lincoln Continental four-door	4,843	4,038
Versailles four-door	3,848	3,828

The 302-cubic-inch engine was standard in the Lincoln line with an optional 352-cubic-inch engine for the Mark VI and the Continental. The CAFE requirement was 20 mpg in 1980 and the Lincolns were ready with many new technical features. The Electronic Engine Control (EEC) regulated fuel-air ratio, the secondary air to the exhaust emission system, the ignition timing, the exhaust gas recirculation flow and the purging of the fuel evaporative emission control canister. The input to the four electronic chips in the EEC was through various sensors located in the engine and various connecting vacuum and electrical lines. The EEC system reacted at the rate of thirty times per second and instantly adjusted the engine to meet both climatic and special conditions. The precise controlling of the air-fuel ratio to 14.7:1 resulted in optimum clean burning of the fuel. During starting and warm-up the EEC automatically provided a richer mixture.

Electronic fuel injection was provided on the 302-cubic-inch engine, again through the use of electronic sensing and metering. The technology of the electronic black box ruled out all but the most sophisticated of mechanics.

Electronic technology was found throughout the cars. On the Mark VI and Continental a keyless entry system permitting door locking and unlocking and deck-lid release from outside the car without a key. Five pushbuttons on the driver's door belt molding were back-lighted for night purposes when the first button was pushed. The first button also turned on the interior lights and the key lock light. The coded sequence of the buttons was then pressed to unlock the car. By pressing the fourth and fifth buttons simultaneously the car was locked. The doors were also locked after all the doors were closed, the driver's seat was occupied, the ignition switch was on and the transmission selector had passed through reverse. The five-digit coding sequence could be changed by the owner at will though the minicomputer retained a permanent code programed at the factory.

An electronic instrument cluster was standard on the Mark VI, and optional on the Continental. Twelve buttons controlled a computer which supplied various readout information including the following functions: speed, in either miles or kilometers per hour; distance to empty tank; various clock functions; and trip log. The fuel gauge was

The new 114.4-inch wheelbase required very tight control of all design elements on the 1980 Continental Mark VI and the successful results are obvious. Overall length of 216 inches meant much overhang. The oval window and fender louvers are instant identifiers of the Mark VI.

divided into segments indicating fuel level by brightness. An empty-fuel gauge flashed at one cycle per second. A low-fuel warning signal was included. The clock functions included time, day, month and date along with a monitor check on eleven car functions and a self-diagnostic test system. The trip log functions were especially interesting and provided 1) distance per gallon; 2) distance traveled since starting, up to 10,000 miles; 3) elapsed time including all time stopped; 4) average speed; 5) remaining miles to destination; and 6) estimated time of arrival based on distance remaining and average car speed.

The monitor check also surveyed brake pressure, alternator, oil pressure and engine temperature. At a lower level of priority the monitor check indicated low washer fluid level, trunk ajar, door ajar, headlamp out, taillamp out, brakelamp out, and miles to empty less than fifty. The word referring to the specific malfunction was flashed to the message center along with a warning tone once every four seconds. Some of the second-level malfunctions were indicated by a chime tone and flashing display.

This extraordinary electronic system provided both entertainment and precisely reliable information to a degree never before offered in an automobile.

Economy was extremely important in 1980 and the new Mark VI and Continental offered a four-speed automatic transmission in which the fourth gear was used as an overdrive ratio with a no-slip power flow. The fourth ratio was a true overdrive, the third gear being 1:1 ratio even though forty percent of the torque was passed through the torque converter.

There were other new features addressing a new decade of smaller cars. The new trunk space was bought at the price of a mini-spare tire. The battery shrank further from 54 to 45 ampere-hour rating though in the Versailles it remained at 53 amp rating. The windshield washer sprayed the whole windshield with a single oscillating jet. The sound system could be offered with six speakers and featured the Dolby system of noise reduction, highly sophisticated quartz tuning, electronic memory and the option of a CB system.

Though there was some nostalgia about the conclusion of production of the last of the 'big' cars, the marketing people were anything but sad. Sales had virtually stopped in May and June as the gasoline crisis reached very serious proportions. Long lines at gas stations throughout the country suddenly made the big Lincoln irrelevant. On August 1, 1978, the inventory of Mark V's had been forty-four days. On August 1, 1979, the inventory was a phenomenal 210 days, almost two-thirds of a year's supply and exceeded only by the Chrysler Cordoba with a disastrous 345 days' supply. A tremendous selling effort by Lincoln dealers was able to shrink the Mark V inventory to 135 days by November 1, 1979, but as late as December, Mark V's were still available in many dealerships. The Continental inventories were smaller and were worked down more easily because there was more and more reason to buy the last big four-door sedan. The Versailles inventory fell from 200 to 108 days between July 1 and August 1, 1979, profiting somewhat from the gasoline crunch because of a more economical image.

The introduction of the 1980 cars was subdued because of uncertain gasoline supplies, high 1979 model inventories and a general concern about the economy. Very high interest rates affected the sales of the high-priced luxury cars. This unfavorable selling climate was particularly distressing for Lincoln because the car was so new and deserved an enthusiastic reception. Those buyers who made the move to the 1980 Lincoln were indeed enthusiastic, but the Wixom plant was temporarily closed in mid-November to balance inventories.

The Lincoln story in the postwar years was a success story in a mighty, competitive battle in which there were few winners. The Lincoln began in a very weak position in 1946, with a car that was basically noncompetitive and running a poor fourth behind Cadillac, Packard and Chrysler. It survived initially because of the pent-up postwar demand but the new-generation 1949 models arrived in mid-1948 just in the nick of time. These great old flathead V-8's were good and solid but Cadillac forged ahead and even Packard made records in 1949 with a car that still managed to retain some echo of its prewar image.

Lincoln struggled for a consistent image in the fifties. The great road cars of 1952-54 were champions in their class but the luxury market was lost because of them. The models of 1955-57 were pleasant enough but set no continuing image, despite the award-winning design of 1956. The road-car enthusiasts who had bought the 1953 and 1954 cars saw the development as retrogressive, as weight and size were added. The true luxury-car buyer still failed to find the Lincoln a suitable alternative to the larger Cadillacs. The problem was compounded by the fact that in the banner sales year of 1955 it was Mercury, not Lincoln, that was ready with a restyled car. Yet Lincoln was doing far better than Packard which soon quietly slipped away into oblivion.

The 1958 Lincoln was a stunning *tour de force* that pleased no one. The previous market was entirely abandoned because the car was incredibly large. But the targeted luxury buyer did not understand the new car and was repelled not only by the tremendous size but by the very sharp and aggressive idiosyncrasies of the various styling blades and cantings. It was a time of styling extremes and the Cadillac descended to its nadir in 1959. The new Imperial, launched rather well in the bubbling market of the mid-fifties, succumbed to the bizarre design emphases of the time and struggled for a consistent styling identification.

This continued to be Lincoln's problem and only with the 1961 Continental did the final success story begin. It was a slow start, with sales building gradually until the two-door Continental opened up new markets. The Mark III began the spectacular success of the Lincoln in the personal car field where it was unexcelled.

The target for Lincoln was always Cadillac, not the Imperial which achieved momentary sales peaks but never really reached the consistent volume level that might have established Chrysler's top car as a major challenger. In this quest the Lincoln was successful because, though it never was able to beat Cadillac on sheer gross volume (in some measure a simple result of limited production capabilities), the Lincoln progressively gained on the Cadillac and in the Mark versus Eldorado competition, was clearly the winner.

The unsettling market of the late seventies caught Lincoln in a somewhat defensive role as General Motors led the downsizing of the luxury car. In particular, the Seville scored an early triumph which the Versailles was unable to overcome in its initial form. The final statement of the great Lincoln Continental and the brilliant Mark V in 1979 represents a pinnacle of American design philosophy.

These great cars are the last automotive reflection of a moment in American history when the grand style and the sense of unlimited power were part of the national dream. That that dream has faded is no reflection upon a motor car that has always stood for greatness and has managed to maintain that image longer than its rivals.

Though the exterior dimensions of the **Mark VI** and Lincoln Continental four-doors are the same, the Lincoln shown above had a narrow rear-quarter window and a vertical rear deck cut-off. The **Mark VI** version replaced the small oval quarter window. The town car sedan as shown added the coach lamps, twin Comfort Lounge seats and other deluxe fittings.

Appendix I
Lincoln and Continental Literature 1946-1961
Compiled by Jeffrey I. Godshall and Autoenthusiasts International

1946:
Catalog, 14 x 9½, full-line, color, 24p.

1947:
Folder, 8 x 6, two-models, color
Folder, 12½ x 9½, full-line, color

1948:
Folder, Continental, color, 2-48

1949:
Folder, 12 x 9, full-line, color
Folder, as above with words "Road Proven"
Catalog, 15 x 11, full-line, color, 32p.
Catalog, 3½ x 7, Quick Facts, b&w&red, 8p.
Catalog, as above in b&w&green with words "Road Proven"
Catalog, 9 x 7½, Hydra-matic, color, 20p.
Catalog, 8½ x 11, Hydra-matic Salesman's Guide, b&w&yellow, 12p.
Folder, 11 x 15, Lincoln/Mercury, sepia&w
Folder, 10½ x 7½, access., green&w
Catalog, 3½ x 5, Quick Facts, b&w&green, 8p.
Folder, 4 x 8, Overdrive, color

1950
Folder, 12 x 8½, full-line, color, 11-49
Folder, 9 x 8½, Lincoln, blue&b&w, 11-49
Folder, 9 x 8½, Cosmopolitan, brown&b&w, 11-49
Folder, 12 x 10, Lido, color, 6-50
Folder, 12 x 9, Capri, color, 6-50
Catalog, 10½ x 8, "Lincoln Mile," color, 12p., 5-50
Catalog, 10½ x 8, "Lincoln Mile," b&w, 12p., 4-50
Catalog, 6½ x 3½, Quick Facts, color, 12p., 11-49
Catalog, 6½ x 3½, Quick Facts, color, 12p., 4-50
Catalog, 8 x 6, engine, color, 12p., 2-50
Catalog, 4 x 8, Hydra-matic, color, 8p., 11-49
Catalog, 8 x 6, access., green&yellow&w, with color cover, 40p., 2-50
Catalog, 3½ x 7, "Lincoln Mile," color, 8p., 5-50

1951:
Folder, 12 x 8½, full-line, color, 10-50
Folder, 11 x 8, Lincoln, b&w&green, 10-50
Folder, 11 x 8, Lincoln, b&w&green, 1-51
Folder, 11 x 8½, Cosmopolitan, b&w&yellow, 10-50
Folder, 11 x 8½, Cosmopolitan, b&w&yellow, 1-51
Catalog, Quick Facts, color, 16p., 10-50
Catalog, 8½ x 6, access., b&w with yellow&grey cover, 36p., 10-50

1952:
Catalog, 11 x 14, full-line, color, 20p., L-52-1 12-51
Catalog, 11 x 14, "Modern Woman," color, 8p., 5-52
Catalog, 11 x 14, "Modern Living," color, 20p., 5-52
Folder, 11 x 14, Capri, color, L-52-3 12-51
Folder, 10 x 12, full-line, b&w&brown, L-52-2 12-51
Catalog, 7 x 4, Quick Facts, b&w&green, 12p., L-52-4 12-51
Catalog, 7 x 9, access., b&w&brown with color covers, 28p., L-52-18 3-52
Catalog, 6 x 9½, V-8, color, 12p., L-52-5 12-51
Mailer/Folder, 11 x 14, "Visibly in Keeping," color, 5-52. Windshield cut out on cover
Folder, 11 x 14, full-line, "For Your Consideration," color, 7-52
Folder, 5 x 9, "Salesman's Eye View," b&w, L-52-15 12-51

1953:
Catalog, 11 x 14, full-line, color, 20p., L-53-101 11-52
Folder, 11 x 14, full-line, color, L-53-103 11-52
Folder, 11 x 14, full-line, color, L-53-103 2-53
Catalog, 11 x 14, power, color, 12p., L-53-105 11-52
Catalog, 8 x 11, Mexican Race, b&w, 12p.
Folder, 6 x 6, "Excellence of Lincoln," color, 3-53
Catalog, 4½ x 9, PowerPacked, b&w&green, L-53-111 10-52
Catalog, 8 x 4½, Quick Facts, b&w&green, 12p., L-53-104 11-52
Card, 5½ x 3, Cosmopolitan, color, L-53-108 11-52
Folder, 11 x 14, "New Dimensions in Modern Living," color with 3-D picture, 7-53
Mailer, 11 x 14, "Member of Modern Family," color, 8p., 6-53
Catalog, 11 x 14, "Cross-Country Mobility," color, 8p., 3-53
Catalog, as above, 5-53
Folder, 10½ x 13½, Mexican Race, b&w
Catalog, 7 x 5, air conditioning, b&w&blue&yellow, 10p.
Folder, 6 x 4, air conditioning, b&w&blue&yellow, LM 7320, 5-53

1954:
Folder, 8 x 11, Road Race, b&w&red, 12-53
Catalog, 8 x 9, facts, b&w&red, 16p., L-54-104 11-53
Catalog, 11 x 14, full-line, color, 20p., L-54-101 11-53
Catalog, 11 x 14, full-line, color, 8p., L-54-103 11-53
Folder, 8½ x 4, air conditioning, b&w&blue, 4054
Catalog, 10 x 14, Road Race, b&w&brown, 8p., 3-54
Catalog, 10 x 13½, "Art . . . Modern Living," color, 12p., 4-54

1955:
Catalog, 7½ x 9, Quick Facts, b&w&yellow, 12p., L-55-102 9-54
Folder, 8 x 11, Road Race, b&w&red, 12-54
Folder, 14 x 11, full-line, color, L-55-101 10-54
Catalog, 11 x 14, full-line, color, 20p., L-55-100 10-54
Catalog, 11 x 14, "On Camera," color, 8p., L-55-104 3-55
Catalog, 11 x 14, "Poise . . . of Champion," color, 8p., L-55-105 3-55

1956:
Folder, 18 x 8, full-line, color
Catalog, 18 x 8, full-line, color, 20p.
Booklet, 8½ x 5, Quick Facts, b&w&blue, 16p.

Continental
Booklet, 9 x 7, "The Continentals," b&w&gold, 20p. plus foldout and covers
Folder, 9 x 10, Mark II, color (gold inside)
Folder, as above, (silver inside)
Book, 13 x 9½, "Continental Story," b&w&green&color, 50p. plus covers, hardbound

1957:
Catalog, 14 x 10, "Smartest Places," color 8p.
Booklet, 8½ x 5, Quick Facts, b&w&green, 16p.
Folder, 3½ x 8½, colors, color
Catalog, 14 x 12, Premiere, color, 12p.
Catalog, 14 x 12, full-line, color, 20p.
Catalog, 14½ x 12½, full-line, color, 20p., plus white covers
Folder, 4 x 8, "Star of Cars," brown&yellow

1958:
Catalog, 10 x 13, Vogue Fashion reprint, color, 8p. plus foldout
Catalog, 15 x 10, Lincoln/Continental III, color, 12p., L-58-02 10-57
Catalog, 14½ x 10, Lincoln/Continental III, color, 24p., L-58-01 10-57
Catalog, 15 x 10, Lincoln/Continental III, color, 28p., L-58-01 with embossed covers

1959:
Booklet, 8½ x 11, "Motoring Comfort," brown&cream, 12p., DM3-59
Catalog, 8 x 10, Lincoln/Continental Mark IV, color, 24p.
Catalog, 9 x 6, access., b&w&blue, 16p. plus covers
Catalog, 12½ x 10, "Pursuit of Perfection," color, 16p. plus foldout, DM4-59
Catalog, 11 x 14, Lincoln/Continental Mark IV, color, 24p. plus special booklet (3 x 4½)
Catalog, 8½ x 11, Mark IV Town Car/Limousine, 12p., b&w&gold, S-I-59, with envelope
Catalog, 14½ x 9, "An Important Message," b&w, 8p. plus covers
Catalog, 12 x 11, "Portrait of Success," color, 16p. plus foldout, DM5-59

1960:
Catalog, 14 x 11, Lincoln/Continental Mark V, color, 24p., LC-100-60 9-59
Catalog, 9 x 7, Lincoln/Continental Mark V, color, 24p., 101-60 9-59

1961:
Folder, 3 x 8½, power differential, b&w&blue, C-9530 11-60
Mailer/Catalog, 8½ x 10, "An Invitation," color, 12p. plus covers with letter, LC61-108
Portfolio, 9½ x 12, Car Life reprint, color & b&w, 12p.
Mailer/Folder, 8½ x 10½, "Pure Elegance," with color insert and 2-year warranty booklet, with envelope, LC61-110
Newsprint, 11 x 13, "Armchair Auto Show," color (Lincoln/Mercury), 12p., 12-4-60
Catalog, 8 x 4, "Confidential Preview," b&w, 16p., LM9-60
Mailer/Folder, 7 x 5, "Honored by Industrial Design Institute," b&w with color insert with envelope

Continental
Catalog, 11 x 12½, color, 10p. plus tissues plus covers
Mailer/Folder, 10½ x 10½, color, LC61-112 with letter
Catalog, 11½ x 8½, color, 20p. plus tissues plus covers plus warranty, 9-60 MD 7019A
Catalog, 11 x 7½, color, 20p. plus covers, 9-60 MD 7019
Folder, 14 x 8½, b&w, LC61-113
Folder, as above without number

Index

Alfa Romeo, 39
Allegheny-Ludlum Steel Corp., 106, 107
Andrade, Julio, 37
Andreson, Wilbur R., 20
Andrews, Keith, 57
Anthony, Earle C., 19
Ash, L. David, 12, 49, 66, 79, 82, 110, 118, 121
Auburn, 10
Automobile Manufacturers' Association, 51

Bendix Aviation, 11, 20
Bennett, Harry, 17, 18, 20, 30
Benton, William, 125
Beyreis, Don, 49
Bijur lubrication system, 59
Blass, Bill, 131, 134, 139, 140, 142, 144
Bloom, Fred, 116
BMW, 140
Bond, John, 52-53
Bordinat, Eugene, 88, 91, 95, 98, 111, 114, 116, 119, 121-122, 124, 141, 143
Borgeson, Griff, 42
Borg-Warner, 36
Bosworth, Charles E., 20

Breech, Ernest R., 20, 30-31, 32, 80
Brezhnev, Leonid I., 125
Bricker, Mead, 20
Briggs Manufacturing Co., 6
Brokaw, Jim, 124, 126
Browning, Albert J., 20
Brunn, Hermann C., 15, 30, 34, 106, 110
Brunn and Co., 15, 30, 41
Buehrig, Gordon, 69, 71, 74
Bugas, John S., 20
Buick models, 10, 25, 27, 40, 52, 69
Business Week, 76

Cadillac models, 15, 25, 27, 28, 36, 37, 40, 41, 43, 50, 51, 53, 56, 57, 59, 60, 61, 69, 70, 71, 73, 75, 77, 80, 81, 83, 86, 87, 90, 94, 95, 96, 97, 100, 103-104, 105, 107, 109, 110, 113, 114, 118, 119-120, 122-123, 124, 127, 128, 129, 131, 132, 133, 135, 136, 138, 139, 140, 142, 143, 147
CAFE. *See* Corporate Average Fuel Economy.
Car Life, 93
Carrera Panamericana, 31, 39, 45, 46, 48, 50, 51, 54, 55, 57, 59, 84, 100
Cartier, 131, 134, 139, 140, 142, 144

Cheek, John, 37
Chicago Auto Show, 108, 112, 118, 119
Chicago World's Fair, 8
Chrysler models, 6, 8, 10, 15, 27, 28, 37, 40, 50, 51, 55, 60, 70, 78, 79, 146
Clark, Cle, 55
Classic Car Club of America, 68
Copp, Harley, 71, 74, 79, 80
Cop-Sil-Loy, 51
Cord, E. L., 6
Corporate Average Fuel Economy (CAFE), 133, 138, 143, 145
Cousins, Ross, 30
Crawford, Ray, 50, 57
Crusoe, Lewis D., 20, 68

Dahlberg, Wes, 121, 122
Daimler models, 81, 87
Davis, John R., 19, 20, 68
Davis Committee, 68, 70
Delahaye, 39
DeLaRossa, Don, 44, 85, 86, 91, 134, 139
Derham coachbuilder, 69, 74, 75
Detroit Automobile Show, 61, 62

Doehler, Robert, 30, 37, 71
Duesenberg, Fred, 6
Duraspark Ignition, 133
Dykstra, John, 80

Earl, Harley, 37
Edelbrock, 50
Edsel car, 77
Eisenhower, Dwight D., 41
Ellington, Duke, 70
Engel, Elwood P., 89, 91, 98, 99, 115
Esper, Al, 35
Estes, Bob, 39
Eucharistic Conference, 101
Exner, Virgil, 78, 82

Farkas, Joseph, 30, 71
Faulkner, Walt, 50, 51, 54, 57
Ferrari models, 50, 51
Feyer, George, 75
Fitch, John, 55
FluidDrive, 27
Fokker Co., 6
Ford, Benson, 25, 28, 44, 50, 56, 61
Ford, Edsel, 6, 8, 9, 10, 11, 12, 15, 17, 18, 25, 56, 62, 68,
    75, 111
Ford, Henry, 6, 8, 70, 92, 96
Ford, Henry II, 18, 20, 24, 29, 30-31, 44, 68, 71, 110
Ford, Walter Buell, 71, 72
Ford, William Clay, 68, 70, 71, 72, 75, 102
Ford Motor Co.
    Advanced Design Office, 110
    Dearborn Proving Grounds, 35
    Executive Committee, 70, 71, 72, 80
    Exposition of Progress, 8
    Facilities
        Long Beach, 51
        Los Angeles, 37
        Metuchen, 37, 52
        Oakwood Boulevard, 77
        Romulus, 50
        Rotunda, 113
        St. Louis, 37, 52
        Wayne, 52
        Wixom, 78, 80, 87, 97, 105, 113, 116, 146
    Interior Design Office, 110
    Models, 16, 31, 32, 64, 77, 78, 89, 93, 106, 110, 112,
        124, 128-129, 133
    Office of the Chief Executive, 70
    Policy Committee, 31
    Product Design, 70
    Product Planning and Styling, 102

Special Design Office, 110
Special Products Division, 25, 32, 70, 71, 72
Special Projects Styling Center, 89
Trade School, 71
Ford Museum, Henry, 75, 95
Frazer Manhattan, 93
Frey, Stu, 118
Fuller, Alvin, 19

Gardner, V., 71, 72
Gilbert, H. H., 35, 38
Givenchy, Hubert de, 131, 134, 139, 140, 142, 144
Gonzales, Jesús Nava, 46
Graham Blue Streak, 6
Granger, Stewart, 76
Greenfield Village, 44, 75
Gregorie, Eugene T., 7, 9, 10, 11, 12, 13, 15, 16, 18, 22,
    23, 30, 31-32, 33, 35, 37, 40, 42, 43, 44, 71, 78, 84
Grisinger, A., 71, 72
Gubitz, Werner, 71

Haldeman, George, 134
Harder, Delmar S., 20, 68
Hendry, Maurice, 69
Henney Co., 41
Hess and Eisenhardt, 90, 94, 95
Hibbard, Thomas L., 30, 35, 38, 42
Hillman, 71
Holley carburetor, 40
Hoover, Herbert, 41
Hotchkiss, 35, 87
Hudson Hornet, 50, 51
Humber, 71
Hydra-matic, 27, 36, 37, 38, 39, 52, 56, 59
    Dual-Range, 47, 49

Iacocca, Lee, 110, 114
Imperial, 60, 61, 62, 66, 67, 82, 83, 84, 94, 95-96, 98, 99,
    107, 109, 114, 120, 124, 126, 127, 128. See also
    Chrysler models.
Industrial Designers Institute, 66, 93

Jaguar XJ-6, 126
Johnson, C. C., 35
Johnson, Frank, 9, 10, 16

Kanzler, Ernest C., 15
Kaufman, I. B. (Bud), 79
Keller, K. T., 50
Kelley Kar Blue Book, 43, 87, 123
Kennedy, Jacqueline, 95
Kennedy, John F., 42, 90, 95

Kenyon and Eckhardt, 55, 112
Kiekhaefer, E. C., 55
Kirkeby, Arnold, 76
Kong distributor, 50
Korf, Bob, 51, 55
Kotten, Chauncey F., 55
Krause, John, 90, 94
Kravre, R. E., 50

Lamm, John, 120
Lancia models, 51, 79
LaSalle models, 6, 10
Laux, Edgar F., 108, 113
Leahy, William, 41
LeBaron Studios, 6
Ledwinka, Hans, 8
Lee, Don, 19
Lehmann, George, 96
Lehmann-Peterson, 96-97, 100, 101, 106, 108, 109, 115
LeRoy, Mervin, 76
Lincoln Continental Owners Club, 75, 76, 113
Liquamatic, 23, 24
Locke Body Co., 6
Lockheed-Wagner, 11
Lodge, Jim, 64
Loewy, Raymond, 70, 71
Lorenz, Paul F., 100, 110
Lund, Robert, 125
Lundy, J. E., 20

MacDonald, Harold, 90, 91
MacPherson, Earle S., 32, 44, 46-47, 49, 78, 90
Mantz, Johnny, 31, 39, 51, 54
McCahill, Tom, 39, 47, 50, 66
McFee, Reginald, 51
McGrath, Jack, 54
McGriff, Hershel, 39
McNamara, Robert S., 20, 80, 89-90
Mercedes-Benz models, 38, 51, 109, 123, 130, 131, 140,
    141, 142
Mercury models, 6, 11, 31, 32, 50, 58, 60, 63, 78-79, 84,
    96, 116, 128, 136, 137, 143
Mexican road race. See Carrera Panamericana.
Michelin, 118, 119
Miller, Arjay, 20
Miller, Logan, 20
Miller, R., 71, 72
Mills, Ben Daivd, 20, 62, 66, 78, 88, 93, 102, 110
Mobilgas Economy Run, 42, 47
Moore, George, 20
Motor Trend, 42, 46, 49, 53, 55, 64, 66, 84, 85, 93, 95,
    96, 118, 120, 123, 124, 129

Multi-Luber, 86
Mundy, Frank, 55
Museum of Modern Art, 68

Najjar, John, 62, 78-79, 80, 81, 82, 83, 84, 85, 88, 89, 91, 94, 110
Nash Motor Co., 80
Neale, Colin G., 89, 91
Nevins, Allan, 17
New York Automobile Show, 96

Oldsmobile models, 37, 39, 50, 51, 55, 69, 109
Oswald, John, 32
Oxtoby-Smith, 112

Packard models, 11, 14, 15, 16, 25, 27, 28, 34, 37, 40, 50, 55, 57, 61, 70, 71
Paris Auto Show, 75
Paul VI, 100, 101
Peter, Henry, 98
Peters, Ralph, 110
Peterson, R. E., 101
Peterson, Robert, 96
Peugeot, 76
Pittsburgh Plate Glass Co., 115
Pontiac Streamliner, 30
Popular Science, 49
Pucci, Emilio, 131, 132, 134, 139, 140, 142, 144

Querfeld, Arthur, 110

Rambler, 87
Rathmann, Jim, 55
Regitko, Martin, 30, 37, 71

Reinhart, John, 69, 70, 71, 72, 74, 77, 82, 83, 91
Reith, Francis C. 'Jack,' 20
Renault, 87
Road & Track, 52, 131
Roberts, Ralph, 6
Rogers National Research, 112
Rolls-Royce models, 70, 80, 87
Roosevelt, Franklin, 41
Ruttman, Troy, 50

Sanders, Bill, 113
Schmidt, William M., 32, 33, 35, 38, 42, 44, 62, 63
Sheldrick, Laurence, 18
Skinner, T. W., 20
Smith, Clay, 45, 50, 51, 54, 57
Smith, Ray, 71
Society of Automotive Engineers, 73-74
Sorensen, Charles, 18
Steinbeck, John, 70
Stevenson, Chuck, 45, 51, 54
Stroppe, Bill, 51, 54, 57
Studebaker models, 8, 70, 71
Sunbeam Talbot, 71
Sure-Track brake system, 118

Taruffi, 39, 50
Tatra Model 77, 8
Teague, Marshall, 51
Thomas, Robert, 71, 89, 91
Thornton, Charles B. 'Tex,' 20
Thunderbird, 77, 79-80, 89-90, 110
Tjaarda, John, 6, 8, 12, 13, 15
Traction-Lok differential, 138
Truman, Harry S., 36
Turbo-Drive, 59, 61, 109, 111

Tuxtla Gutierrez. See Carrera Panamericana.

United States
    Office of Price Administration (OPA), 14, 24
    Secret Service, 23, 41, 109, 115-116
    War Production Board, 20
    White House, 27, 37, 39, 41, 42, 94

Vanden Plas Princess, 136
Veasey, D. R., 92
Viland, Les, 42, 47
Volkswagen models, 79, 87, 142

Wagner, Paul, 74
Walker, George W., 31-32, 44, 56, 71, 72, 78, 89
Wall Street Journal, 105
Walton, Harry, 49
Ward, Roger, 54
Warner Brothers Studios, 50
Warner transmission, 23
Waterhouse, Charles, 32
Weibel, A. M., 18
Williams, A. L., 76
Williams, Walker, 68
Willoughby Co., 30
Willys Aero, 58
Woron, Walt, 46-47, 53, 55, 66
Wright, Frank Lloyd, 70
Wright, James O., 20

Yntema, Theodore O., 68
Youngren, Harold T., 20, 31, 36, 44, 59, 68

Zimmerman, Frank E., 106-107, 108